Phyllis Webb and the Common Good

PHYLLIS WEBB

AND THE COMMON GOOD

Poetry / Anarchy / Abstraction

Stephen Collis

Talonbooks
Vancouver

Talonbooks
P.O. Box 2076, Vancouver, British Columbia, Canada V6B 3S3
www.talonbooks.com

Typeset in Adobe Garamond and printed and bound in Canada.
Printed on 100% post-consumer recycled paper.

First Printing: 2007

The publisher gratefully acknowledges the financial support of the Canada Council for the Arts; the Government of Canada through the Book Publishing Industry Development Program; and the Province of British Columbia through the British Columbia Arts Council and the Book Publishing Tax Credit for our publishing activities.

Library and Archives Canada Cataloguing in Publication

Collis, Stephen, 1965–
Phyllis Webb and the common good : poetry, anarchy, abstraction / Stephen Collis.

Includes bibliographical references and index.
ISBN 978-0-88922-559-6

1. Webb, Phyllis, 1927– —Criticism and interpretation. I. Title.

PS8545.E22Z62 2007 C811'.54 C2007-900768-6

Contents

Disinterest: An Introduction

Phyllis Webb is a poet around whom archetypes tend to cluster. The reclusive artist. The distraught, borderline suicidal sapphic woman poet. The lonely Canadian in the wilderness, cabined in the cold—shacked up alone Tom Thomson style. There is of course some truth to these mythic associations, but, of course, they do not come close to telling the whole story. This cartoon biographical version of Webb must be bracketed aside here at the beginning—if not cast out entirely—so that we may focus instead on a more public and engaged Webb, a poet who forms a key part of, and who, as it turns out, has been so concerned with, our "common good." I will be polemical: if we are writing now on the West Coast of Canada we are all of us writing in some sense "after Webb"—both chronologically (though still very much alive, Webb has given up writing) and in terms of our debt (what she has given to poetry which we should not forget).

The Days of the Unicorns

I remember when the unicorns
roved in herds through the meadow
behind the cabin, and how they would
lately pause, tilting their jewelled
horns to the falling sun as we shared
the tensions of private property
and the need to be alone.

Or as we walked along the beach
a solitary delicate beast
might follow on his soft paws

until we turned and spoke the words
to console him.

It seemed they were always near
ready to show their eyes and stare
us down, standing in their creamy
skins, pink tongues out
for our benevolence.

As if they knew that always beyond
and beyond the ladies were weaving them
into their spider looms.

I knew where they slept
and how the grass was bent
by their own wilderness
and I pitied them.

It was only yesterday, or seems
like only yesterday when we could
touch and turn and they came
perfectly real into our fictions.
But they moved on with the courtly sun
grazing peacefully beyond the story
horns lowering and lifting and
lowering.

I know this is scarcely credible now
as we cabin ourselves in cold
and the motions of panic
and our cells destroy each other
performing music and extinction
and the great dreams pass on
to the common good.[1]

The unicorns were (to borrow from the title of Timothy Findley's novel) "not wanted on the voyage," or at least, chose not to go, rejecting the advantages and burdens of salvation.[2] And yet—stepping out of the purely imaginary—they seem to need "our fictions" to make them "real." Contending gestures of joining and rejecting flood Webb's work. The unicorns "follow," seeming to need "consolation," and yet ultimately they "need to be alone." Webb's own joining—what will here be referred to as a "poetics of response"—can be seen in this poem's response, and near merger with, one of Rilke's "Sonnets to Orpheus";[3] her rejection in its near-elegiac celebration of the pre-lapsarian and—here comes that archetypal Webb again—her anarchist islanding and ultimate abandoning of poetry for the (more material) opacities of abstract painting. Always both "Making" and "Breaking," twin masks separate and inseparable.

~

The Poet and the Public Sphere

On the surface Webb, in her isolation, might seem someone supremely disinterested in the public sphere. This is an illusion. Her own sense of her oeuvre is that it is anything but voluminous—but her slim books speak volumes. If there is a sense of abandoned projects hovering as ghosts on the margins of her books ("poems of failure," long silences, retreats and removes), it is a purposeful abandonment, an anarchist's abdication of positions of power and authority. It is not psychic vulnerability, but intellectual and political commitment of a complex sort. Here is a telling example.

In the early 1970s, Webb proposed a course at the University of British Columbia on "Mind and Marketplace: Consuming Concepts."[4] The focus was to be on the idea of obsolescence, intellectual fads, "the rise and fall of culture heroes; the fate of 'movements,' and the absorption of dissent." While there were to be "no required texts," Webb did provide a reading list that included R. D. Laing (*The Politics of Experience*), Norman O. Brown (*Love's Body*), Alvin Toffler (*Future Shock*), Kate Millett (*Sexual Politics*), Franz Fanon (*The Wretched of the Earth*), as well as texts by Paul Goodman, Herbert Marcuse, and (apparently to be featured prominently) the only recently translated Michel Foucault. She proposed that "a new list will be created by the group to replace the original. The aim of the workshop is to become obsolete in eight weeks and understand why." What fascinates in this is Webb's almost poststructuralist interest in work that challenges the constructedness of social power—at the same time as she takes this to its logical conclusion: that the critique of authority must not in turn set itself up as a new authority.

Her "course" was to be an intellectual "vacation" at the very intersection of knowledge and power.

There are other examples of Webb's moves into and strategically out of the public sphere. Early on, in the mid-1950s, there is her interest in the relationship between poet, publisher, and public, resulting in several versions of an essay entitled "The Poet and the Publisher," in which she notes that "it is eminently clear that this relationship [between poet and public] has broken down."[5] The idealistic Webb, here in her early twenties—not long after having run as a CCF candidate in the 1949 B.C. provincial election—writes to E. J. Pratt of her hopes for "regaining a wide public for poetry."[6] The possibility of academic graduate studies coming out of this project was eventually abandoned, but her activities as a radio broadcaster, culminating in her work as an executive producer for CBC Radio in the mid-1960s, grow out of this concern with poetry and the public sphere. The fruit of her work with the CBC—beginning with *University of the Air* (the utopian institution, we might say, with which she maintained her longest affiliation) in 1964—was the program *Ideas,* which still airs to this day. This ambitious project of putting some of the most challenging and topical figures of art, politics, and philosophy on public radio was only abandoned when, as Pauline Butling hypothesizes, Webb came to "recognize her own co-optation to the nationalist project."[7]

This is the Webb of interest here—the Webb committed to "the common good," the Webb who was forever engaging and retreating, who found herself "on the waiting list to join the crew" of the first Greenpeace voyage to Amchitka in 1971, but who, either not wanted on that voyage, or retreating from the too-public display of protest, wrote about it instead, from her island enclosure, in that most public of Canadian periodicals, *Maclean's.*[8]

Disinterest

Poetry is language that we notice. That is one place to begin. When words "thicken" and rough round the edge, when a writer in awareness works with the way words sound, opens to degrees of opacity, we are well on our way to poetry. Take a chemical analogy (there is a good tradition for doing so): Poetry is language in its purest, and therefore most unstable, form—or so a student once taught me—a volatile chemical compound that may explode—if we are lucky.

> **'Hanging Fire'**
>
> *Furioso,* flame-eyed Flamenco, castanets' death
> rattle.
>
> Guru from the frozen North heats up shamanically,
> her two big feet *Southbound.*
>
> As lights go out, crisis of lambency.
>
> 'Dresden/China' – or thereabouts.
>
> A curtain of fire drops over the overview,
> glass-like substances, 'fragments of quartz'.
>
> They leap and hang in the air. Firebugs.
> Organic memory goes up in smoke.
>
> *Action.* Smiling. Acidulous. Eating its heart out.[9]

The "curtain of fire" that is poetry "drops over the overview" criticism would provide. As language "thickens" and troubles smooth referentiality (and it is the contention of this book that all poetry tends in this direction, to vastly varying degrees—or what then is the distinctness of, the interest specific to, poetry?), it challenges our "capacity to read, interpret, or critically respond to it in conventional ways"[10]—we respond unconventionally—we respond in kind—we thicken into language, "leap and hang in the air" with the poem. This is where we must go now, in interest.

"The proper response to a poem is another poem," Webb writes in *Hanging Fire.*[11] In this admonition to anyone who would write *about* poems this study finds its genesis: all that follows flows from this stricture. What is appropriate to the poem? What is proper? What is criticism's "interest," and how does it differ from the poem's? What sort of criticism is proper to a poetry that already sees itself as a response to other poetry—already performing a critical function? Cannot criticism itself also be "creative"? What would such a criticism look like?

> **PROPER** (adjective)—of the required type; suitable or appropriate: *an artist needs the proper tools.* [predic.] (**proper to**) belonging or relating exclusively to. [archaic] belonging to oneself or itself; own: *to judge with my proper eyes.*
> ORIGIN Middle English: from Old French *propre,* from Latin *proprius* "one's own, special."

To offer the required type of response, to judge with one's own (proper) eyes, to take up one's proper tools, to make this one's own and (simultaneously) to belong to this as its own, to judge (as has so often been the critic's task) but to judge in a prose seeing with poetry's own special eyes—this study would with much interest respond to the singular poetry of Phyllis Webb.

~

Matthew Arnold, one of the founders of modern literary criticism, writes in his essay "The Function of Criticism at the Present Time" that "Creative literary genius does not principally show itself in discovering new ideas; that is rather the business of the philosopher."[12] Poets have time and time again proved the falsity of this statement. Phyllis Webb is one of them—a philosophical poet par excellence, addressing the big ontological questions, metaphysical to her bones.

> Give us wholeness, for we are broken.
> But who are we asking, and why do we ask?
> Destructive element heaves close to home,
> our years of work broken against a breakwater.[13]

The debate between poetry and criticism—poetry and philosophy—is at least as old as Plato, who banished the poet from his ideal republic, and accused poets of being, essentially, poor readers of poetry.[14] Matthew Arnold is one of the great inheritors and perpetuators of this debate. "The critical power is of lower rank than the creative," Arnold admits, but he goes on to note that creativity may be exercised "in other ways than in producing great works of literature or art."[15] Is he opening the door for the blending of the critical and creative that would allow for Webb's "proper response"? Many others have mined here.

> STEPHEN SCOBIE: poetry can *think*.
>
> ROBERT CRAWFORD: writing verse ... is a critical as well as a creative Activity.
>
> LORNA KNIGHT: the roles of poet and critic are interdependent.[16]

However we choose our separations and joinings, Arnold is clear: not all epochs are conducive to the creative power and "the creation of a modern poet, to be worth much, implies a great critical effort behind it"; "Criticism first; a time of true creative activity, perhaps ... hereafter, when criticism has done its work."[17] This is, of course, in Arnold's interest—he has given up poetry for criticism—an expression of his interests and investments. And this in the essay that is famous for his championing of the concept of "disinterest":

"keeping aloof from what is called 'the practical view of things.'"[18] By "practical" here Arnold means political—the public sphere of worldly affairs—swept out of the domesticated critics' kitchen. Webb is no domestic, as creator or critic. Her work sweeps into the wilds of politics, philosophy, economics—all the places Arnold would keep both critic and creator from, and into which we must follow here.

"Most literary criticism is based on calculations of interest," writes poet and scholar Susan Howe.[19] Her caution should not be read as an endorsement of Arnoldian *disinterest.* She is critical of calculations of returns on investments. Her own (proper) *My Emily Dickinson* is conceived as a gift in return for a gift already received—a different economy of tribute and thanks that is marked in other ways by its *interest* (its enthusiasm for its subject). But then criticism is supposed to be anything but enthusiastic.

> FRANK O'HARA: If you cover someone with earth and grass grows, you don't know what they looked like anymore. Critical prose makes too much grass grow.[20]

I come not to bury Phyllis Webb.

> Speak to that violet
> or call to the light
>
> and what is given back
> is not echo
> but the mute substance
> of the work of love[21]

All this is to declare the "interestedness" of this study, one aspect of which is in a particular (proper) sort of response to poetry—the "function of criticism at the present time," as this (poet) critic would have it. "I am not a disinterested scholar," Robert Duncan writes of his obsession with the work of the poet H.D., for it is in her poetry that his "deepest responsibilities in work have been conceived."[22] The goal is "a book of continuations not conclusions." The guides, *via a poetics of response, to a criticism of response*, are several—Duncan on H.D., Howe on Dickinson—but Webb herself provides an excellent example of a poetic criticism in her essay on Robin Blaser, "The Crannies of Matter." George Bowering has noted the similarity between Webb's approach in this essay and Susan Howe's in *My Emily Dickinson.*[23] Allowing her prose a certain poetic opacity or "texture," relying on the juxtaposed fragment and "Notes, Impressions, Guidelines, and Data Clusters," Webb creates something of a "serial essay" form to properly respond to Blaser's serial poetry in the "Image-Nations" sequence.[24] The attempt here, in this laying of critical cards on the scholarly table, is to follow suit.

~

> ROBERT DUNCAN: Responsibility is to keep / the ability to respond.[25]

To "*keep* the ability to respond" is to keep it in, into, the future—it is of and for the future that we write. "Futurity," writes Webb, "is tact": sensitivity to others, related to touch.[26] To respond is to return the other's touch, or to retain the other's touch into the future—to hold a hand out beyond the individual life, into the beyond of both space and time—"*dear beings*," writes Robin Blaser, "*I can feel your hands.*"[27] A response poetics/criticism is open-ended and future-oriented—to open texts, to follow lines of flight out of them, to touch and to join and to continue them. Fusion. Anyone writing on another one who wrote is in some sense striving towards futurity, striving to continue, to touch, to be the other's other hand—"a shadow following the / hand that writes."[28] Here are three related dicta:

> SUSAN HOWE: What is writing but continuing.
>
> RACHEL BLAU DUPLESSIS: *A poetics gives permission to continue.*
>
> SUSAN HOWE: My precursor attracts me to my future.[29]

Which brings us to the question of literary influence. "This whole question of literary influence is a very untidy one. It hovers between plunder and awe," Webb writes introducing a radio reading in 1969.[30] But she announces that she is "going to read poems that were written in response to other poets," confounding the Bloomian notion of anxiety and repression. Harold Bloom, in *The Anxiety of Influence*, argued that as poets seek above all else the cachet of originality, they disguise and repress all evidence of literary borrowings and influences—they present themselves, in other words, as *disinterested*. Webb, however, reads and writes differently. She is interested in the "imaginations companions," in "[t]he work [which] is kin."[31] We see her reading in her writing, and it is not evidence of repression, but of devotion to "benevolent influences."[32] In the words of Rachel Blau Duplessis, one sees in Webb a "refusal to play the game of belatedness"—an awareness that "the ground can never be cleared of the prior."[33]

All of this suggests something about (literary) property and propriety. For Bloom poetry is "property," and the "commodity in which poets deal" is originality.[34] Counter this with Webb's echoing of the anarchist Pierre-Joseph Proudhon: "[P]roperty is theft."[35] And another, for closeness of collage: "What I put into words is no longer my possession. Possibility has opened. The future will forget, erase, or recollect and deconstruct every poem."[36]

  Have I struck

The right note?
  I exit the scene
    paring my fingernails.

The field surges behind me
  with fun & names
    disrupting the bloody text.[37]

Poetry, as a "proper response" to poetry, undermines all notions of literary property—it is proper here to appropriate, if such appropriation is as much a devoted response—a "keeping" into the future, a fusion-with that makes reading and writing blur. Webb's work points steadily towards the idea that the poem is not a hoardable commodity but a shared response-ability, an aspect of the commons and our "common good." The gradual dissolution of the lyric "I" traceable over the course of her writing career mirrors both the development of avant-garde poetics across the century and the anarchist inflected notion of the poem as a *common property*—an effect of language (the commons) and not the self (the private). Our notions of "intellectual property" are not necessarily part of what is proper to the poem, which has its own sense of what is "proper," and what is "property."

At the end of every poem the writer "exit[s] the scene," and the reader enters. This gesture is taken to another level, however, when the writer "exits" writing altogether—when she stands outside her oeuvre as such, nonchalantly (or nervously?) "paring" her fingernails, or cleaning a brush before the "surging field" of a new medium.

This Exploratory Surgery

Webb is, of course, not without her anxieties, and has been very open about this. The prior is not always a friendly haven, and "our inheritance" may very well be "our distress."[38] This may be because Webb, as a woman, looks back on a tradition mostly male, which figures her gender as material and not maker. The openness to anxiety, however, has in part resulted in a critical tradition that has too often been too quick to read her as a neurotic or hysteric (and to read *her*, rather than her *work*), projecting again gendered stereotypes, containing and dismissing the work of this uncontainable poet.[39] Many critics—and Webb herself—note affinities to Emily Dickinson. "I refuse to publish because I refuse to write," Webb here making and breaking the connection to the reluctant-to-publish-but-very-willing-to-write Dickinson.[40] And in mentioning her "critical wounds," or the "exploratory surgery" she would perform on Robin Blaser's work, we might recall Dickinson thanking her "preceptor," T. W. Higginson, for the editorial "surgery" he performed on her poetry.[41] This comparison is mentioned here mainly because the critically dangerous temptations in responding to Webb's work are similar to those many critics of Dickinson have faced. These temptations reside in the potential answers to a series of questions, which really boil down to one repeated question: why didn't she (Dickinson) publish; why her (Webb's) long silences, her eventual cessation of writing altogether? The temptation is of course psychobiography, an approach taken to women writers far more often than to men (because it has made them easier to contain and dismiss), and which Webb herself decries in an essay from 1993, noting how the poet "become[s] a sociological phenomenon whose secret life has become an almost more dramatic gift than the poems, become the sacrificial meal we seem to hunger for."[42] Obviously this is one of Webb's most striking anxieties: that we may focus on her anxieties, and not her words. The proper response is the proper response.

While gender per se is not the focus here, the importance for contemporary avant-garde writers (many of them men) of work by women is remarkable—the ground-breaking we can now trace (indirectly) from Emily Dickinson through H.D. and Marianne Moore and Gertrude Stein on along other unconnected branches to poets like Susan Howe, Rachel Blau Duplessis, and Juliana Spahr in the United States and Phyllis Webb, Lisa Robertson, and Lissa Wolsak here on the Canadian West Coast. Webb's "embarrassment" over "the dominance of male figures" in her response poems meets in the shift of generations a contemporary sense of the crucial work being done by women poets.[43] Joseph Boone and Michael Cadden may have some explanation in *Engendering Men*: "[T]here now exists an entire generation of male critics, many of whom, having been educated by 'first generation' feminist scholars, have in turn been 'engendered' by feminism."[44] (Thank you Smaro Kamboureli.) But it is never as simple as it seems.

If women writing have—through "a denial of competition and aggression"—formed "non-hierarchical forms of mutuality," then we would all benefit by being led by women into such mutuality.[45] If this is a form of appropriation (the male critic assuming the discourse of feminism) then *this* male critic is as much appropriated as appropriating. Duplessis goes on to note that "I cannot prove that only women, that women only, use this aesthetic"—"what we have been calling (the) female aesthetic turns out to be a specialized name for any practices available to those groups ... which wish to criticize, to differentiate from, to overturn the dominant forms of knowing and understanding with which they are saturated"—performing instead "non-hegemonic practices" in a "decentered universe." This is an apt description both of Webb's mature poetics and, in fact, the poetics of response.

Webb's work is a bridge one can walk across to a more complete understanding of the fractures, rifts, and shifts in twentieth century North American poetics. In this sense Webb's poetry is here read as it conjoins (and simultaneously diverges from) various twentieth century literary movements and moments, this being what accounts for "the tension between modernism and postmodernism in her work" and which makes Webb "a modernist whose writing nevertheless provides an opening into postmodernism."[46] To further pursue Scobie's terms and analogy, we can read her modernism (*Even Your Right Eye* and *The Sea Is Also a Garden*), locate the introduction of the first wave of postmodernism via the New American poetry (*Naked Poems* and eventually *Wilson's Bowl*), and ultimately read her late work in relation to the development of postcolonialism (*Water and Light*) and even aspects of language poetry (*Hanging Fire*). Her work weaves a web across numerous conceptual divides: the (porous) boundaries between poetry and painting, poetry and politics, modernism and postmodernism, the lyric and the long poem, the ontologies of the self and the other, even CanLit and American avant-garde poetics. Indeed, the attempt here is to bring Webb in from the CanLit cold, as it were, to restore her to her rightful place in the Image-Nation of radical, philosophically engaged poetries that have flourished throughout twentieth century North American literature.[47]

What is striking about Webb's oeuvre is the play between change and continuity—the Olsonian "what does not change / is the will to change."[48] The changes across decades of writing, it is part of this study's argument, mirror changes in the methods and approaches of the twentieth century avant-garde. But these changes or aesthetic shifts can also be registered as *changes in the poetics of response.* What shifts or is altered over Webb's career in writing is the *way* in which she responds and the *what* she responds to—a honing of her response-abilities, the general trajectory of which this book attempts to follow. At first, in the early work, it is the response of modernist allusion and quotation. This aspect of her work can be seen as evolving into a more engaged and direct response to the other poem / the otherness of the poem read. These arguments are taken up in the first chapter, in which a theory of the poetics of response is elaborated. A further refinement comes as the response capacities of poem-to-poem come to be applied *within her own work*, leading to the serial poem as response-sequence. The politics of this federative poetic form is discussed in the second chapter, where the possibilities of an anarchist aesthetics are explored. Finally, the response in Webb's work is to the very otherness of language itself—that ground of otherness we so completely inhabit that it in turn inhabits us and inward and outward responses become indistinguishable. Here we move ultimately beyond the poem, following Webb, into the realm of abstract painting, and returning from that point beyond the written word, to explore the possibilities of an abstract poetry—the subject of the final chapter.

Some final declarations of interests and intents are in order. While I am wary of the "possessiveness" of the first-person pronoun, I will "own" these objectives as part and parcel of my (hopefully proper) response to the poetry of Phyllis Webb. Thus it is necessary to note that my "interest" is partisan and hardly "disinterested." I am attempting to pay tribute to the most startling poet the Canadian West Coast has produced; much more than I could ever give is her due. She positioned the poem as an intellectual site for discovery, and employed it to unearth everything from the Salt Spring Island shoreline to abstract painting and the Persian ghazal. We can now enter the field of the poem, seeing it as part and parcel of our common, intellectual being—the commons itself, that "field" which "surges" behind the work of every great poet—and approach through its unfenced parameters some ontological or epistemological complexity.

Of interest here is the problem of the lyric: how the lyric "I" evolves and is perpetually posited and problematized throughout Webb's oeuvre so that it becomes clear that it is not so much a final and complete "death of the lyric" that is enacted, but the revelation that the lyric is—in each iteration—a movement beyond the threshold of the self, a "pure hole in the world," in Emmanual Levinas's terms, where the poet stands "tend[ing] the silence" of being.[49] This means that, in many respects, more than the poetry of Phyllis Webb is at stake here: it is *the ontological status of the poem itself* that this book is in search of—the poem as it has (perhaps) always existed, but more importantly and accurately, the status of the twentieth (and now twenty-first) century poem, which has abdicated so much that has seemed historically characteristic of the poem (rhyme, meter, narrative—even clear referentiality), and which has slipped from any pretensions to a position of cultural centrality (recall Webb's concerns over the poet's presence in the public sphere)—but which has actually turned more squarely than ever towards the other at the heart of the poem's ontology. Thus, philosophical flights and digressions out and away from Webb's poetry are necessitated throughout—but the poetry always returns as the ground and substance of these explorations, for her poems, above all else, remain of great interest.

Of interest here is a poet whose books are all singularities, entirely unique (as in the sense of being discrete), and which nevertheless respond to, are in dialogue with, and ring changes upon each other—over nearly forty years of publication. Webb's work, for all its internal differences, forms a cohesive whole. It is not a failure. It evolves its own principles and follows these through to their poetic conclusions.

Of interest here, and taken quite seriously, is Webb's anarchism—her claim to being "a law-abiding anarchist."[50] Stephen Scobie is right when he claims that "The great weakness of Webb criticism has been to present her as inward turning and solipsistic, to the exclusion of [the] political world."[51] We will attempt to see what Webb's poetic politics is, as it is present in the politics of poetic form, at the very least. Here I will draw upon (and argue with) such recent theorizations of anarchism's cultural meaning as David Weir's *Anarchy and Culture*, in which he argues for "the structural resemblance of much of twentieth century culture to the political model anarchism provides."[52]

And finally, of perhaps central interest here is the fact that this is a poet who became a painter—that the trajectory of Webb's career is *towards abstraction*, towards the visual surface. The presence of painting and painterly abstraction, as John Hulcoop was the first to note, has been a part of her project from the beginning. In this regard the focus will be, in the final chapter especially, on *Hanging Fire*, Webb's least read book (by critics, who seem to have stopped writing about Webb when she stopped writing poems). In an interview with Smaro Kamboureli Webb calls *Hanging Fire* a "transitional book"—transitional, that is, to the medium of painting.[53]

But before we get too carried away, there *are* the poems.

Notes

1. *Wilson's Bowl* (Toronto: Coach House Press, 1980), 84–85.

2. The poem occupies a place of convergence for a number of interesting literary responses. For instance, Findley's novel *Not Wanted on the Voyage* acknowledges "Phyllis Webb, whose poem, *Leaning* [from *Water and Light*], was the book's initial impetus."

3. Sonnet II, 4. See chapters one and two for further discussion of this poem.

4. A typescript of the course outline is in Webb's papers at the National Library of Canada. I am indebted to Pauline Butling for this discovery. Quotations following in this paragraph are from the typescript.

5. "The Poet and the Publisher," *Queens Quarterly* 61 (Winter 1954–55), 508. Another version was published in *Writing in Canada: Proceedings of the Canadian Writers' Conference, Queens University, 28–31 July 1955*, ed. George Whalley (Toronto: The Macmillan Co., 1956), 78–89.

6. Letter dated July 27, 1951. Webb Papers, National Library.

7. Pauline Butling, "Phyllis Webb and CBC Ideas: Intersections of the personal and political," typescript, 21.

8. "Protest in Paradise," *Maclean's* 86 (June 1973), 38–39, 73–77. The article is on Greenpeace "propaganda minister" Ben Metcalfe.

9. *Hanging Fire* (Toronto: Coach House Press, 1990), 35.

10. Sianne Ngai, *Ugly Feelings* (Cambridge, Mass.: Harvard University Press, 2005), 336.

11. *Hanging Fire*, 57.

12. Matthew Arnold, "The Function of Criticism at the Present Time," in *Essays in Criticism, First Series*, ed. Sister Thomas Marion Hoctor (Chicago: University of Chicago Press, 1968), 10.

13. *Selected Poems: The Vision Tree*, ed. Sharon Thesen (Vancouver: Talonbooks, 1982), 46.

14. Aside from Plato's discussion of poetry and poets in *The Republic*, which I will return to in chapter two, I have in mind here the resolution of *The Phaedrus*, where Plato has Socrates tell his interlocutor that "lucidity and finality and serious importance are to be found only in words spoken by way of instruction"—that is, in the words of a philosopher ("a lover of wisdom")—and sends this "message" to "Homer and other poets." This is part of Plato's privileging of speech over writing. See *Phaedrus and Letters VII and VIII*, trans. Walter Hamilton (Markham, Ont.: Penguin Books, 1973), 101–02.

15. Arnold, "The Function of Criticism," 10.

16. Stephen Scobie, "The Poet of the Mind," in *Inside the Poem: Essays and Poems in Honour of Donald Stephens*, ed. W. H. New (Toronto: University of Toronto Press, 1992), 246. Robert Crawford, *The Modern Poet: Poetry, Academia, and Knowledge Since the 1750s* (Oxford: Oxford University Press, 2001), 1. Lorna Knight, "'Oh for the Carp of a Critic': Research in the Phyllis Webb Papers," *West Coast Line* 26: 2 (Fall 1992), 120.

17. Arnold, "The Function of Criticism," 11, 18.

18. Ibid., 18.

19. *My Emily Dickinson* (Berkeley: North Atlantic Books, 1985), 13. My thoughts on the relation between poetry and criticism have been deeply affected both by the examples of works like Howe's *My Emily Dickinson* and Duncan's *H.D. Book*, but also by essays such as Ron Silliman's "The Dysfunction of Criticism," Charles Bernstein's "Artifice and Absorption," and Robert Crawford's *The Modern Poet.* Silliman attributes the continued separation of the critical and the creative, in part, to poets' "equating critical discourse per se with the bureaucratization of writing," but notes that there is a counter tradition which "proposes the critical essay as an art act in and of itself" (186–87). See "The Dysfunction of Criticism: Poets and the Critical Tradition of the Anti-academy," in *Poetics Journal* 10 (June 1998), 186–87.

If, as in Walter Pater's formulation, "All art aspires to the condition of music," then criticism, in this counter-tradition, humbly aspires to the condition of poetry.

20. Frank O'Hara, *The Collected Poems of Frank O'Hara*, ed. Donald Allen (New York: Knopf, 1971), 510.

21. Phyllis Webb, *The Vision Tree*, 39.

22. From an unpublished preface to *The H.D. Book*, The Poetry/Rare Book Collection, university libraries, State University of New York, Buffalo.

23. I owe this to Phyllis Webb herself, in conversation with the author, May 2, 2005. Webb did not read Howe's book, though it was mentioned to her by Sharon Thesen in a letter dated February 18, 1986 (National Library). The idea of a "serial essay" comes from Susan Howe's "Heterologies" essay, where she notes that—after quoting Robin Blaser on the serial poem as being "like rooms, lit and then dark"—"I think that essays can also be like rooms, established in concepts intuitively arrived at." See "Heterologies: Community of Form in Practice and Imagination," in *The Recovery of the Public World: Essays on Poetics in Honour of Robin Blaser*, ed. Charles Watts and Edward Byrne (Vancouver: Talonbooks, 1999), 218.

24. Phyllis Webb, "The Carnies of Matter: Texture in Robin Blaser's Later 'Image-Nations,'" in *Nothing But Brush Strokes: Selected Prose* (Edmonton: NeWest, 1995), 60.

25. *The Opening of the Field* (New York: Grove, 1960), 10.

26. *Even Your Right Eye* (Toronto: MacClelland and Stewart, 1956), 44.

27. *The Holy Forest* (Toronto: Coach House Press, 1993), 118.

28. Phyllis Webb, *Wilson's Bowl*, 13.

29. Susan Howe, *The Birth-mark: unsettling the wilderness in American literary history* (Hanover and London: Wesleyan University Press, 1993), 143. Rachel Blau Duplessis, *The Pink Guitar: Writing as Feminist Practice* (New York: Routledge, 1990), 156. Susan Howe, *My Emily Dickinson*, 97.

30. "Radio Talks: from the Phyllis Webb Papers, National Library," *West Coast Line* 25:3 (Winter 1991–92), 98.

31. Phyllis Webb, "Imaginations Companion," in *Nothing But Brush Strokes*, 45; *Hanging Fire*, 38. The phrase "imagination's companions" (with an apostrophe) comes from Sharon Thesen's poem "Postscript to Duncan McNaughton," but clearly has its origin in Robin Blaser's idea of "great companions." Thesen, *The Pangs of Sunday*, (Toronto: McClelland & Stewart, 1990), 5. Whether a mistake or not on Webb's part, I am reading the implied possessive into her "imaginations."

32. Phyllis Webb, "Palpable Relations," in *Talking* (Montreal: Quadrant Editions, 1982), 83.

33. Duplessis, *The Pink Guitar*, 128–29.

34. Harold Bloom, *The Anxiety of Influence* (Oxford: Oxford University Press, 1973), 64.

35. Webb, *Water and Light: Ghazals and Anti Ghazals* (Toronto: Coach House Press, 1984), 50.

36. Howe, *My Emily Dickinson*, 13.

37. Webb, *Hanging Fire*, 66.

38. Webb, *Even Your Right Eye*, 55.

39. John Hulcoop, for instance, while normally a redoubtable champion of Webb's work, concedes in his introduction to her 1971 *Selected Poems* that there is "a measure of truth" to the psychobiographical tradition of seeing her poetry as "neurotic, narcissistic and morbidly self-obsessed" (*Selected* 7).

40. Webb, *Wilson's Bowl*, 37.

41. Ibid., 9. "The Crannies of Matter," in *Nothing But Brush Strokes*, 57. The Dickinson letter is her second to Higginson, dated April 25 1862. See *Selected Letters*, ed. Thomas Johnson (Cambridge: The Belknap Press, 1958), 172.

42. Webb, "Poetry and Psychobiography," in *Nothing But Brush Strokes*, 91.

43. Webb, *Wilson's Bowl*, 9.

44. Joseph Boone and Michael Cadden, *Engendering Men: The Question of Male Feminist Criticism* (New York: Routledge, 1990), 2.

45. Duplessis, *The Pink Guitar*, 6–16. The succeeding citations in this paragraph are from the same source.

46. Stephen Scobie, "Leonard Cohen, Phyllis Webb, and the End(s) of Modernism," in *Canadian Canons: Essays in Literary Value*, ed. Robert Lecker (Toronto: University of Toronto Press, 1991), 67–69. While I think the modernism/postmodernism distinction can still be instructive in some cases, I tend to agree with Marjorie Perloff when she calls this supposed divide "the tired dichotomy that has governed our discussion of twentieth-century poetics for much too long." Perloff goes on to suggest that "the real fate of first-stage modernism was one of deferral"—and thus that what we have been calling "postmodernism" is really a kind of return—after the interruption of New Criticism and its (in Ron

Silliman's terms) "distortion of modernist principles"—to the heart of the modernist project. In this sense, I am arguing, one of the truly instructive aspects of Webb's example is that her work embodies the *enduring* tradition of the twentieth century avant garde, in a more accessible form than many readers find some of the more syntactically thorny poets. See Marjorie Perloff, *21st Century Modernism: The New Poetics* (Malden: Blackwell Publications, 2002), 1–3 and Ron Silliman, "The Dysfunction of Criticism," 186.

47. I am thinking of Robin Blaser's idea of a "pacific nation"—an imagined community existing outside the conceptions of actual nations. See Blaser's preface to the first issue of *Pacific Nation*, vol.1, June 1967. The poetics of modernism and the long twentieth century avant garde are transnational, even supra-national. There has been a steady interchange—particularly on the West Coast—between, for instance, the San Francisco Renaissance poets (Duncan, Blaser, Spicer) and Vancouver poets such as George Bowering, Daphne Marlatt, Fred Wah, and, I am trying to point out, Phyllis Webb. This is the restoration I am attempting here: Webb has too long been associated with an eastern, centrally CanLit tradition, when her enduring ground has clearly been the West Coast poetics I have just outlined. The association of Webb with an eastern Canadian aesthetic is in part attributable to some of the same poets I am here trying to associate her with (a *Tish* poet such as Frank Davey, for instance). In private conversation Webb has said that the *Tish* poets were suspicious of her "eastern Canadian association," but that she was "much closer to them than they thought" (May 2, 2005). Interestingly, Webb claims she first "got the American influence" in the east, in the 1950s, reading poets central to the poetics I am tracing here, such as Pound and Williams, and meeting Robert Creeley and Cid Corman—all before the origins of *Tish*.

48. Charles Olson, *Selected Poems*, ed. Robert Creeley (Berkeley: University of California Press, 1997), 5.

49. Emmanuel Levinas, *Humanism of the Other*, trans. Nidra Poller (Chicago: University of Chicago Press, 2003), 39, 61.

50. Phyllis Webb, "Phyllis Webb's Canada," in *Talking*, 12.

51. Stephen Scobie, "Leonard Cohen, Phyllis Webb, and the End(s) of Modernism," 63.

52. David Weir, *Anarchy and Culture: The Aesthetic Politics of Modernism* (Amherst: University of Massachusetts Press, 1997), 5.

53. Smaro Kambourelli, "'Seeking Shape. Seeking Meaning': An Interview with Phyllis Webb," in *West Coast Line* 25:3 (Winter 1991–92), 34.

ONE The Poetics of Response

'There *Are* the Poems'

> An editor asks me to put it all down: the reasons I write. And I thought 'it' was a gift. Homo ludens at play among the killing fields of dry grasses. Playful woman making a space to breathe. 'There are the poems,' Sharon says, she means, between the critical flash. There *are* the poems, like fists wearing birthstones and bracelets, her 'roses & bliss'. Or they're like legs running, bounding over the fields of force, momentum, for a quick roll in Darwin's tangled bank. And there are the poets doing what? And why, the editor asks. What does he want? Contributions to knowledge? Civilization and its discontents? Chaos among the order – or, oh yes, french doors opening onto a deck and a small pool where we can watch our weird reflections shimmering and insubstantial? The proper response to a poem is another poem. We burrow into the paper to court in secret the life of plants, the shifty moon's space-walks, the bliss, the roses, the glamorous national debt. Someone to talk to, for God's sake, something to love that will never hit back.[1]

It is by strange and untraceable paths that one poet finds her way to another, seeking what she needs. It is wayward, unpredictable, governed as much by chance as by personal proclivity. Strange attractors of the imagination's companions. But we can see by poems their arrival there—the presence of passages read if not always passages followed. This much is certain: "[T]he future will forget, erase, or recollect and deconstruct every poem," and in so doing we may see "[a] poet's admiring heart born into voice by idealizing a precursor poet's song."[2]

Marianne Moore once wrote: "A good stealer is *ipso facto* a good inventor."[3] Phyllis Webb credits Moore with having taught her a "trick … which is to incorporate quotations into the body of the poem."[4] We could add Eliot's remark, too, in this argument by accumulation, that "the most individual parts" of a poet's work "may be those in which the dead poets … assert their immortality most vigorously."[5] And finally Len Diepeveen: "In their new context the appropriated voices help to create a poetry less derivative than much poetry that contains no overt borrowing."[6]

Webb's "'There *Are* the Poems'" is a prose-poem statement on poetics that denies the possibility—or at least the desirability—of such a statement. It is also a meditation on response and responsibility, the writer's relationship with other writers (the title quotes poet Sharon Thesen), and the ontological status and epistemological capacities of the poem as such. It is also a "quoting poem" (to borrow from Diepeveen once more), from a book of poems (*Hanging Fire*) that are responses—to quotations, dictations, and other impingements of the outside—"the vast other that language also holds," in Robin Blaser's words.[7] The answer to Webb's editor's request for "the reasons I write" is that *there are the poems*—both Webb's own poems, here presented as though speaking for themselves, without the intruding "critical flash" of secondary reflection and self-awareness, and *other poems*: poems written by other poets (such as Thesen) to which Webb can respond in kind and enter into dialogue with—"Someone to talk to … something to love." Poems are tokens of the between, the milieu in which self and other, author and reader, meet and exchange. They are, as will be argued below, about *proximity* and *continuity*: Webb responds because the other is there (proximate), and so that writing (the between / the exchange / the self's involvement with the other—the other's involvement with the self) will continue.

~

Let us pause a moment longer over this poem that underwrites much of what will be argued in this book. The tangled lines of response here are more complex than they may at first seem, and this complexity is instructive. There is Webb's response to the editor's question, and to Thesen's suggestion of an answer. In addition to these obvious rejoinders, there is the presence of lines quoted from Thesen's poem "Praxis," itself something of a poetics statement in poetic form:

> Unable to imagine a future,
> imagine a future better
> than now, us creatures
> weeping in the abattoir
> only make noise & do
> not transform a single fact.
> So stop crying. Get up. Go out. Leap
> the mossy garden wall
> the steel fence or whatever
> the case may be & crash
> through painted arcadias,
> fragments of bliss & roses
> decorating your fists.[8]

In Thesen's poem, a sense of poetry's incapacity ("Unable to imagine a future") is met by the poem's "fists" crashing through "fragments of bliss & roses"—the traditional adornments of a poetry safely enclosed in its "garden." Webb's "'There *Are* the Poems'" is thus both a comment on the poetics of response and itself a response poem, taking up Thesen's theme of poetry's lack ("What does he want," Webb asks, "[c]ontributions to knowledge?") and its "proper" vocation (to crash through boundaries and "burrow into the paper"; to embody the energy of "[c]haos among the order"). Thesen and Webb respond to the long-standing sense that poetry requires a supplement—that it needs another discourse to step in and speak on its behalf when it comes to the larger social tasks of "imagining futures" or assessing its place and purpose (the "reasons" for writing). This recalls the American poet H.D. (to whom we will turn later in this chapter), whose long poem *Trilogy* is largely a response to the claim that "poets are useless"[9]—that poetry has no *practical* consequences.

There is, however, still a further response in "'There *Are* the Poems'" to the critical/creative dynamic: on a typescript version of the poem amongst Webb's papers in the National Library she has written the header: "after reading Aretha Van Herk's 'review' piece in The Malahat issue on Jiles, Thesen, Hartog."[10] Van Herk's ficto-critical essay—"An Armchair (Reader's) Companion to Club Cars and Ladies Crossing Canada by Train or Will the Real Picara Please Leave Town (Please Haul Ass)"—is similarly written out of a response poetic, merging with the piece it "reviews" (Paulette Jiles's *Sitting in the Club Car Drinking Rum and Karma-Kola*) more than seeking critical distance and disinterest. We are here in the space of *proximity* and *continuity*. The other text is *proximate* in that it is not directly written about (it is, rather, "a neighboring," as Emmanuel Levinas writes, "a side by side, an alliance");[11] similarly, the other text is *continued*, rather than analyzed, the complexity of its materials and ideas added to, rather than reduced/explained. Texts are not closed in the continuous gestures of response—they are re-opened and extended.

Finally, there is yet another possible response embedded in Webb's poem: her "french doors opening onto a deck" recalls Duncan's quotation of Gustave Stickley's *Craftsman Homes* in "The Architecture, Passages 9:" "'French doors opening out upon a porch.'"[12] In Duncan's poem a clear analogy is being drawn: the poem as architecture, spatially laid out in rooms one passes through—rooms in which the poet resides with his "bookcases," upon which "glimmering titles [are] arrayd," or in which he listens to "strains of *Mahagonny* on the phonograph."[13] Thus in Webb's "'There *Are* the Poems'" Duncan's "The Architecture" may hover as one of the now numerous others being invoked and responded to—a room within the spreading architecture of her poem. Her "french doors" reveal "a small pool where we can watch our weird reflections"—the poet's self reflected in another poet (her architecture opening onto Duncan's, and his onto hers in the poem's spatial between), or the other within the self revealing the strange truth that "I am an other." The poem's plural lines of response similarly reveal that the poet herself is multiple, "stitched of responsibilities," in Levinas's phrase.[14]

The poem's responsive architecture is indeed complex and multiple, but it is just this complexity that answers the editor's question: why write? Because there are others—there are poems because there are other poems—and poetry is a responsibility for and towards the other, a responsibility *to respond.* We are already veering off into philosophy, as we will continue to do in the following section, before returning to Webb's poetry in any kind of detail; this is necessary in order to consider the ontological conditions and implications of the poetics of response. Webb is a stridently philosophical poet, with one eye always fixed on the essential questions of existence. But her sense of the social is also of interest here, and inseparable from the ontological investigations and claims made in her poems. For Webb, *the poem is response*, and thus *it is alterity.* It expresses, in Levinas's terms, a "desire for others," which is the very basis of "sociality."[15] The politics of the poetics of response is closely related to a Levinasian ethics of the other, a *joining-with* fundamental to being and the poem (which will be associated, in the next chapter, with Webb's anarchism).

The argument of this book, however, is as much about the lyric and *the evolution of the lyric towards the sequence and abstraction* as it is anything else. In this movement it is possible to track the expanding and thickening relationship of the (lyric) self to (poetic and linguistic) otherness—the self as implicated and imbricated in the otherness of the works of other poets and the givenness of language itself.[16] In the following sections of this chapter we will move from a broadly philosophical investigation of Webb's poetic ontology to explore her early (modernist) response via quotation and literary allusion, and her subsequent movement towards a more direct response to other poets and poems in some of her middle and later works.

~

I. The Poetics of Response

1.1 "**The proper response to a poem is another poem**" implies, for one thing, *call and response* as the central poetic matrix—the very crux of the poetic act. Poetry begins in listening. It begins with receptivity. It hears a question and answers with its poem. But this is an extra-ordinary form of listening and hearing, incorporating but also extending far beyond the operations of the ear.

> HEIDEGGER: [The call] calls without uttering anything. The call discourses in the uncanny mode of *keeping silent*.[17]
>
> LEVINAS: [I]t would be necessary to think of language as a question.... The question is *posed*; it is posed in view of a response.[18]

The call to which the poet responds is the call of the very ground of language itself, echoing most recognizably in its self-conscious uses by poets. It is read as much as it is heard, and produces a writing that is as much a reading as a listening.

1.2 This, the first principle of the poetics of response, implies both similarity and difference—a response in kind that is nevertheless *of* a different kind. Repetition with variation. Poems respond to poems but they are different poems, working transformations and variations on the prior. At one level: *fusion with* another—so that, if you want to locate this poet's poetics or criticism, you will have to look for it in her poetry. At another level: radical alterity / *separation from* the other—the other poem presents an irreconcilable otherness that, denying the possibility of full understanding, allows only for response.

~

2.1 **"Responsibility is to keep / the ability to respond."** Duncan's focus on "ability" positions response as an *act* (a process, not a thing as such)—but it is an act paradoxically held in reserve, at the ready, in potential. Its locus is in the *keeping* of that ability. This may imply practice (keeping in shape, in working order, honing) but it also implies a holding of something prior (we already *have* what we *keep*) for a potential future (when we may need to respond). This is, according to Levinas, an "awaiting without something awaited," a state of being "held-in-awakening" or "vigilance."[19] It is an *objectless* keeping-open, what Duncan figures as *tendance*, the ancient Greek cultic form of worship he derives from Jane Ellen Harrison and which he expresses most succinctly in a letter to H.D.: "'Poetry' is a womb of souls, which we as poets attend."[20] Poets exercise their responsibilities in their *attending to Poetry*—awaiting the call to which they will respond. Duncan's focus on the *keeping* of responsibility shifts the focus of poetry from the produced poem to the process of awaiting Poetry—a move towards the silence surrounding poetry which can be seen in Webb's often remarked upon long silences and absences.[21] Poetry is as much its light matter as it is its dark, as much its sounds as it is its silences. It is words and what escapes, or at least awaits, surrounds, words. Thus, Duncan's *keeping* reveals an essential paradox at the heart of poetic response: what Sianne Ngai calls "a condition of utter receptivity," linking it to Gertrude Stein's "open feeling," is both the condition for response and "an obstruction of response."[22]

2.2 That responsibility is prior suggests that it is itself some basic aspect of being. Certainly at least, as Levinas maintains, "responsibility is anterior to all the logical deliberation summoned by reasoned decision."[23] It is "an-archic responsibility"—outside of the human construction of order—without any ascertainable origin, or beyond origins, always already we are responsible, always already with and in the face of others.

2.3 We do not control or deploy responsibility at our will (it is one of our "given" capacities—its "inscription in being is made without our choice"),[24] but we can *keep* it and attend to it, as opposed to, say, repressing or escaping or denying it. Thus the poetics of response implies the opposite of Bloom's "anxiety of influence" theory: the other (prior poem) does not invoke "the immense anxieties of indebtedness," but is a *gift* that we recognize in our response.[25]

~

3.1 **Poetic response-ability does not resolve the relationship between self and other**, but rather, reveals this relationship in all its complexities and contradictions.[26] Robert Duncan's mammoth and unpublished *H.D. Book* is, amongst other things, a tract on poetic responsibility. As a reader's as much as a writer's autobiography, it sees *self* in intimate relationship with *other*—that (much as Levinas contends) the self is little more than its responsibilities and its response-abilities. Responsibility, as Duncan unwinds its complexities, points in the two unresolved directions referred to above. On the one hand, responsibility implies a merging of self and other, to the extent that, in *The H.D. Book*, H.D.'s aims become Duncan's aims: "to fight for her cause that I saw as my own."[27] On the other hand, responsibility implies a separation of self and other; it is based upon an "exchange" in which something coming from outside triggers a response from inside: "Certain imperatives in what we know give us responsibilities in what we make up.... To respond *is* to recognize imperatives"—"we are creatures of an exchange."[28]

> LEVINAS: Between the one that I am and the other for whom I answer gapes a bottomless difference, which is also the non-indifference of responsibility.[29]

3.2 Poetry's response thus lies in the intersubjective. Levinas is close to Duncan and Webb on responsibility when he notes that "knowledge of the other also demands sympathy or love, ways of being that are different from impassive contemplation."[30] The sentiment is similar to what has here been referred to as Duncan's erotics of criticism, an approach Levinas locates in the "interhuman" and which "lies in a non-indifference of one to another, in a responsibility of one for another."[31] Heidegger's *Dasein* (being-there) is always already a "being with others,"[32] and Jean Luc Nancy, clearly taking his lead from Heidegger and Levinas, suggests that "if Being is being-with, then it is, in its being-with, the 'with' that constitutes Being."[33] But the distinction between *being-with* others and *being others* is tricky. Levinas notes that "The other individuates me in the responsibility I have for him," and that "The 'me' [moi] only surfaces in its uniqueness in responding for the other"; elsewhere he sums up this problematic by quoting poet Paul Celan: "*Ich bin du, wenn ich ich bin*" ("I am you, when I am I").[34] What might we conclude? That self is not other but that self is so very close to other, in the drawing nearness of listening and response, where the answer of the self is completely dependent upon the question of the other, that they become virtually indistinguishable, parts of a larger process. Webb wondered, "Why do I so often feel that something or someone else is writing the poem?"[35] Because in key ways, "something or someone else" *is,* and the act or writing, as Allen Grossman contends of the art of reading, "begins with this ontological assertion"—"that something not the self is."[36]

3.3 Of Jack Spicer's "After Lorca," Robin Blaser has noted that the temptation is to distinguish "what is Lorca's, what is Jack's," with the result that one "wind[s] up in the joining. The book proposes ... the lack of separation, that one poet is the other"—"They stream into one another."[37] Sometimes my response to another is such a pure fusion with the other—their voice becomes mine, my poem a re-articulation of theirs. At other times I am deeply aware of the jointure between myself and another, between their words and mine. At this point response can begin as "horizon" (here is my limit, beyond is beyond) or "companionship" (I hear the call of another and respond), both of which relate to the issue of *proximity*.[38] Radical intersubjectivity *subtends* both possibilities, and truly something or someone else sometimes does write my poems—one may not always be aware of another's words in one's own but they are there just the same, echoing, echoing—reminding that no *one* can in fact "own" words.

3.4 To return, momentarily, to the question of criticism, one could propose that for poet-scholars like Duncan, academic criticism, based upon concepts of "objectivity" and "disinterested" separation of the selfhood of the critic from the otherness of the creative author, is keyed into one version of responsibility—what Charles Bernstein refers to as the "tone lock" of academic criticism.[39] Duncan as liminal poet-scholar unearths the secreted other of academic disinterest—the desire for fusion and merger with the other, an erotics of criticism. "[T]hese things she loved," Duncan writes of his introduction to contemporary literature, including the work of H.D., by his high school English teacher, "she gave me to love."[40] Another implication of Webb's "proper response to a poem" is that poetry *has* a secondary, critical, or even scholarly function—that a primary responsibility of poetry *is to respond* to other poems. The basis of the argument that the poetic and critical functions are separate and mutually exclusive is found in the "calculations of interest" Susan Howe critiques. The poetics of response is a counterbalance to the claims of critical disinterest.

This critical capacity of poetry is the subject of much of this chapter, but for now we could turn to Webb's "Poetics Against the Angel of Death" as a brief example.

I am sorry to speak of death again
(some say I'll have a long life)
but last night Wordsworth's "Prelude"
suddenly made sense – I mean the measure,
the elevated tone, the attitude
of private Man speaking to public men.
Last night I thought I would not wake again
but now with this June morning I run ragged to elude
The Great Iambic Pentameter
who is the Hound of Heaven in our stress
because I want to die writing Haiku
or, better,
long lines, clean and syllabic as knotted bamboo. Yes![41]

The very title of the poem as "Poetics" suggests its theoretical bent, and its claim that "last night Wordsworth's 'Prelude' / suddenly made sense" places us directly in the midst of a critical pronouncement. The poem's critique of Wordsworth, however, is largely imbedded in the structure and diction of the poem. The "elevated tone" of "private Man speaking to public men" that Webb's speaker has come to understand is undercut by her own poem's beginning with a personal apology, presumably to her own critics ("I am sorry to speak of death again"), and its ending on a note of unrestrained enthusiasm ("Yes!"—also the last word of Joyce's *Ulysses,* the close of Molly Bloom's outpouring of feminine consciousness). Wordsworth's poetics is literally *contained* (enclosed, bracketed, set aside) by Webb's own—just as the ten syllables of the phrase "clean and syllabic as knotted bamboo" are contained in the longer line "long lines, clean and syllabic as knotted bamboo. Yes!"[42] Webb responds to Wordsworth and the response is, in this case at least, a critical response, assessing and critiquing the prior poetic. Distance is in many ways asserted—but it is a distance that incorporates a certain amount of fusion and identification.

4.1 **Response implies proximity.** Plato debarred poets from his ideal republic for just the sort of fusional response we have been discussing here. In *Preface to Plato*, Eric Havelock summarizes Plato's discomfort with the poetics of response: "By his [the poet's] portrayal he can unlock a corresponding fund of sympathetic response in us and evoke a wide range of our emotions. All of which is dangerous, none of it acceptable."[43] The danger Plato sees lies in poetry's tendency towards identification and merger through *mimesis*.[44] Poetry is doubly mimetic (and thus doubly damned), imitating other imitations, rather than the pure and originary Ideas: it imitates the speech of others (as dramatic dialogue/monologue or as lyric address), and it imitates prior poetic models. In either case, the self comes into too-close proximity with otherness, and the distance (disinterest) upon which epistemology relies (a self knowing separate objects) is dissolved.

4.2 Steve McCaffery, in his essay on Levinasian ethics, describes the proximity poetic response relies upon and which separates it from the kind of pure knowing Plato sought: "The poem, understood as one sense of the ontological plot Levinas describes, must convolve both writer and reader in a tangle beyond the potency of an epistemic unwinding."[45] The responsive "tangle" of self and other disallows clear "epistemic unwinding." Poetry, speaking from the heart of being, comes directly from the "with" Nancy describes as "being singular plural"—an experience of being simultaneously one and many, both self and others. This proper speaking of poetry is proximity, what McCaffery calls "the language before language" (209): the *keeping* and *attending* of response; the fact that something other is there to which we must respond, for which we are unavoidably responsible; poetry not as self-expression but as the expression of being's singular plurality. Prior to meaning, poetic response is "the initial relation of a reader to a text," which is "one of proximity, not knowing" (210). The proper response to a poem—not "contributions to knowledge," but a "bounding over the fields of force."[46]

4.3 Such "bounding" is continuing. Proximity breeds response (I sense the other: call: call back—"Little Cousins," Emily Dickinson writes in her last letter, "called back").[47] The proximate text, McCaffery argues, is "a constant producer not of critiques but of new speakings" ("Scandal" 212). The proper response, once again. And such a response is not exactly "dialogue and interaction," McCaffery writes, but "solidarity gained precisely by taciturnity and prelingual receptivity" (212). Poems are neighbours, proximate speakings. Jack Spicer, calling the solitary poem a lonely "one night stand," insisted that "There is really no single poem"—"They cannot live alone anymore than we can."[48]

4.4 As both horizon and companion, the poem (as McCaffery writes of Levinasian ethics) "establishes a connection between neighborly parties, separating writer from reader and equally bringing both into proximity"—"both writer and reader acquire their reality through the text's intervention as a third term" ("Scandal" 212). As both gap and tangle, the proximity of response occupies the intersubjective crossroads. It is the chiasmus Susan Knutson sees as so characteristic of Webb's poetry—the "criss-cross" which "moves the focus from the centre of the self to the essence of the other."[49] The response poem (returning to McCaffery) settles in "the space of the hyphen in the Bubrian I-Thou relation" ("Scandal" 214). It is the "with" of being singular plural.

5.1 **The lyric is *the* genre of response**, and the problem of the relationship of the self and the other is the problem of the lyric. The poem-as-response troubles our usual association of the lyric with the self and self-expression: something more than the self is obviously being given expression in such a poetic.[50] Despite making many contradictory statements regarding this key issue, Grossman, in "Summa Lyrica," calls the lyric "the genre of the 'other mind,'" which may be willfully misread here as "the other's mind."[51] Certainly there is no denying the fact of so-called self-expression, but it is the argument here that what we normally call self-expression is wholly dependent upon the call or question of an otherness no self can enclose or incorporate but which is nevertheless "so near to the heart" it stutters and shudders as though it were us. It may be, as Grossman argues, that the lyric "derives historically from the ancient choral poems and from the chorus of Greek tragedy.[52] The namelessness of the speaker in lyric is a residue of the namelessness of the collective" ("Summa" 271). Thus "the 'I' in lyric is both singular and collective" (242)—singular plural—a speaking subject fallen into "the ground of language as a collective possession" (240). The traditional apostrophic I/you dynamic of the lyric (Webb's realization of Wordsworth's "private Man speaking to public men")—which patrols and reifies the boundaries between self and other—can thus be transformed into an I/we dynamic in which the poet's being is figured in both the call (of the multiple other "I" also belong to as "we") and in the personally locatable response (as in Webb's response to, in the current example, Wordsworth). Pauline Butling argues much the same about Webb's use of pronouns, seeing a "collaborative" matrix in the I/we relation.[53]

5.2 The I/we (self/self-as-and-amongst-others) dynamic implies a politics that will be described here (in the next chapter) as anarchist: maintaining a balance (or at least a paradoxical simultaneity) between individual autonomy and the realization of dependence upon and embeddedness in the commons. It is here, perhaps in paradox and an impossible demand (both/and!), that the lyric and responsive matrix of self and other achieve their closest yet not-yet-resolved resolution. The subjectivity implied in the poetics of response is anarchist. It simultaneously protects and projects both autonomy and collectivity.

5.3 GROSSMAN: The poem is an occasion, across vast reaches of space and time, for the performance of the ceremony of hospitality in which the stranger is greeted and the contracts of sociability are recovenanted. This is because the poem as a common place is like a festive table where persons renew their relation to the substance of being in colloquy. The poem has no other life than the relationships it facilitates ("Summa" 284).

WEBB: "Who is this I investing my poems?…

> *I* am the mask, the voice, the one who begins those lyrical poems, *I wandered lonely as a cloud*….
>
> *Listen*: Do you hear the *I* running away from the man in the green hat? Look again. *I* is off and diving into Fulford Harbour to run with the whales. *I* spout. *I* make whalesong. Passengers on the ferry swarm to starboard to see me disporting myself. *I* / *we* know they are out to get us. Yes, they are mad for education. They'll pen us up at Sealand and we'll die. We don't build big and we can't shoot. *I* commits suicide in the watery commune, the vocal pod. *We* swims on."[54]

~

6.1 **The question of death is at the heart of the question of response and responsibility**, as Heidegger, Levinas, and possibly Webb's noted obsession with death make clear. "Death is the no-response," Levinas writes—the absence of responsive and receptive keeping-open—however, death is also a question—"a pure interrogation mark," the most difficult "uncanny" call-that-is-not-a-call to respond to.[55] In death, the reciprocal call and response of self and other merge into the collective workings of language, that "common place." This is Grossman's contention: that "death is the condition of access to the collective [language], and the death of the individual is the condition of the life of the collective" ("Summa" 241). Levinas too finds it "necessary to think of language as a question" and sees death as the "pure question mark." So we have a constellation of concepts—death, language (as question/call), the collective. Death as the call/question to which response is held (kept) in abeyance, waiting, attending, open—that which inevitably and for the time in which response remains a possibility continues to be a question with an impending and possible response—this is of course a figure of futurity. The death at the heart of response is *of* the future and despite all movements towards merger of the self into other "the other is the future."[56] Seen in this light Webb's "Poetics Against the Angel of Death" is a response that is a keeping of the ability to respond (the poem projects future forms for the poet to try) and thus a keeping of death at bay (as an open and ongoing question: "I am sorry to speak of death again"). A "Poetics Against the Angel of Death" is necessarily and simultaneously a poetics of response. More can be elaborated here about characteristic aspects of Webb's poetics.

6.2 SUICIDE: Webb's famous morbidity ought to be read as another *keeping*, another move "against" death as the no-response. In "To Friends Who Have Also Considered Suicide" one might see Heidegger's insistence that death "must be understood *as a possibility*, it must be cultivated as a possibility, and we must *put up with* it *as a possibility*."[57] The poem's opening line—"It's still a good idea"—places suicide/death *in the future*, as a *possibility*. The poem does not lobby for suicide but for its "contemplation" (its "idea" and "concept"). It is as much a poem about the possible and the future, about response and responsibility, as it is a poem about the possibility and means of taking one's own life.

> But there's no shame
> in this concept of suicide.
> It has concerned our best philosophers
> and inspired some of the most popular
> of our politicians and financiers.
> Some people swim lakes, others climb flagpoles;
> some join monasteries, but we, my friends,
> who have considered suicide take our daily walk

> with death and are not lonely.
> In the end it brings more honesty and care
> than all the democratic parliaments of tricks.[58]

6.3 FAILURE: "[T]here is in this responsibility a failure or undoing"—attributable to the fact that "[r]esponsibility cannot be stated in terms of presence. Responsibility for the other in me is an exigency that increases as one responds to it."[59] Responsibility is the *keeping* of the ability to respond; related to Heidegger's notion of being (by way of which we are our responsibilities), being is similarly future-oriented, always "being-ahead-of-itself," and thus characterized by a "lack of totality."[60] Achievement, wholeness—if these are usually assessed as poetic values (of the lyric at least) then the poetics of response is a poetics of failure. It is rather an open possibility we keep if we would be in close proximity—as close as we can be—to language, the collective, death and the future. To all our others. "Futurity is tact." Touch the hem of the weaving of our world of words. It is not not yet just out of reach.

~

7.1 **Despite the orientation of responsibility *towards* the future and *for* the future, the responses of poets are *to* the past and prior**—most often, to other poets and poems that have gone before.

> BLASER: The extraordinary nature of language is that it attaches to the prior, to the before one, and to the after one [and this] duplicity is especially the business of poetry.[61]

A response poetics does not feel an inhibiting anxiety of influence. Responsibility is influence, in many respects—a poetry built out of poetry, a listening to the ground of language as it echoes in the responses of other poets. Poetry as an echo not an origin. Poetry as language's response to its own call—

language, which is everywhere and everything, trying to find an outside from which it can hear itself and respond to itself. "Every atom belonging to me," Whitman writes in *Leaves of Grass*, "as good belongs to you."[62] No single particle molecule or DNA strand marks me as unique. What makes me me is the particular *combination* of molecules and DNA strands. I am largely repetition, a quotation. I am singular plural. I am proximate. In the poetics of response this condition is embraced.

II. "Eyes" That Are "I"s: Pearl and Mollusk, Eliot and H.D.

The allusion to and quotation and incorporation of the work of other writers and poets—which so marks twentieth century avant-garde poetics (beginning with the modernists)—is the most basic, or at least obvious, form of the poetics of response: something read triggers writing; the poet turns from the page she is reading to the page she is now writing, and continues. The early Webb of *Even Your Right Eye* (1956) and *The Sea Is Also a Garden* (1962) is every bit the late-modernist, crafting poems out of a dense field of allusions and references. Many writers are named directly in the poems (Marvell, Yeats, Gide, Stendahl, Blake, Clare, Wordsworth). More often than not the allusions are, well, more allusive: appropriations and responses that amend as they merge with source material. While Yeats's name appears with perhaps the greatest frequency, and William Carlos Williams stands prominently over *The Sea Is Also a Garden* (as the source of its epigraph and title), the argument made here is that the two poets the early Webb is most productively read against—that is, prior poets to whose work her own can be seen as responding to—are T. S. Eliot and H.D., neither of whom is named or quoted directly.[63]

This is a bit disingenuous. Eliot is nowhere named, but everywhere suggested. And while the trajectory followed here is from the more noticeable Eliot influence to the less explicit H.D. response, it should be admitted at the outset that there is a decided lack of manifest evidence for the impact of H.D.'s work on Webb's.[64] Webb was, however, deeply affected by Robert Duncan, with whom she spent a considerable amount of time in the early 1960s—years during which he was working intensively on *The H.D. Book*—so much news of H.D. must have reached Webb through the oracular Duncan. Ultimately, it is the similarities between Webb and H.D. that are more interesting than any direct influence. Both are Island poets. Both have been seen as "borderline" personalities, ever close to collapse, failure, dissolution of the self. Both were, early in their careers, solitary women amongst turgid male-dominated avant-gardes. Both were critically attacked for just these reasons, and long bore the scars of these attacks. Indeed, the body of criticism that developed around their work, prior to their (re)discovery by feminists, is remarkably similar in tone and intent.

Readers who have continued to insist upon "the somewhat solipsistic character"[65] of Webb's poetry miss her struggle with the lyric self and the relation of this struggle to Webb's response to the other embodied in her poetic inheritance. Even Liza Potvin, in an otherwise convincing feminist reading of the poetry, falls into this trap: "[F]or the very reasons she is rejected by mainstream [male] critics"—her supposed "self-indulgent solipsism and exhibitionism"—"she may be celebrated as a poet of the feminine voice."[66] Here Potvin does not disagree with Webb's early male critics: she simply re-values what they have said. Nevertheless, Potvin is on to something when she notes that "When men write about despair, they are considered great existential poets.... When women write of despair, they are being melodramatic, bitchy, hysterical, vain."[67] This double standard is clarified by reference to a poet such as T. S. Eliot. If Webb had created a J. Alfred Prufrock to speak her poems of despair, there may have been less grounds for accusations of "solipsism" (although those accusations would no doubt have been made just the same, given Potvin's comments above). But her poems' speakers are just as much masks and personae as those of any other poet's (see her prose poem "Performance," for a highly self-conscious commentary on this). A young poet beginning to write in the 1940s and '50s could not but feel the (often oppressive) shadow of Eliot's influence. But Eliot was an important example and guidepost for the early Webb *because he too* was a poet struggling with his responses to his inheritance and the difficult relationship between his lyric self and the otherness he met as a talented individual reader of a tradition.

~

From self-doubting Prufrock who, having "heard the mermaids singing," does "not think that they will sing to me,"[68] to the evocation of Dante's Ugolino near the close of *The Waste Land*—

I have heard the key
Turn in the door once and turn once only
We think of the key, each in his prison
Thinking of the key, each confirms a prison
(*Collected* 79)

—Eliot's poems famously give voice to the isolation of the self from the otherness of the social and historical world surrounding it. The frustrated attempts of the self to know what is outside its prison are often figured in failures of sight and speech:

Rhapsody on a Windy Night

I could see nothing behind that child's eye (27)
....

She winks a feeble eye (27)

The Waste Land

I could not
Speak, and my eyes failed, I was neither
Living nor dead, and I knew nothing (64)
....

(Those are pearls that were his eyes. Look!) (64)
....

(Another hid his eyes behind his wing) (66)

....

"You know nothing? Do you see nothing? Do you remember
Nothing?" (67)

Compare Webb's own pervasive "eyes" in *Even Your Right Eye*:

chokes and enchants my eyes[69]
....
our prismed eyes divide such light
as this world dreams on
and rarely sees
(EYRE 23)
....
and eyes deal only death
(26)
....
the whites of our eyes falling
(33)

* * *

...
Her eyes have failed as life failed
(*Vision* 37)

Webb's "eyes," pervasive in her early poems, are, like Eliot's, in some distress, unable to perform as they should, or revealing only strangeness and alienation. They are failed, falling, flawed in focus. There are other allusions to Eliot in the early Webb—her "corpse is moving in the early spring" from "Sacrament of Spring" (EYRE 21), evoking *The Waste Land*'s "corpse you planted last year in your garden" (*Collected* 65), her "madman captive in a leaf's embrace / the poet wildly shakes his tree" from "Two Versions" (*Vision* 32) with its echoes of Eliot's "Rhapsody" where "Midnight shakes the memory / As a madman shakes a dead geranium" (*Collected* 26), and the use of Eliot's term "objective correlative" in "Standing" (EYRE 45)—however, the eyes have it, and one must read Webb's "eyes" as a response to Eliot's. Thus Webb, following Eliot, connects her "eyes" with "pearls," as in "Marian Scott"—"*pearl* smoking whiteness, and then *eye*" (*Vision* 36, my emphasis)—and more directly, via a slightly modified and inverted quotation in "Beachcomber": "those are eyes that were her pearls."[70] Webb's response raises what is hidden in Eliot's "eyes" to the surface: the "eyes" (with a nod to Louis Zukofsky)[71] are "I"s: "this earthly eye / (it is I)" (*Vision* 26). The tradition of the lyric has of course long located poetic perception in a single detached observer. The eye (I) may be a pearl but the pearl is hidden from view. One consequence is that the eye (I) cannot see (know) itself, although it tries, projecting itself, as Prufrock does, as "formulated, sprawling on a pin" (*Collected* 15), or as a pearl—a perfect and dead outcast from an oyster's shell (recall Prufrock's "sawdust restaurants"), a fashioned and finished product, a bit of psychic grit the ego forms around in order to have done with it.

Take the pearl away from its ground (sea/shell) and it is an image of self-contained perfection, a small cosmos in and of itself, a "still point of the turning world" (*Collected* 191). Replace the eye/I with the perfect pearl and the self "dies" (Webb: "[T]he self is a grave." [EYRE 23]). The lyric's pearl-like self-containment is a ruse; the self cannot be and be self-contained: its being lies in interstices of call and response, self and other, proximity and the "with" of singular plurality. By the time Webb comes under Eliot's influence in the 1950s his work represents both the poem as pearl—the New Critical "well wrought urn" with its "achieved harmony"[72]—and the lyric self as disconnected talking corpse with "pearls" for "eyes," cut off from its social ground and the outside it no longer sees.

~

Here is perhaps the key poem in *Even Your Right Eye*:

… Is Our Distress

This our inheritance
is our distress,
born of the weight of eons

it skeletons our flesh,
bearing us on
we wear it,
though it bares us.

The eye's lid covers
the I aware,
the hand hovers
over, then plunders
emerging despair.

Here is our overture then
where prayers of defeat are sown –
inheritance, bright with death
spangled with bone

(EYRE 55)

Skeleton, eye / I, bone. The pearl as skeletal excretion, glittering calcinate architecture, as the self is here stressed, pressured, plundered, until it too is excreted as beautiful "bright" (but dead) bone. Our (literary) "inheritance," robbing and plundering, leaves us a skeleton. Or, if we are lucky, a pearl. But what inheritance? John Donne, perhaps, his "bracelet of bright hair about the bone" from "The Relic" hovering behind Webb's closing lines. But Eliot would hide in that allusion too—the Eliot who similarly references Donne's lines, in the "Prufrock" poem: "Arms that are braceleted and white and bare / (But in the lamplight, downed with light brown hair!)" (*Collected* 15). And the collocation of "bone" and "eye" is every bit as common in Eliot as in Webb. Eliot (or any other significant influence), Webb is saying, can impoverish, can whittle us down to bone. But bone can itself be "bright," and the poem, though lifeless, may still stand, may still inspire response. Diana Relke may be right when she argues that the early Webb "made poems that enacted contradiction in order to expose the bankruptcy at the heart of the late modernist aesthetic."[73] One does not come away from these poems with a sense of open possibilities and abundant poetic directions for a poetic career just getting off the ground. The difficulty may be that while Webb is being drawn into writing responses to her reading, her reading is presenting her with mostly unresponsive corpses whose cold pearl eyes stare out but do not see her—there is no exchange, no real call to respond to. Only the much commented upon "death" of the lyric.

~

But in every turning away there is a lingering joining. Is Eliot a horizon or a companion for Webb? It seems Eliot is the sort of poet who prompted many of his readers to ask this question.[74] The "message" Webb sends "Prufrock" in "New Year Message for J. Alfred Prufrock" is ambiguous, double, but indicates at least the proximity of Eliot's work, and the fact that it continues to produce "new speakings" that are both kinds of critiques and poetic responses.

> The road is long for us, Mr. Pru-
> frock, in 1952.
> Figuring yourself all
> smartened up, unshocked, since O so
> long ago unfrocked of all mysteries,
> merriment and imaginary mermaids—
> to soothe you I will comb your hair
> and part what is left to care—
> and would it be, perhaps, unkind
> if one should find your bright
> politics now quartered in the socio-
> sexual structure of the corner bank?
> But they are there, I fear, and you
> now take your tea aware with lemon
> and run to shun the measurements
> of coffee. Oh yes, oh yes,
> J. Alfred P., I can sense, indeed
> foresee that here in this year
> of yellowing words you will walk
> strict with conservative love
> telling birds not to bother you
> and the stars to settle their own affairs.[75]

While the poem lightly mocks Eliot's persona, particularly in terms of his sexual repression—enacting a metaphoric "unfrocking"—it nevertheless includes its speaker in Prufrock's predicament ("The road is long for *us*"), and ultimately expresses a similar sense of belatedness as Eliot's poem ("this year / of yellowing words").

~

The turn away from Eliot is never unequivocal, never final. But we do begin to see a shift in *The Sea Is Also a Garden* (1962). The sort of diminishing influence which "skeletons our flesh" (or results in "yellowing words") becomes "the bone-blooming skeleton" of an enabling sense of influence—a fecund source which could prompt productive response. The pearl of the poem as inherited object, the pearl of the self become object and objective, is not an end in itself, not complete, final, dead. Now that "bright" "bone" "blooms" again, revealing itself part of a responsive process, not a plundered product. In the shift from *Even Your Right Eye* to *The Sea Is Also a Garden*, the pearl as by-product of oceanic life is replaced by the sorts of sea-creatures that themselves produce pearls.

We see the turning of the Eliot influence to use in the reversed quotation from "Beachcomber": "those are eyes that were her pearls."[76] This follows the "beach-cleaner" who "combs the left-overs / of burnt-up yesterday's savage sunbathers"—another obvious reference to the fact of literary influence (as well as another embedding of echoes of Eliot's "Prufrock"—his spat-out "butt-ends" of days and the mermaids "combing" the waves). But now the pearls that had replaced eyes are themselves replaced by eyes once more, and the poet's local habitat is visually embraced:

> but the sea and mountains casually show
> Vancouver has a fine enough view
> to challenge the world in any part.

Eliot is given his firmest reprimand and dismissal when, in the poem "Flux," Webb writes:

Who would call me to still centers
needs a lesson in desire.
I am fire's ephemeral
boast on Heraclitean air.[77]

Despite this poem's vestigial formality (the quatrains etc.), the New Critical perfection of "still centers" is largely given up for elemental flux and the first stirrings of a truly open poetics. The shift so indicated might be figured as the poetics of William Carlos Williams (standing as he is behind the title of Webb's second book) coming to replace that of T. S. Eliot. However, we will now turn to the significance of H.D.'s poetry and poetics as Webb looks for a "corrective" to the still and centered Eliotic "pearl." As already noted, there are no direct allusions to H.D.'s poetry in Webb's work. She must have read her, briefly if not thoroughly, but the leavings of this reading are not necessarily obvious. Perhaps this is to exercise what Julianna Spahr has called an "aesthetics of joining" by creating "a bridge that joins two things together,"[78] but the poetry of Phyllis Webb and H.D. cries out for such a bridge, and even leaves the shadow of a foundation one can build upon. Both poets gave expression to lesbian desire. Both endured the romantic thralldom of male mentors. Both chose a form of exile and abdication. We can bring them into proximity; despite the distance of horizons, they can be read as unconscious companions.

~

The title of H.D.'s 1916 *Sea Garden* is a ghost in Webb's (and Williams's) *The Sea Is Also a Garden.* A Spectre haunting. A poetry within the poetry.

Consider, first, in *Even Your Right Eye*, the poem "Sprouts the Bitter Grain":

Hot, the wind threatens my trees with weather
. . . .

And Oh, I call

Oh, to the gods of the temperate climes,
Praise me, destroy these criminal branches,
Bring me – soft – the weather of meadows.
(EYRE 19)

And H.D.'s "Sheltered Garden":

I want wind to break,
scatter these pink-stalks,
snap off their spiced heads,
fling them about with dead leaves
. . . .
O to blot out this garden
to forget, to find a new beauty
in some terrible
wind-tortured place[79]

Consider, too, "Propositions," the second poem in Webb's *The Sea Is Also a Garden*:

I could divide a leaf
And give you half
(*Vision* 44)

And H.D.'s "Garden":

If I could break you
I could break a tree.

If I could stir
I could break a tree –
I could break you.
(HD 24–25)

I could divide a leaf, I could break a tree. When one poet's work arrives at the same place as another's, we can at least claim the significance of a confluence, if not an outright influence. "Breaking" and "Making," Webb titles two poems early in *The Sea*

Is Also a Garden: "Give us wholeness, for we are broken" (*Vision* 46). The apostrophic plea to unnamed powers is typical of both poets. They both appropriate a choral "we," sometimes reduced to an equally plural and public "I." They both address an outside "you" who is both a threat and a guardian, a horizon and a companion. They are both women, both poets, and both were critically attacked for being so, for, as it was seen, exposing the "unseemly" frailties and wounds and anxieties and passivity of their gendered positions.[80] The most significant connection, however, is in their choice of images for an enabling vision for female creation. They both turned to the sea.

~

Webb's poem "Bomb Shelter" reveals a number of convergences with H.D.'s long poem *Trilogy*. Webb might be seen to speak for both poets when she claims that

> Nakedness is our shelter.
> Bones are only temporal
> Yes, there will be splinters.
> Yes, there will be cancers
> To split this partial temple.[81]

Trilogy also opens with the image of the "split" "temple"—

> there, as here, ruin opens
> the tomb, the temple; enter,
> there as here, there are no doors:
>
> the shrine lies open to the sky.
> (HD 509)

—and goes on to reveal the brutal results of an attack which "skeletons the flesh" down to the nakedness of bone:

the bone-frame was made for
no such shock knit within terror,
yet the skeleton stood up to it:

the flesh? it was melted away,
the heart burnt out, dead ember,
tendons, muscles shattered, outer husk dismembered,

yet the frame held.

(510–11)

Webb's "Bomb Shelter" similarly offers a strange survival:

But, like Saint Sebastian,
in love with our destruction,
at least await deliverance
from a familiar essence.
Flesh, sheltering all within,
bodied forth the architect,
nor will he go till he deploys
skin's widowed, gross philosophies.

However, her poem envisions no hard "frame" yet—it is the "flesh" that is "sheltering all within," the flesh which seems to stand without bone and even outlive bone ("Bones are only temporal"). Yet elsewhere in *The Sea Is Also a Garden* "the bone-blooming skeleton" is invoked, the calcinate "coral orchard" of submarine life (*Vision* 43). In "Bomb Shelter," too, the speaker imagines a "swim dark in phosphorous seas," but the need for some sort of bony "frame" returns in "A Tall Tale":

"Under the waters, under the waters wise,
all loving flesh will quickly meet demise,
the cave, the shadow cave is nowhere wholly safe
and even the oddest couple can scarcely find relief:
appear then to submit to this tide and timing sea,
but secrete a skilful shell and stone and perfect be."

(*Vision* 53)

The fact of skeletal survival and fleshly dangers, the reduction to bone and the production of exoskeletal architectures (recall both poets' "temples"), the turn to the (archetypally feminine) sea for a sheltering analogue—all this is in *Trilogy* too:

> the shell-fish:
> oyster, clam, mollusc
>
> is master-mason planning
> the stone marvel:
>
> yet that flabby, amorphous hermit
> within, like the planet
>
> senses the finite,
> it limits its orbit
>
> of being, its house,
> temple, fane, shrine
> ....
>
> be indigestible, hard, ungiving.
>
> so that, living within,
> you beget, self-out-of-self,
>
> selfless,
> that pearl-of-great-price.
>
> (HD 513–14)

A skilful shellfish. A master mason. We can only wander down the paths between poems and with our pearl eyes enact joinings that are pre-prepared. The shift from produced pearl to producing shellfish—from product to process, the most convincing distinction between a New Critical modernism and a poststructural postmodernism—is an enabling and empowering move for a female poet who herself has typically been figured not as poet-producer but as poem-object. Poem and poetic (lyric) self are fashioned not as finished goods to be displayed but as processes "living within" (and living in the "with"), a bi-valvular life where what is taken in from outside the shell may produce the pearl of a self-out-of-self worked and hidden from sight within. Webb's movement from exposed skeleton to withholding exoskeleton (shellfish) is paradigmatic of her development of the poetics of response. In this regard the shell's enclosing and withholding should not be read as a shutting out of the other and outside; rather, it is the creation of a space for the outward to grow inward. The exposed/finished/dead Eliotic pearl of "spangled" bone gives way to H.D.'s mollusc which "unlocks the portals / at stated intervals" and which "opens to the tide-flow" (HD 513), taking in, and *keeping*, the calls to which it is the (ongoing) response.

This ongoingness can be further illustrated by turning to Webb's next collection, *Naked Poems* (1965). Here it is clear Eliot has not completely disappeared as a poet to whom she is responding. His call is *kept* and Webb *continues* the dialogue. John Hulcoop has compared Webb's "yellow chrysanthemums" and "stillness / in jade" (*Vision* 83) to Eliot's "stillness, as a Chinese jar" (*Collected* 194), and Liza Potvin refers to Eliot as one of the poets whom the various fragments of the *Naked Poems* "address."[82] H.D. is possibly here again too, her poem "The Gift," which begins

> Instead of pearls—a wrought clasp—
> a bracelet—will you accept this?
>
> (HD 15)

echoing in Webb's

> *you brought me clarity*
>
> *Gift after gift*
> *I wear*
>
> *Poems naked*
>
> *in the sunlight*
> *on the floor*
>
> (*Vision* 79)

Pearls or poems, or "pearl poems" threaded on her "narrative line,"[83] it is the *giving* and the *linking*—an aesthetics of joining—

that is significant for both poets. Eliot and H.D. are no longer contending forces or even counter-weights by the time Webb writes *Naked Poems.* They are now both continuing active responsive possibilities echoing in the sea-shells of Webb's poems. And despite Hulcoop's invocation of the "pearl poem," Webb's small naked lyrics are perhaps better seen as shells "listening for / the turn of the tide" (*Vision* 88). Or at least as "bone blooming" star fish—the cryptic epigraph hanging over the *Naked Poems (star fish / fish star)* which may itself have some source both in Eliot's "starfish" from "The Four Quartets" and H.D.'s *Trilogy* once again:

> The river is within us, the sea is all about us;
> The sea is the land's edge also, the granite
> Into which it reaches, the beaches where it tosses
> Its hints of earlier and other creation:
> The starfish, the horseshoe crab, the whale's backbone;
> The pools where it offers to our curiosity
> The more delicate algae and the sea anemone.
> It tosses up our losses, the torn seine,
> The shattered lobsterpot, the broken oar
> And the gear of foreign dead men. The sea has many voices,
> Many gods and many voices.
>
> (*Collected* 205–06)

> Now polish the crucible
> and in the bowl distill
>
> a word most bitter, *marah*,
> a word bitterer still, *mar*,
>
> sea, brine, breaker, seducer,
> giver of life, giver of tears;
>
> now polish the crucible
> and set the jet of flame
>
> under, till *marah-mar*
> are melted, fuse and join

and change and alter,
mer, mere, mère, mater, Maia, Mary,

Star of the Sea,
Mother.

(HD 552)

Whoever would see Webb as a solipsistic poet misses the "many voices" that echo within her resonating and responsive poems, misses the "fusing" and "joining" of her responsive poetics. Misses the clearest fact, of these early poems especially, that this is a poet at grips with *Poetry* more than struggling with *her self*, a beachcomber gathering the gear of dead men to see what a woman now might wear—a poet creating a self-out-of-self, which is a self *outside* the self, something, as Nancy writes, "the very law of which is 'relation.'"[84]

~

III. Horizons and Companions

When Webb writes a poem that is in its entirety a meeting with and response to another poet or poem then something different than, more than and more complex than mere allusion or citation is at work. Webb *alludes* to Eliot repeatedly, but—other than the uncollected "New Year Message for J. Alfred Prufrock"—no single poem can be summed up as—and, perhaps more importantly, no poem *announces itself as*, in its *address*—a response-to-Eliot poem. But such poems, addressed to other named poets, abound in Webb's canon. Even she refers to these as simply "poems that were written in response to other poets."[85] Earlier such poems were discussed as forms of poetic-criticism: poems that perform critical functions, poems that we should be reading in a sense as part of the body of criticism on the poet in question.[86] Several more of these will be read here, as we track how they hover somewhere between "plunder and awe," to borrow Webb's own dialectic for these poems. They are not only critical pieces; they also have a *tributary* function.

A *tributary* poem is a poem which *flows out of (and perhaps even back into) another source or feeder poem.* It is also, simultaneously, a poem that *pays tribute* to a previous poem.

Such poems are so prevalent in Webb's canon, from beginning to end, that they should be thought of as the very framework of her output: "Marvell's Garden," "Two Pears: A Still Life," "Poems of Dublin," "Poetics Against the Angel of Death," the "Poems of Failure" and the "Portraits" from *Wilson's Bowl*, "Lines from Gwen. Lines for Ben," the entirety of *Water and Light*, "Gwendolyn MacEwen," and "Bronwen's Earings" in *Hanging Fire.*

~

This can be taken one step further. Webb's poems "written in response to other poets" ought to be read as analogous to Robin Blaser's notion of "Great Companions"—the company and "Image-Nation" of the "imagination's companions." Despite the presence of a certain degree of angst and even critical rejection, particularly in her early response poems, these critical poems are always as well tributary poems, naming masters and guides and the poets and poems Webb's own work has grown in communion with. In their apostrophes, Webb's poems, like Blaser's, declare (both to the reader and the other poet addressed or invoked), "I desire / you as companion of poems."[87] The poet addressed/invoked in a poem of this sort brings forth both contradictory possibilities of "plunder and awe," for the other poet is one of

> those opposites
> who are companions
> and also horizons in one another's
> eyes
>
> (*Forest* 113)

"Eyes" that are "I"s. Companions and limits. Proximity and continuation. Webb herself has written at length on Blaser, and there is obviously much that is shared by the two poets. In Blaser's citations of other authors Webb sees a "mutual exchange" of "gifts, of energies."[88] In "Image-Nations 5 (erasure," Blaser positions the other in complex relation to the self: a "companion," but also a "horizon." There is "a translation of oneself into the Other" where one

is
 so
  delicately
   perched among words
(*Forest* 114)

but that other remains an outside *inside*:

the Belovéd is the murmur
inside the work
at the edge
 of the words
(117)

The other addressed is an outside *inside* the poem, a translation of self into other that sits perched amongst the words of the responding poem. The responding poet, anticipating both plunder and awe, performs both plunder and awe. The poet finds both horizon (here is my limit) and companions (my words exist in intimate relationship with these other words / words of another).

~

For Robert Duncan

"In myself I am desolate"
but the other self, "the poet self"

threads a melodic theme out of griefs
and snows, goes to wisdom and gladness.
We listened intently. We were a room.
We were a silence waiting for the high
absolute note of a fixed star to enter
our ears. It entered. We went forward
together in that sadness that wills us.

In myself I know we were together
knew we were going.

In the narrow chamber separating the self
from the self we listen alone to a bell
echoing in virtue, applauding itself
in absolute time. By virtue
of this bell the selves keep distant
respect each for the other, know
their longing for music.[89]

It is an unpublished poem—a response to a poet who is a key companion of Webb's poetics. Separate and yet together, two responsive chords, Duncan and Webb, the self and the other self (the other—outside—*inside*), "distant respect" (Duncan in Berkeley and Webb in Toronto)[90] and the proximity of the "bell" both poets "listen alone" to in the room they form by their poetic jointures. This poem's "I" is thoroughly contained (in the opening quotation marks and the short middle stanza), the rest of the poem given over to the plural—a "crowd of one who writes," as Duncan describes his writerly self in the preface to his book *Letters.*[91] This crowd includes more than Webb and Duncan (two hardly make a crowd): there may be echoes of Rilke here too—the silence into which "a tree" ascends "in the air" of the first of the "Sonnets to Orpheus," compressed together with the "waiting" "star" that gives way to the violin yielding "to your hearing" in the first of the "Duino Elegies."[92] "We were a room"—a poetic architecture, a passage between, joining in response.

Of Webb's response poems, "Marvell's Garden" and "Rilke" have probably received the most critical attention. We will try to move fairly quickly here. Brenda Carr, Pauline Butling, and Diana Relke are all correct in locating Webb's "male mentor" poems in their gendered dynamics, the "contestatory practice whereby Webb resists the prescriptions of masculinist culture."[93] But they miss something else in focusing on this side of what Webb herself calls a "contradiction." Marvell is resisted but he is also embraced. There is as much plunder as awe at work. A declaration of both horizon and companionship:

> Marvell's garden, that place of solitude,
> is not where I'd choose to live
> yet is the fixed sundial
> that turns me round
> unwillingly
> in a hot glade
> as closer, closer I come to contradiction,
> to the shade green within the green shade
> (*Vision* 33)

Much of this first stanza obviously declares horizon. And it leads, in the next two stanzas, into a clear critique of Marvell's notions of "solitude" and idealism ("he *did* care more for the form / of things than for the thing itself"). However, as the poem unfolds the speaker's attitude to Marvell becomes more ambiguous:

> But then I saw his luminous plumèd Wings
> prepared for flight,
> and then I heard him singing glory
> in a green tree,
> and then I caught the vest he'd laid aside
> all blest with fire.
> (34)

This is unquestionably an expression of awe. As Webb writes in her introduction to a reading of her response poems, Marvell "spoke to me. I listened. And I remembered."[94] He is one of the reasons she "caught" up and donned the poet's "vest." But the contradiction does not resolve and Webb's critics are right to emphasize the speaker's distress over the model of isolation—and the exclusion of women from the poetic preserve—that Marvell holds up as an ideal in his poem. Webb's poem offers a reverse–mirror image of Marvell's: her "shade green within the green shade" reflecting and refracting his "green thought in a green shade."[95] *His garden* becomes *my walls*—Webb becomes Marvell, but in doing so Marvell becomes a twentieth century woman anxious about the exclusions of patriarchy and the idealism which separates ideas from things and the walled self from the world without. There is a "mutual exchange," a difficult and ultimately still contradictory attempt to "tear together this world and his" (*Vision* 33).[96] Marvell is Webb's companion, but he is also a horizon—a limit she would argue beyond. Like Eliot, Marvell is too much the poet of the "still point," the self-enclosed pearl cut off from the cycles of exchange.

~

In "Rilke," the German poet is presented in similar fashion—as limit *and* companion:

> Rilke, I speak your name I throw it away
> with your angels, your angels, your statues
> and virgins and a horse in a field held
> at the hoof by wood. I cannot take so much
> tenderness, tenderness, snow falling like lace
> over your eyes year after year as the poems
> receded, roses, the roses, sinking in snow
> in the distant mountains.[97]

This poem enacts a number of contradictions. The opening lines "throw" away Rilke's name and his "angels," seemingly drawing a horizon and making a poetic declaration of independence. Presumably, these angels are those from the opening lines of Rilke's

"Duino Elegies": "Who, if I cried out, would hear me among the angels' / hierarchies?"[98] But in throwing them away, Webb re-enacts Rilke's apostrophe, perhaps even answering his question: "Who … would hear me … ?" Phyllis Webb, that's who, responding rejecting and reconfiguring.

The "throwing" of Rilke's name also recalls the advice of the speaker of the first Elegy, who commands "Fling the emptiness out of your arms / into the spaces we breathe." What happens when we throw a poet's name to the wind? The birds, in Rilke's poem, "will feel the expanded air with more passionate flying." The poet, in poetry's "vision tree," is such a bird, perched in another's words.

In the closing lines of Webb's "Rilke," the speaker finds herself contained in much the same way as the speaker in "Marvell's Garden" does:

> This page is a shadowed hall in Duino Castle.
> Echoes. The echoes.
> I don't know why I'm here.

Webb's speaker is trapped once again, but now is even less certain about the enclosure a prior poem has proffered. However, there may be another echo once again—this time of the last line of one of Rilke's great poems—in Webb's "I don't know why I'm here." This would be the German poet's "Archaic Torso of Apollo," which ends with the sudden and unexpected non sequitur "You must change your life."[99] Webb's "Rilke" has this same suddenness of closure, a turn away from the rest of the poem, a turn toward the observing self, which has to this point hidden behind the pearl-white object of focus, or had its "eyes" (I's) covered with "snow." If this allusion is hovering here then one of those "statues" thrown away at the beginning of Webb's poem comes back at its end. Horizon is also companion. The poem which attempts to escape the gravity of its precursor poem is inevitably drawn back into its orbit. We are a room. Listening. Together.

There are other responses to Rilke. His possible presence in the poem "For Robert Duncan" has already been noted. He also shadows "The Days of the Unicorns," which can be seen as a response to another of Rilke's "Sonnets to Orpheus." In Rilke's sonnet, the unicorn—"the animal that never was," but which is "nourished" by "the mere possibility of being"—occupies a "space hollowed out" by "love."[100] A "room" that "we" are, a garden for "meeting," the unicorn's space is in the aesthetics of joining, the "with" of poetic response where one writer in affection and enthusiasm reads another. Rilke's unicorn stalks out of his poem and into Webb's—but here we step outside of rooms (Webb's "cabin" of the self) into a sort of commons (outside "the tensions of private property") where poets borrow freely from each other imaginative possibilities of "the common good."

~

In both "Marvell's Garden" and "Rilke" there is, following Blaser once again, a "greater language" or commons both poets' words are "fragments" of, a "continuous / *carmen*"—an eternal song or garden[101] where poets dead and alive still meet and walk together, forgetting, erasing, recollecting, and deconstructing each other. This preserve can reveal itself as a great colloquy, an imagined community for the perpetual exiles that poets so often feel themselves to be. But it can also reveal itself as a male preserve, in which the gendered biases of language rise to the surface, and the poet is seen as a man, the woman as a muse.

> SUSAN HOWE: How do I, choosing messages from the code of others in order to participate in the universal theme of Language, pull SHE from all the myriad symbols and sightings of HE.[102]

Webb's response poems to her female contemporaries—Atwood, MacEwen, Bronwen Wallace—tend to take the form of poetic correspondences addressing more the poet than the poetry. The exception, perhaps, is "Letters to Margaret Atwood," which, while addressing Atwood directly as a friend, does engage critically with some of Atwood's writing and ideas. Even more importantly, the response to Atwood prompts some thoughts on Webb's own poetics:

> After survival, what? The sedition in my own hand, will it be written down legibly, will I sign it and hand it over for someone else to fulfill? Or will I open like a Venus fly-trap to catch fat spies from the enemy lines and feed myself forever on them on them on them? They really aren't worth my exotic trouble but I can't eat money and I want for once to be useful.[103]

What is so interesting here is the continuing presence of the contradictory impulses of plunder and awe, despoilment and gift. Will my mother eat me or feed me? Will I feed or devour my young? How can we survive the cannibalism of poetic creation, where poems must feed on other poems, Venus fly-traps catching fat poet flies? And after survival, what? Satisfactory failures. Poems breaking and making. But gender makes and marks a difference. Is the vision of poetry as an agonic struggle between "strong" poets a masculine projection? Are women poets on the margin of literary history forced to fight each other over scraps? Webb, here, ultimately wants "to be useful," but in poetry "useful" can mean being devoured by another. In the foreword to *Wilson's Bowl* Webb writes that, to this point in her career, she has "been denied access to inspiration from the female figures of my intellectual life" by "the domination of a male power culture." The woman poet is a horizon Webb wants to make a companion, but still moves under ambiguous pressures and clouds of "an evil weather." There are still, even after 1980, few women in Webb's canon of responses. Yet she does attempt to escape the "male power culture" through other means.

~

Webb's most extensive, fully articulated response to another poet is that contained in *Water and Light* (1984)—a response to the Urdu poet Ghalib (1797–1869), his English-Canadian adaptor, John Thompson, and the ghazal form both precursors worked in. In this complex, multi-layered response, Ghalib stands as a shell containing the echoes not only of John Thompson, but of his various translators, as well as other poets to whom Webb has responded, here and elsewhere in her work—a chamber of echoes right down to the associative structure Webb employs to move from stanza to stanza, image to image, poem to poem throughout the long sequence. A comprehensive reading of all the subtle shifts, tags, allusions, appropriations, and sub-textual connections within *Water and Light* is beyond the scope of the present discussion; what we can attempt is to pick a path through its intricacies, eyeing its responsive chords. In so doing we will sidestep what is arguably the best-known section of the book—the sequence "I Daniel," which has already received solid critical attention.[104] We will "learn by going where [we] have to go"—to borrow a phrase from Theodore Roethke, borrowed again by John Thompson. We will trace the reverberations of responses within responses, which is the very fabric of this, Webb's most complexly allusive work.

~

The ghazal (and it is significant that, in this case, the response is more *to a poetics* than to any single poet—a broadening of response towards language itself) is described by John Thompson as follows:

> The ghazal proceeds by couplets which (and here, perhaps, is the great interest in the form for Western writers) have no necessary logical, progressive, narrative, thematic (or whatever) connection. The ghazal is immediately distinguishable from the classical, architectural, rhetorically and logically shaped English sonnet.
>
> The link between couplets (five to a poem) is a matter of tone, nuance: the poem has no palpable intention upon us. It breaks, has to be listened to as a song: its order is clandestine.[105]

Webb first learned of the ancient Persian form through Thompson's imitations in *Stilt Jack* (1978), and it is clear that the ghazal would have attracted her for similar reasons: "the freedom it allows—the escape, even, from brief lyric 'unity.'" The structure of the ghazal is paratactic, the stanzas treated as discrete units, their appearance together in the same poem dependent upon no systematic syntax or semantics, no system of subordination. Webb is closest to the true ghazal form in the initial poems in the sequence:

> Ten white blooms on the sundeck.
> The bees have almost all left. It's September.
>
> The women writers, their heads bent under the light,
> work late at their kitchen tables.
>
> Winter breathes in the wings of the last hummingbird.
> I have lost my passion. I am Ms. Prufrock.
>
> So. So. So. Ah – to have a name like *Wah*
> when the deep purple falls.
>
> And you have sent me a card
> with a white peacock spreading its tail.[106]

There are no necessary connections between the stanzas. Rather, the present absence of connection is what we most notice—the breach, gap, silence—the outside of the poem. But there are some hints. The mention of Eliot's "Prufrock" (this example has been chosen as a further instance of this ongoing response—another response to Eliot within the response to Thompson/Ghalib) in the third stanza may lead, by association, to the following stanza's "So. So. So," if we choose to hear behind this the "O O O O" stutter of *The Waste Land*'s "Shakespeherian Rag" (*Collected* 67). If that connection is not tenable, then surely there is a tidy juxtaposition between Eliot in the third stanza and Fred Wah in the fourth: two poets, one modern the other postmodern, one distant/dead/already a canonical "classic," the other local, immediate, alive—a contemporary. A further connection between the stanzas may be that the "you" of the fifth and final stanza is Wah, a friend as likely as any other to have sent a postcard. Certainly the syntax—the final sentence beginning with "And"—suggests a continuity of sorts with the subject of the previous stanza.

The point is that, no matter how close Webb's response is to the ghazal of Ghalib, her poems are "anti-ghazals" which increasingly defy "some of the traditional rules, constraints, and pleasures laid down so long ago."[107] Webb is "simultaneously loving and subversive," "simultaneously affirming and denying the connection."[108] So the ghazal is, once again, both horizon and companion, both an other wholly other and an other whose merger is sought. Here is an example of how the form begins to evolve in Webb's hands:

> My soul, my soul, who said that?
> as the rain stumbles over my mental horizon
>
> horizon which wavers, creates the mirage
> of a café in Milano where
>
> Mary, he says, what shall we do tonight?
>
> Tonight, tonight, love, what shall we do tonight?
> The mirage settles into rain falling
>
> into the harbour and onto the day I own
> feeding the heat of dry September
>
> September and the cats restless, hungry
> in view of winter, in view of cold
>
> cold as the curse of mere matter, *Mére*
> matter, the subject family, the repeated
>
> word ready to pounce out of thunder
> out of the rain-forest where leap the wild, bereft deer.
> (*Water* 46)

The connections between stanzas are very different here, far less subterranean. They are formed by refrains, by repetitions of key words (horizon horizon / tonight tonight / September September / cold cold—"the repeated / word ready to pounce"). But there are other weavings with previous poems: "September," the "rain," "Mary," "the harbour," "the cats" all take us elsewhere in the collection: they are refrains between poems, responsive chords plucked across the pages. Eliot, too, is here in response once again, the repeated "what shall we do tonight" recalling *The Waste Land*'s "'What shall I do now? What shall I do?'" (*Collected* 67), and of course there is the "thunder" speaking and bringing rain. Returning to the poem's internal connections, the "Mary" of the third stanza (breaking the couplet form with its singularity) connects to the "*Méré*" (mother) "matter" (*mater*) of the seventh.[109] This also recalls—to return to an earlier argument—H.D.'s similar word play in *Trilogy*:

> mer, mère, mere, mater, Maia, Mary,
>
> Star of the Sea,
> Mother.
>
> (HD 552)

These examples have been chosen in part because of the echoings within echoings they contain. Webb follows Thompson into Ghalib and finds Eliot and H.D. once again. A poem of response becomes responsive on ever-increasing levels, to ever-increasing depths, breaking down the *disconnective* structure of the ghazal with which the original response began, revealing voice to be voices, the lyric self to be others, being to be singular plural.

The pattern of responses within responses, of playing upon multiple chords, is seen again in the second section in *Water and Light*, entitled "The Birds." Here is the mention of "Mary," recurring later in the text—a ghazal dedicated to poet Mary Melfi. The response to Ghalib—his frequent birds and mirrors—reveals a fold within a fold, a response to Melfi (again, juxtaposing past and present, "classic" and contemporary), whose poem also contains birds and mirrors:

> If a horde of flamingos
> were to walk out of my mirror
> while I was combing my hair

I'd stop everything.
I'd be content to watch their show

but what's there in the mirror,
that spy, is just another container
which I throw about from room to room.
I aim it perfectly in front of the television set
with or without its wrappers.

I hate to see that container,
that colossal can,
combing its hair,
copper wire,
but I'd never hate to see flamingos.
Whose fault is that?[110]

Webb's ghazal begins with a line taken directly from Melfi's poem:

I'd never hate to see flamingos
walking out of the mango patch.

What should I tell her who can see
in the mirror the chance of a bird

standing on one pink leg?

(*Water* 27)

For good measure, here are two stanzas from Ghalib's poem, in William Hunt's translation (the first stanza of which forms the epigraph to Webb's section "The Birds"):

No one denied you your memory of wings:
those clouds, although faces, are not your own.

I stay in, but cannot avoid the talk about love;
captured in the broken mirror, I find the rainstorm.[111]

All three poems use similar imagery, all three evoke the surreal shifts of direction common to dreams. Webb uses the typical I/you apostrophe of the ghazal to respond to Melfi, assuring her that she is, after all, "the Queen holding a mummified cat" (*Water* 27)—a reference to the title of Melfi's book. If we are to read Webb's response to Ghalib in a similar vein to her other responses to "male mentors," then her moves in *Water and Light* suggest a different sort of "corrective." For starters, as already noted, the response here is more to the form and its poetics than to any single practitioner. Ghalib comes filtered to Webb through Thompson and the translations of the likes of Adrienne Rich. What is more, Webb, following the ghazal's fractured and associative formula, is able to fold responses to other poets—many of them women—within the structure offered her by male predecessors (Ghalib/Thompson). Indeed, the ghazal may be, as Susan Glickman argues, an "androgynous" form, combining long, "masculine" lines with "feminine" gaps.[112] Webb uses the ghazal, Glickman suggests, "to unite her public and private voices, her extroverted 'male' concerns and her shadowy 'female' ones." Instead of the Wordsworthian "private Man speaking to public men" of an earlier response poem, Webb here combines the two into the feminist-inspired notion that the private is public. This is figured overtly, in the pop cultural reference of the opening ghazal of "The Birds," in which "Yoko Ono was seen in the Empress Hotel today. / She can never be seen for herself alone again" (*Water* 25), as well as in the more covert situation of the Melfi poem, where Webb reaches through Ghalib and his translator Hunt to touch and unite with a contemporary woman's very private moment of vision and distress—her capture within the "container" self, reflected in its lyric mirror.

However multiple the response is in *Water and Light*, Thompson and Ghalib do frame its echoing chamber. Thompson is evoked, muse-like, in the opening ghazal—"(calling stone-dead John Thompson)" (*Water* 9)—and Ghalib is similarly addressed in the last: "Ah Ghalib, you are almost asleep" (61). On the book's contents page, the title of each sequence is appended with an epigraph from *Ghazals of Ghalib*, thereby creating a ghazal-collage no more or less disjunctive than any of Ghalib's own. While there is a complex and subtle interplay between epigraph and sequence, we will now to turn to the responsive exchanges between Webb's work and another of Hunt's translations of Ghalib:

> We lean in the full moon as would a circle of gods
> passing a window. Together our voices rise in song.
>
> To those below, our lamp is mistaken for a star.
> But the true stars lie at the bottom of the bowl.
>
> Her voice spirals to me from the other side of moons.
> Her expression tells me of secret springs, jewels, ice.
>
> How long will I stand alone against the broken walls?
> Once I watched how a star fell behind her blue gown.
>
> There is no message that will satisfy the mystery I sense.
> Even secret letters from my home arrive here torn open.[113]

The resonances here work in a number of directions. Elements from this poem appear scattered throughout the opening sequence, "Sunday Water." The "sun" and "wall" in one poem (*Water* 14), and in another, the "moon," "star," and the hint of the alchemical formula *as above, so below* from Ghalib/Hunt's second stanza in Webb's "And down here, trappings of 'as above'" (18). More interesting still, this alchemical image—and alchemy, perhaps, as symbolic transformation, would be a better image for the responsive changes Webb is working on her source materials—also evokes the image of the bowl from "Wilson's Bowl" where the "Moon floats," and which "cups a sun."[114] So we might imagine Webb finding this image in Ghalib, seeing her own "bowl" reflected in it, and responding to it periodically, throughout her book. But also of interest is what from an a-chronological perspective may be characterized as *Ghalib's response to Webb.* Response is multi-directional and implies a fairly fluid, non-linear conception of time as a spatialized "with"—like the ghazal, its "order is clandestine." In the poetics of response the past is still present and may itself still respond to what has come after it. This is in part because in response authority passes from authors to readers, and reveals authors as readers—so that important connections are made, as it were, after the fact. In the fluidities of reading, nothing is ever finished, per se.

> EZRA POUND: All ages are contemporaneous.
>
> T. S. ELIOT: [T]he past should be altered by the present as much as the present is directed by the past.
>
> ELIZABETH GROSZ: [T]he inherent capacity for time to link, in extraordinarily complex ways, the past and present to a future that is uncontained by them and has the capacity to rewrite and transform them.[115]

We have not yet exhausted Hunt's version cited above, or Webb's responses to it. The speaker(s) *lean* out a "window" in the first stanza. Near the end of *Water and Light*, there is one poem that, unlike any others, has a title separate from its sequence title: "Leaning." Here again we have a speaker "leaning" out of a window. In Webb's poem it is the Leaning Tower of Pisa, the spiral staircase of which ("climbing into the curvature") mirrors the "voice spirals" of the Ghalib/Hunt poem. Both poems also imply cosmic considerations, with "Einstein and Bohr" in the former and the falling stars and "the other side of moons" in the latter. Thus the very fabric of time is perhaps in question here—"secret letters" arrive already "torn open," and dead "Authors," as the previous poem in Webb's sequence tells us, with a nod to William Blake, "are in Eternity"—as well as all over the poems that close out Webb's book:

> The Authors are in Eternity,
> or so Blake said,
>
> but I am here, feet planted
> on the ground;
>
> I am listening to the song
> of the underground river.
>
> I go down to the same river twice,
> remembering, always remembering.

I am you in your jewel-domed reading room,
I am you in your kayak skimming.

I stand in one place risking almost everything.
I weep for the last notes.

The river-stones are polished
by the blue-veined hands of Ishtar.

Poor Fishstar! Yet – all is not lost.[116]
(*Water* 57)

In "The Authors Are in Eternity" ghazal, Webb's speaker addresses several such authors (including Coleridge) with the phrase "I am you," suggesting fusion with the other. In "Leaning," this phrase is modified to "You are in this / with me too," suggesting not fusion, but a more social sense of companionship. Here in this poem Williams—"the ice-pond Brueghel's figures are skating on" also present in his "Pictures from Brueghel"—and Rilke—"(Rodin in Paris, his amanuensis, a torso ...) / I must change my life"—are two of the poets, keys from Webb's writing past, who are "with" the speaker. But, as elsewhere in *Water and Light*, these are echoes within the echoes of Ghalib, and it is Ghalib himself who is most "with" Webb over these final poems. In "Leaning," Webb's speaker's "sick head" is "on the table where I write" (*Water* 58), while in the following poem (the last in the book) it is Ghalib who is "almost asleep, / head on the table" (61). In addressing Ghalib directly, as Webb's speaker does in her final ghazal, Webb not only makes her response to Ghalib overt, she also further merges with him ("I am you") in that Ghalib's poetry is itself filled with various self-addresses to "Ghalib" and "Asad," identities that turn out to be pen names for the poet Mirza Asadullah Beg Khan. Thus, when Webb addresses "Ghalib" *in Ghalib's voice*, in a poem imitating Ghalib's ghazal, she is also addressing herself. Separation and merger, horizon and companion, the responsive relationship flutters between these poles—Blaser's "moth in the piano," the "lyric voice loose" in "*an impossible body.*"[117]

This self-address is also imitated in Webb's use of the figures of "Fishstar" and "Ishtar" throughout *Water and Light*. This is her

"Ghalib," her poetic alter-ego or *nom de plume*, the inscription of which into the closing lines of a ghazal being one of the form's conventions. When Webb "signs" a poem "Fishstar," she both repeats and personalizes Beg Khan's use of "Ghalib." Companionship and horizon are marked in complex ways here. Webb's linking of her Fishstar with the Babylonian goddess Ishtar is a further divergence from Ghalib: her persona has a divine provenance, but one carefully chosen, located at the Persian roots of the ghazal itself. Furthermore, Fishstar has several interesting sources and associations within Webb's own *oeuvre*, making her all the more powerful a personal deity/self. The name first occurs in the gnomic epigraph to *Naked Poems* as a mirror image—

star fish

fish star

—the mirroring suggesting the doubleness of reflection and the possibilities of a Steinean "bottom nature" or unconscious inner self. Such doubling and mirroring also recalls the later image of the Bowl, which captures the cosmos in the sea beneath (as above/so below), or the chiasmal tangle of proximity. Tracing backwards once again, we might see the origins of this stellar sea goddess in the mysterious closing lines of the early poem "To Friends Who Have Also Considered Suicide": "the bright crustaceans of the oversky" (*Vision* 54). We might also find that one possibility of Fishstar's provenance is as a response to the lines cited above from H.D.'s *Trilogy*, where the mother goddess is invoked as a "Star of the Sea." Not quite her "Prufrock," but a personae just the same, Fishstar as Ishtar allows Webb to "dance / into Persia" (*Water* 9)—a transitional self opening doors to merger, fusion, borrowing, and appropriation. That Webb's speaker can stand back and address Fishstar, even correct her ("but I tell you, / *Fishstar*, the colour was not / Peacock blue" [30]) again positions us in a place where response involves both companionship and horizon, the intersubjective proximity of self and other and a simultaneous separation of the same. To engulf and gulf.

In *Water and Light*, two assertions of Webb's source-poets are proved.

> ADRIENNE RICH [translating Ghalib]: Poetry is just really a way of meeting poets.
>
> JOHN THOMPSON: The poet [is] a cinder never quite burned out.[118]

Certainly for Webb, always attuned to the voices within the voices she reads, the poem is a place for "meeting poets": "We are a room," a garden, a "continuous *carmen*." Thompson's lingering "ember," too, sounds like a perfect epigraph for a practitioner of the poetics of response, where poets breathe onto the still warm coals of prior poems, re-igniting the Heraclitean fire of verse again and again, "hanging fire," which is a kind of keeping, awaiting, anticipating the call of the other echoing in the shell of the word.

Notes

1. Webb, *Hanging Fire*, 57.

2. Susan Howe, *My Emily Dickinson*, 13, 76.

3. From a notebook, quoted in Leonard Diepeveen, *Changing Voices: The Modern Quoting Poem* (Ann Arbor: University of Michigan Press, 1993), 1.

4. Webb, "Polishing up the View," in *Talking*, 50.

5. T. S. Eliot, "Tradition and the Individual Talent," in *Selected Prose of T. S. Eliot*, ed. Frank Kermode (New York: Harcourt Brace Kovanovich, 1975), 38.

6. Diepeveen, *Changing Voices*, 4.

7. "The Practice of Outside," in *The Collected Books of Jack Spicer* (Santa Rosa: Black Sparrow Books, 1975), 309.

8. Sharon Thesen, *The Pangs of Sunday* (Toronto: McClelland and Stewart, 1990), 27.

9. H.D., *Collected Poems, 1912–1944* (New York: New Directions, 1983), 517.

10. Phyllis Webb Papers, National Library and Archives of Canada. The issue of *The Malahat Review* referred to is no. 83 (Summer 1988); Van Herk's essay

appears on pp. 115–26. Webb's short essay on Thesen, "Imaginations Companions," appears in the same issue (83–88).

11. Emmanual Levinas, *Humanism of the Other*, trans. Nidra Poller (Chicago: University of Chicago Press, 2003), 19.

12. Robert Duncan, *Bending the Bow* (New York: New Directions, 1968), 27.

13 Ibid., 26.

14. Levinas, *Humanism of the Other*, 67.

15. Ibid., 29. It should be noted right off the top that, first, there are of course limits to the poetics of response (I am not trying to fashion a totalizing theory which answers all questions about poetry). While I would argue that all poetry participates in a matrix of call and response at some level (which may be as simple as saying "poetry comes from somewhere"), not all poets develop this into a self-conscious praxis (actively "listening" and "responding" to their various sources). Second, with Webb as the specific example, it should be kept in mind that she did not leap from the womb of poetry with a fully formed poetics of response in hand. She has always been a poet who "read in order to write," but her responsive strategies definitely developed over her writing career, and at first, in the early work, they are no more or no less complex than any young writer working through her given field of influences.

16. Levinas writes: "In desire the ego goes out to Others in a way that compromises the sovereign identification of the ego with oneself." Ibid.

17. Martin Heidegger, *Being and Time*, trans. John Macquarrie and Edward Robinson (New York: Harper and Row, 1962), 322.

18. Emmanuel Levinas, *God, Death, and Time*, trans. Bettina Bergo (Stanford: Stanford University Press, 2000), 128.

19. Ibid., 139, 22.

20. Duncan to H.D., January 2 1960, in *A Great Admiration: H.D. / Robert Duncan, Correspondence 1950–1961*, ed. Robert Bertholf (Venice: Lapis Press, 1992), 22.

21. "The poem or work of art tends the silence, lets the essence of being be." Levinas, *Humanism of the Other*, 61.

22. Sianne Ngai, *Ugly Feelings*, 253.

23. Levinas, *Time and the Other*, trans. Richard A. Cohen (Pittsburgh: Duquense University Press, 1987), 111. Steve McCaffery summarized Levinas's position: "Prior to all categories and actions of an ego and prior to all knowing is an ethical relation to an Other." See "The Scandal of Sincerity," in *Prior to Meaning: The Protosemantic and Poetics* (Evanston: Northwestern University Press, 2001), 206.

24. Levinas, *God, Death, and Time*, 175.

25. Harold Bloom, *The Anxiety of Influence*, 5. As in the introduction, I am keying on Bloom's use of financial metaphors ("indebtedness") related to private property and the accumulation of poetic "capital." Bloom writes that "Where generosity is involved, the poets influenced are minor or weaker" (30). He, in contrast, is only interested in "strong poets," though he fails to define a "strong poet" beyond the tautology that such a poet feels the anxiety of influence and sees the other poet/poem as a threatening depletion rather than a "generous" donation.

26. It is possible that, at its heart, responsibility maintains a paradoxical form of "irresponsibility" which figures in the poet's desire for fusion with the other. Susan Howe: "[N]ot to explain the work [of another], not to translate it, but to meet the work with writing.... [A] kind of *fusion*." *The Birth-mark*, 158 (my emphasis). These contradictory impulses of responsibility are very much the subject of Jacques Derrida's discussion of the concept in *The Gift of Death*. Elaborating on, and of course deconstructing, an essay by Jan Patočka, Derrida notes that responsibility originates in the gap between two concepts of the mystical: a "daimonic" and "orgiastic" experience of fusion with the other, and a Christian sense of separation from and standing before the other in which the very otherness of the other and the selfness (singularity) of the self is emphasized. Fusion with the other is defined as "irresponsibility" as it elides the separate self-consciousness that could actually *feel responsible*. However, as the concept has evolved historically and as pagan daimonism has given way to Christian theology, the concept of fusion with the other has not been erased but subsumed and incorporated, for "history never effaces what it buries." Thus the "secret of responsibility would consist of keeping secret, or 'incorporated,' the secret of the demonic and thus of preserving within itself a nucleus of irresponsibility." This might be seen in Duncan's "A Poem Beginning with a Line by Pindar," which describes the *keeping* of the unitive secrets of "animal life," "before our histories," that hovers behind or within our separate responses to the world:

Finders Keepers we sang
when we were children   or were taught to sing
before our histories began   and we began
who were beloved   our animal life
toward the Beloved,   sworn to be Keepers

See Derrida, *The Gift of Death*, trans. David Wills (Chicago: University of Chicago Press, 1995), 20–21. Duncan, *The Opening of the Field*, 68.

27. Duncan, *The H.D. Book*, Part II, Chapter 7, *Credences* 1:2 (1975), 62.

28. Duncan, preface to *The H.D. Book*, Robert Duncan Papers, The Poetry and Rare Book Collection, SUNY Buffalo, 5.

29. Levinas, *Humanism of the Other*, 6.

30. Levinas, *Entre Nous: On Thinking-of-the-Other*, trans. Michael B. Smith and Barbara Harshav (New York: Columbia University Press, 1998), 5.

31. Ibid., 100. See also Nick Crossley, *Intersubjectivity: The Fabric of Social Becoming* (London: Sage Publications, 1996). Crossley argues that "recognition of other (autonomous) subjectivities or consciousnesses is fundamental to any ethical relationship. We enter into ethical relations to the extent that we recognize that they exist in their own right" (3). But "by entering into dialogue [with others], subjects transcend their individuation and become components of a larger whole" (8). Crossley locates this "larger whole" in language (14), and distinguishes two modes of the intersubjective. The first he calls "radical" intersubjectivity. This "involves a lack of self-awareness and a communicative openness towards the other." Fusion and merger. The other he calls "egological" intersubjectivity, which "involves an empathic intentionality which experiences otherness by way of an imaginative transposition of self into the position of the other" (23). Distance and desire. Subjectivity (which is really intersubjectivity—self and other are "relational terms") "swings between" the two modes: "sometimes we are deeply engrossed with others, too engaged to be aware of either ourselves or them. At other times ... we can become sharply aware of both, constituting them as reflective and reflexive aspects of experience" (71).

32. Heidegger, *Being and Time*, 281.

33. Jean Luc Nancy, *Being Singular Plural*, trans. Robert D. Richardson and Anne E. O'Byrne (Stanford: Stanford University Press, 2000), 30.

34. Levinas, *God, Death, and Time*, 12, 20, 175. Levinas's translator Bettina Bergo renders Celan's German as "I am you, if I am I."

35. Webb, "The Muse Figure," in *Nothing But Brush Strokes*, 4.

36. Allen Grossman, "Summa Lyrica," in *The Sighted Singer: Two Works on Poetry for Readers and Writers* (Baltimore: Johns Hopkins University Press, 1992), 250.

37. Blaser, "The Practice of Outside," 305–06.

38. The terms are Blaser's (see section III of the present chapter). Clearly a "companion" is more proximate than a "horizon," but both relate to the joinings and divisions of the intersubjective push and pull.

39. Charles Bernstein, "The Revenge of the Poet-Critic or The Parts are Greater Than the Sum of the Whole," in *My Way: Speeches and Poems* (Chicago: University of Chicago Press, 1999), 10.

40. Duncan, *The H.D. Book*, Part I, Chapter 2, *Coyote Journal* 8 (1967), 34.

41. Webb, *The Vision Tree*, 60.

42 The ten-syllable phrase "clean and syllabic as knotted bamboo," while not iambic pentameter, is nevertheless carefully metered and, indeed, "syllabic." I scan it as a four-stress line: a trochee, an iamb, and two anapests.

43. Eric Havelock, *Preface to Plato* (Cambridge, Mass.: Harvard University Press, 1963), 5–6.

44. Whitman's poetic-politics of the "merge" can thus be read as answering, in some distant and indirect sense, Plato's eviction of poetry from his politics for just this reason. Poetry punctures the boundaries philosophy has traditionally placed around knowing.

45. McCaffery, "The Scandal of Sincerity," 206. Subsequent references to this work are cited parenthetically in the text as "Scandal."

46. Webb, *Hanging Fire*, 57.

47. Emily Dickinson, *Seletced Letters*, ed. Thomas H. Johnson (Cambridge Mass.: The Belknap Press, 1958), 330.

48. Jack Spicer, *The Collected Books of Jack Spicer* (Santa Rosa: Black Sparrow Books, 1975), 61.

49. Susan Knutson, "Chiasmus, Chasm, Chi: Phyllis Webb's Semantic Geometry," in *West Coast Line* 25:3 (Winter 1991–92), 120. This chiasmal "criss-cross" may be related to Webb's current obsession, as a painter, with the material form of the crossword puzzle. See chapter three.

50. Robin Blaser, writing of Jack Spicer, suggests "that one had first to learn to use the I and then to lose it," and that, for Spicer at least (though I would argue that much the same holds true for Webb), "This becomes an attack on the 'subjective aim' and assurance of a whole culture." Blaser, "The Practice of Outside," 271–321. One loses the "I" by moving into dictation and the outside. Webb moves steadily in this direction, arriving there most completely in *Hanging Fire*, her final book and final, and most explicit, statement of the poetics of response. For a good discussion of the links between the loss of the lyric "I" in contemporary avant-garde poetics and poststructuralist theory, see Marjorie Perloff's essay "Language Poetry and the Lyric Subject: Ron Silliman's Albany and Susan Howe's Buffalo," *Critical Inquiry* 25:3 (Spring 1999), 405–34.

51. Grossman, "Summa Lyrica," 211. Further references are cited parenthetically in the text as "Summa."

52. This is certainly clear in the case of the modernist lyric, as the origin of H.D.'s imagism in her translations of Euripides demonstrates. See Eileen Gregory, *H.D. and Hellenism: Classic Lines* (Cambridge: Cambridge University Press, 1997).

53. Pauline Butling, *Seeing in the Dark: The Poetry of Phyllis Webb* (Waterloo: Wilfred Laurier University Press, 1997), 76. Butling similarly traces Webb's attempts to "escape the I/you enclosure of the lyric" (78).

54. Webb, *Hanging Fire*, 67.

55. Levinas, *God, Death, and Time*, 9, 14.

56. Levinas, *Time and the Other*, 77.

57. Heidegger, *Being and Time*, 306. The emphasis is Heidegger's.

58. Webb, *The Vision Tree*, 23.

59. Levinas, *God, Death, and Time*, 185.

60. Heidegger, *Being and Time*, 279, 288.

61. Blaser, "The Practice of Outside," 290–91.

62. Walt Whitman, "Song of Myself," *The Complete Poems*, ed. Francis Murphy (New York: Penguin Books, 1977), 63.

63. In making this assertion I am returned once more to Harold Bloom's "anxiety of influence" theory, which suggests that poets overcome the oppressive influences of their predecessors by subsuming and repressing their example into hidden allusions and appropriations. I have already been critical of Bloom; I should clarify that I do not deny that there is such a thing as anxiety of influence, but I do question its totalizing pervasiveness and the conclusions Bloom draws from his theory. Anxiety over being influenced does not necessarily indicate an agonic sense of competition and contest with other poets. It can simply and I think obviously be part and parcel of the process of coming to terms with what Allen Grossman calls the "recognition of recurrence" and what I am here calling the poetics of response. While Webb does express anxiety over her influences in her early work (as when she refers to "our inheritance" as "our distress" and "the weight of eons" [*Even Your Right Eye*, 55]), and while anxiety does coalesce around particular allusions to Eliot's work, I think the reasons for this anxiety are very specific, relate directly to the workings of the poetics of response, and involve the problematics of the lyric's self/other nexus.

64. When asked directly about H.D., in the summer of 2004, Webb discounted H.D. as an influence on her work (private conversation with the author). Nevertheless, she clearly read her, and certainly read poets who were readers of H.D.—including Marianne Moore, Duncan, A. M. Klein, and others.

65. George Woodcock, "In the Beginning Was the Question: The Poems of Phyllis Webb," *Queen's Quarterly* 93: 3 (Autumn 1986), 529.

66. Liza Potvin, "Phyllis Webb: The Voice That Breaks," *Canadian Poetry* 32 (Spring/Summer 1993), 45.

67. Ibid.

68. T. S. Eliot, *Collected Poems 1909–1962* (London: Faber and Faber, 1974), 17. Subsequent references to the same edition are cited parenthetically in text as *Collected*.

69. Webb, *Even Your Right Eye*, 19. The following references to this same work are cited parenthetically as EYRE. Where the poem is available in *The Vision Tree* I use that text instead, with parenthetical references cited as *Vision*.

70. Webb, *The Sea Is Also a Garden* (Toronto: Ryerson Press, 1962), unpaginated. The poems in this book are numbered: "Beachcomber" is poem 15.

71. I have in mind Zukofsky's book *I's (pronounced eyes)* (New York: Trobar, 1963). My reading of Webb's eyes also owes something to Zukofsky's reading of Shakespeare's "definition of love" in *Bottom: On Shakespeare* (Austin, Texas: The Ark Press, 1963). Zukofsky writes that Shakespeare's embodied love is "Amor, identified with the passion of the lover falling short of perfection—discernment, fitness, proportion—at those times when his imagination insufficient to itself is an aberration of the eyes" (15). Later, working from Ludwig Wittgenstein's *Tractatus Logico-Philosophicus*, Zukofsky writes: "*Looking* has its own logic, but (it may be inferred from Wittgenstein's *looking* logic) he who *looks* is still the philosophical *I*, the metaphysical subject, the limit—not a part of the world" (89). Webb, I am arguing, identifies a similar problem—the I as eye and limit.

72. Cleanth Brooks, *The Well Wrought Urn: Studies in the Structure of Poetry* (New York: Harcourt Brace, 1947), 195.

73. Diana Relke, "Feminist Ecocritique as Forensic Archaeology: Digging in Critical Graveyards and Phyllis Webb's Gardens," *Canadian Poetry* 48 (Spring/Summer 1998), 75–76.

74. Duncan, after years of denying that Eliot was one of his "imagination's companions," finally and publicly admits in "Orders, Passages 24" that "Eliot was one of them, I was / one of his"—one of the poets in his "chrestomathy." *Bending the Bow*, 78.

75. This is an uncollected poem, originally published in *Civ/n* (1953), 17.

76. Webb, *The Sea Is Also a Garden*, poem 15.

77. Ibid., poem 28.

78. Juliana Spahr, "Spiderwasp or Literary Criticism," in *Telling It Slant: Avant-Garde Poetics of the 1990s*, ed. Mark Wallace and Steven Marks (Tuscaloosa: University of Alabama Press, 2002), 409.

79. H.D., *Collected Poems 1912–1944*, ed. Louis L. Martz (New York: New Directions, 1983), 20–21. Subsequent references to this book cited parenthetically in text as HD.

80. In *Trilogy*, the appearance of Mary Magdalene at Kaspar's door is described as "unseemly," a trespassing of the feminine upon a masculine preserve (HD 591).

81. Webb, *The Sea Is Also a Garden*, poem 6.

82. John Hulcoop, "Phyllis Webb and the Priestess of Motion," *Canadian Literature* 32 (1967), 31. Potvin, "Phyllis Webb: The Voice That Breaks," 51. References to Webb's *Naked Poems* are cited from *The Vision Tree*.

83. Hulcoop, "Phyllis Webb and the Priestess of Motion," 30.

84. Nancy, *Being Singular Plural*, 45.

85. Webb, "Radio Talks," 98.

86. Ron Silliman, in his essay "The Dysfunction of Criticism," cites Robert Grenier's review of Robert Creeley's *A Quick Graph*, from the first issue of *This*

magazine (1971), where Grenier proclaims that "a kind of critical writing which does not now exist will have to be made dominant: one in which the intention to say something is accomplished in a form possessed, first, of all the self-sufficient factness of the actual poem/prose being discussed … in the work that matters … there will have to be no essential difference between criticism and poems" (quoted in Silliman 180). Silliman's invocation of Grenier is not entirely approving, and Grenier's insistence that such a critical-poetic merger will "have to be made dominant" is a little too proscriptive, but nevertheless, his words do seem to point in the direction much of language poetry did in fact evolve in, and even appears prophetic in light of the subsequent work of poets such as Susan Howe and Charles Bernstein. It should go without saying that Webb's response poems are not examples of language poetry, but there is a shared sensibility, with Grenier's comments here cited by Silliman, that poetry, and the sort of critical response "proper" to it, forms a semi-"autonomous literary act" (Silliman 179).

87. Blaser, *The Holy Forest*, 306. Subsequent references to this edition cited parenthetically in text as *Forest*.

88. Webb, *Nothing But Brush Strokes*, 60. As to what the two poets share, see, for instance, Webb's review of *The Holy Forest*, which closes with a citation from his "Moth Poem": "I said 'master.'" Here, via citation, Webb names Blaser "master." See "A Bow to the Numinous," *Books in Canada* 23:3 (April 1994), 27–28.

89. Webb Papers, National Library of Canada.

90. The poem closes with Webb's name and address, listed as "83 Isabella St., Apt. 34 / Toronto 5, Ont." Webb Papers, National Library.

91. Duncan, *Letters: Poems 1953–56* (1958; reprint Chicago: Flood Editions, 2003), X.

92. Rilke, *The Selected Poetry*, ed. and trans. Stephen Mitchell (New York: Random House, 1982), 151, 227.

93. Brenda Carr, "Genre Theory and the Impasse of Lyric?: Reframing the Questions in Phyllis Webb's Lyric Sequences," *West Coast Line* 25:3 (Winter 1991–92), 71. See also Relke, "Feminist Ecocritique as Forensic Archaeology: Digging in Critical Graveyards and Phyllis Webb's Gardens," especially 76–81: "Webb's poets negotiate with many gardeners, gatekeepers, and muses—all aspects of Father Culture—for a place to put down roots and grow." In *Seeing in the Dark*, 19, Butling writes that "Marvell's Garden" "allegorizes the woman writer's personal and social losses on entering a traditionally male space."

94. Webb, "Radio Talks," 98.

95. Andrew Marvell, "The Garden," in *The Oxford Book of Seventeenth Century Verse*, ed. Sir Herbert Grierson and G. Bullough (Oxford: Clarendon Press, 1934), 752.

96. In a radio talk typescript, in Webb's papers in the National Library, titled "Flowers and Garden of Summer" and dated to the period of her Marvell poem,

she notes that "Gardens in literature generally serve two purposes: People meet in them, or people retreat to them" (4–5). She then mention's Marvell's "Garden" which, she claims, "speaks of retreating but is a meeting" (6). The poem as meeting place is an early version of Webb's poetics of response.

97. Webb, *Wilson's Bowl*, 32.

98. Rilke, *The Selected Poetry*, 151.

99. Ibid., 61.

100. Ibid., 241. I am indebted, here, to a variety of sources for this connection. First, a letter found in Ottawa, from Nadine Gordimer to Webb, put me on to the presence of an allusion to Rilke. Webb then confirmed the reference, and, after checking with John Hulcoop, sent me to the correct poem. The joinings around this poem extend into its reading here, where I am indeed a "crowd of one writing."

101. By happy coincidence—or "rime," as Duncan would say—Blaser's Latin "*carmen*" (song) also evokes the possibility of the Arabic "*carmen*" (garden): "[A] hillside villa with an enclosed graden hidden by high walls," as Ian Gibson describes the *carmen* of Granada in his biography, *Federico Garcia Lorca, A Life* (New York: Pantheon, 1989), 36. This poetic meeting place—whether song or garden—where a living poet can join a dead poet, is the archive.

102. Howe, *My Emily Dickinson*, 17–18.

103. Webb, *Wilson's Bowl*, 38.

104. See, for instance, Stephen Scobie's excellent essay "I AND I: Phyllis Webb's 'I Daniel,'" *Open Letter* 6: 2–3 (Summer/Fall 1985), 61–70, or Butling's discussion of the poem in *Seeing in the Dark*, 43–46.

105. John Thompson, *Stilt Jack* (Toronto: Anansi, 1978), 5.

106. Webb, *Water and Light*, 12. Subsequent references to this work are cited parenthetically in text as *Water*.

107. Webb, preface to *Sunday Water: Thirteen Anti-ghazals* (Lantzville: Island Writing Series, 1982), unpaginated.

108. Douglas Barbour, *Lyric/Anti-Lyric: Essays on Contemporary Poetry* (Edmonton: NeWest Press, 2001), 108, and Stephen Scobie, "I AND I: Phyllis Webb's 'I Daniel,'" 63.

109. Webb's mother's name was Mary. There is something to be made—beyond the scope of the present argument—of female poets working with the mythological valences of their mothers' names: H.D.'s mother Helen, Susan Howe's mother Mary.

110. Mary Melfi, *A Queen Is Holding a Mummified Cat* (Montreal: Guernica Editions, 1982), 7.

111. *Ghazals of Ghalib*, ed. Aijiz Ahmad (New York: Columbia University Press, 1971), 46.

112. Susan Glickman, "Proceeding before the Amorous Invisible: Phyllis Webb and the Ghazal," *Canadian Literature* 115 (Winter 1987), 56. If the form of the ghazal is somehow "androgynous," or even "feminine," then it may be so in Rachel Duplessis's terms, cited in the introduction: "non-hierarchical forms of mutuality." Duplessis, *The Pink Guitar*, 6.

113. *Ghazals of Ghalib*, 40.

114. In a letter to Butling, Webb comments on her lasting interest in the alchemical formula: "As above so below has thrummed away at me for a very long time, probably dating from the time when I first studied Marvell and the metaphysicals who were into correspondences." Letter dated November 11 1986, Webb Papers, National Library. The connection to Marvell is interesting in the context of present discussion of response poems—and looking ahead, Webb's mention of the as above/so below is in response to Butling's enquiry into the "fish star / star fish" emblem to which I will turn shortly.

115. Ezra Pound, *The Spirit of Romance* (1920; reprint New York: New Directions, 1968), 5. T. S. Eliot, "Tradition and the Individual Talent," in *Selected Prose of T. S. Eliot*, ed. Frank Kermode (New York: Harcourt Brace Kovanovich, 1975), 39. Elizabeth Grosz, *Becomings: Explorations in Time, Memory, and Futures* (Ithaca: Cornell University Press, 1999), 7.

116. One of Webb's divergences from the ghazal form is, obviously, her occasional use of single lines (breaking the couplet pattern). Typically, she employs a single line at the close of a poem, suggesting a pause or breach in the ghazal mid-couplet.

117. Blaser, *The Holy Forest*, 39, 362. Webb cites these lines both in her review of *The Holy Forest*, and in her Blaser essay, "The Crannies of Matter." It is, once again, a point of convergence for the two poets, and I cannot help associate Blaser's "glass in *an impossible body*" with the crystalline structures of Webb's "Images in Crystal" and "The Glass Castle" as an "image for the mind" (*Vision* 50)—a mind now revealed as multiple, *singular plural*.

118. *Ghazals of Ghalib*, 108. Thompson, *Stilt Jack*, 24.

TWO Poetry and Anarchy

To welcome multitudes—the miracle of deeds
performed in unison—the mind
must first renounce the fiction of the self
and its vainglory. It must pierce
the dreamplate of its solitude, the fallacy
of its omnipotence, the fairytale
aprilfools recurring every day
in speeches of professors and politicians.
—Edwin Rolfe, "Credo"

Obsessed, bewildered

By the shipwreck
Of the singular

We have chosen the meaning
Of being numerous.[1]
—George Oppen, "Of Being Numerous"

These excerpts, from two socialist poets, give polemical expression to the main thrust of Webb's anarchist poetics: the movement from the (lyric) self to the multitude of others. The poem is a place of commoning (sharing), of communion.

When shall we break this vase of perfect silence
into the scattering chips of dialogue!

So passionately this vase holds us,
as water, inwardly and at one level.

> But the word, the word is a wafer of communion
> and speaks to the flesh, being of it.
>
> Then the time and the courage for destruction?
> In this small poem I offer my breaking wafer.[2]

In this unpublished, early poem—"And Again the Theme of Perfection and Destruction"—Webb appears to apply the anarchist notion of creative destruction—something similar to Bakunin's "The passion for destruction is a creative passion, too!"[3]—to the New Critical notion of the poem as a well-wrought urn ("this vase of perfect silence"). Poetically, Webb cannot yet (this is the early 1950s, the apex of New Criticism's influence) envision a poetry of "scattering chips of dialogue," but it's coming, and will arrive with her *Naked Poems* in 1965. Her critique of the small, perfect closed poem comes from within just such a poem, and any potential "destruction" or "breaking"—out away from the enclosure of this limited "inward" and isolate "level"—is just that: potential, virtual, out beyond the poem's tidy limits, a futurity, a communion with as yet no community. There is a similar issue with Rolfe's poem "Credo," which renounces "the fiction of the self" from within the enclosure of the self's own domain: the short, solitary lyric poem of passionate self-expression. Oppen, writing some thirty years after Rolfe (and, interestingly, about the same time as Webb's *Naked Poems* and her aborted beginning of "The Kropotkin Poems"), can move from "the shipwreck / Of the singular" to a poetics "Of being numerous" in the serial poem's formal apparatus, in which "part[s]" are arranged in "an infinite series"—the politics of which will be discussed in this chapter.[4] So far as an anarchist aesthetics is conceivable, the serial poem would appear to be the anarchist form *par excellence*—the formal analogue of anarchism's decentralist philosophy.

~

But isn't anarchism the philosophy of unrestrained individualism? Why poetry *and anarchism*, and why begin with two socialists?

Propose first a sort of "necessary" (albeit hypothetical) affinity between poetry and anarchy—as "aesthetic" practices and modes of social being—Herbert Read's notion that "the poet is necessarily an anarchist."[5] Considering the long history of poetry's relationship with centres of power and social structure—the epic poet as repository of a people's myths and celebrator of its (usually military) heroes, the medieval and renaissance court poet pandering after patronage, even up to the institutional place of the creative writing industry and the nationalist expectations placed upon contemporary parliamentary poets laureates—this gesture may seem willfully utopian, if not downright deluded.[6] But seen from another angle, there is at least one obvious and initial family resemblance: poetry, as it is commonly conceived, is one of the most private and solitary of practices—a medium, we assume, for self-expression, autonomy, and enactments of individuality. Anarchism—in its common conception (when not written off as mindless destruction) as a philosophy of unbridled and uncompromising individual liberty—might meet poetry on the ground of the sacrosanct and self-enclosed subject: here we are separate and alone, and express our singularity most intimately and absolutely.

This is not, ultimately, the anarchism in mind here (and thus one reason to begin with two socialist poets)—as the argument of this book thus far should have demonstrated a similar lack of interest in outmoded notions of the isolate (lyric) self. The self, we have maintained, is always already found amongst others, *is*, in some essential and inseparable sense, *an other*—or at least, can only be found in the interstices between self and others. The politics of this ontological *being-with* are anarchist, and an anarchist poetics is an exploration of the between and of relational space. Obviously this implies something other than a destructive death drive or a no-holds-barred, *laissez-faire* individualism.

> HERBERT READ: This question of the relation of the individual to the collective society of which he is a member is the fundamental issue, in art as well as in politics.[7]

There is, in fact, an anarchist spectrum which, while never abandoning the individual, nevertheless stretches from a coarse atomism at one extreme, all the way over to a fully elaborated communism at the other.[8] Thus, looking towards the communist end of the anarchist spectrum (and it is significant here that there have been proponents, such as the Russian Peter Kropotkin, of "anarcho-communism")—in the nineteenth and early twentieth-centuries at least (before the advent of state socialism)—it was clear that socialism and anarchism were not mutually exclusive or even contradictory ideologies. They were complementary, parts of an oppositional whole.

> PIERRE-JOSEPH PROUDHON: To make a man free is to balance him with others.
>
> ALBERT PARSONS: We contend for communism and anarchy.... Politically we are anarchists, and economically, communists or socialists.
>
> EMMA GOLDMAN: [The] individual and social instincts ... [are] to be understood, not as foreign to each other, but as closely related and truly harmonious.[9]

Indeed, as Sean Sheehan has recently argued, the communist end of the anarchist spectrum "has its metaphysical underpinning in Marx's philosophy."[10] In this view, Marxism, in its most basic approach (and most recognizable in Marx's early philosophical writings), embodies a "social ontology" which implicates the subject in the object, self in other, in "dynamic relationship" (61). The very future of social struggle, Sheehan maintains, depends upon a "return to Marx though anarchism" (159).

It might be worth pausing at this point to note that Webb, who describes having "brought [herself] up as a Marxian [*sic*],"[11] chose to attempt to write a book called "The Kropotkin Poems," and not "The Stirner Poems," or even "The Marx Poems," for that matter. She didn't choose an arch individualist (Max Stirner, a key influence on the individualist-anarchist strain and advocate of "egoism"), nor the grand collectivist (Marx)—but a synthesis of the two—a political philosopher who consistently posited the importance *both* of the free individual *and* the collective and communal, upholding simultaneously the

> tendency towards integrating labor for the production of all riches in common, so as finally to render it impossible to discriminate the part of the common production due to the separate individual; and second, a tendency towards the fullest freedom of the individual in the prosecution of all aims, beneficial both for himself and for society at large.[12]

Webb, though always concerned with the politics of isolation—"I am studying," she writes in a note amongst her "Kropotkin Poem" papers, "how I may compare the prison where I live and the world"[13]—and part of her interest in Kropotkin is clearly in his experiences as an isolated prisoner—nevertheless chooses to explore the communist wing of anarchism. The implications of this choice are the concern here in this chapter, for they have much to tell us about Webb's path through and beyond the lyric.

Thus it is here that we can return to the question of the lyric and the self/other relationship implied by an ontology of (in Jean Luc Nancy's terms) *being singular plural*—an ontology that also finds expression in Kropotkin's anarcho-communism—taking the formal and ontological issue directly into poetry's social sphere (as far as it is possible to speak in such terms).[14] The serial poem similarly embodies Nancy's notion of the *singular plural*, as individual lyrics are "federated" into a centreless whole. But—to borrow Laura Riding's phrase—"anarchism is not enough," and the serial poem may, ultimately, not in and of itself be the vehicle for escaping the wider issue of *representation* (both aesthetic and political)—of the iconic and the representative as such—that Webb came up against in her struggles with Kropotkin and anarchism through the late 1960s and into the early 1970s—in fact, throughout her long silence between the publication of *Naked Poems* in 1965 and *Wilson's Bowl* in 1980, amidst which lies the wreck of "The Kropotkin Poems."

~

I. Abdication and the Commons: Versions of Poetic Anarchy

If a full history of the relationship between poetry and anarchy were to be attempted, it would need to begin—at the very latest—with Plato's dismissal of the poet from his ideal republic.[15] This is the originary moment for poetry's incompatibility with the state—its being declared out of order—and the badge of its inherent subversiveness. From Plato on, one could contend, poetry has had to defend itself against accusations of disorderliness, and one could divide poets into those who have tried to smooth over poetry's disorders (Sidney) and those who have embraced the same (Shelley). The point here, however, is simply that anarchism may have something to tell us about poetry (and poetry something about anarchism), and that there is a reasonably long tradition of linking certain poets with anarchism. The concern in this chapter, ultimately, is to develop a clearer sense of the tradition Webb's poetry should be read within, to better understand the politics of her poetic form, and the potential anarchist aesthetics of a poet whose work is clearly absorbed with the problem of political anarchism.[16]

Thus, we will first focus on two of Webb's twentieth century precursors whose work exemplifies the two extreme poles of anarchist ideology: the individualist and communist strains. Laura Riding, author of *Anarchism Is Not Enough*, shares much with Webb's tendencies towards isolation, refusal, silence, and, ultimately, abdication and literary suicide.[17] Riding clearly exemplifies an individualist form of literary anarchism. Robert Duncan, whose direct and considerable influence on Webb's introduction to an open poetics in the early 1960s we have already noted, is a poet absorbed with the idea of "the commune of poetry," as he writes in *Bending the Bow*—the book that gives his fullest expression of poetic anarchism.[18] If Riding is the individualist, then Duncan, describing himself as "a crowd of one who writes," is the anarcho-communist of twentieth century poetics.

Webb embodies the tension between these two anarchist poles, which often reveals itself in her penchant for paradox, as in "The Days of the Unicorns," where the poem's third-person "we" *shares* "the need to be alone." Both singular and plural, a "society of islands"[19]—it may be best to understand this tension by reading Webb alongside poets where these conflicting extremes may be more clearly analyzed in isolation.

~

Poetry, for Riding, is a form or enactment of autonomy, and thus at times a cognate for anarchism. Writing, with collaborator Robert Graves in their landmark *A Survey of Modernist Poetry* (1927), Riding has this analogy between poetry and anarchism in mind:

> The whole trend of modern poetry is toward treating poetry like a very sensitive substance which succeeds better when allowed to crystallize by itself than when put into prepared moulds.... Modern poetry, that is, is groping for some principle of self-determination to be applied to the making of the poem—not lack of government, but government from within.[20]

Sounding not unlike Henry David Thoreau demanding not "no government, but *at once* a better government"—a Jeffersonian government "which governs least," or perhaps even "not at all"[21]—Riding is here squarely on anarchist turf, arguing not for chaos (she discredits complete "laissez-faire ... anarchy" further on in the same passage) nor "lack of government," but self-government: autonomy. This linking of poetry and anarchism (as autonomy, not disorder) is further elaborated in her next book, *Anarchism Is Not Enough* (1928).[22]

Opening with a discussion of what she refers to as "the Myth" all children are born into—a concept combining epistemology, ideology, and basic sociality, "the universal sense of duty, the ethics of abstract neighbourliness"—Riding argues that "Poetry ... is essentially not of the Myth.... It has no system, harmony, form, public significance or sense of duty" (*Anarchism* 10–11). Poetry, happily, it seems in Riding's scheme, "is perhaps the only human pursuit left still capable of developing anti-socially" (32). It is "properly an art of individualization" (114)—"narrow ... broken, quick.... Poetry is personal" (118)—it is autonomy and anarchy. And although "anarchism is very nice," Riding does not think "that anarchism is enough" (67–68). It soon becomes clear (if one takes the trouble to untangle the purposeful obscurities and strange, anti-systemic turns of her "system") that if anarchism is not enough, then neither is individuality, nor poetry—"Nothing is enough" (132).

~

What can be defined can be delimited, controlled. Knowledge is power. A pure anarchism would resist the very notion of a name, of an "ism," of an ideology as such that would *represent* (and thus limit) its nexus of desires and demands. The true rebel rebels even against rebellion.[23]

~

The World and I

This is not exactly what I mean
Any more than the sun is the sun.
But how to mean more closely
If the sun shines but approximately?
What a world of awkwardness!
What hostile implements of sense!
Perhaps this is as close a meaning
As perhaps becomes such knowing.
Else I think the world and I
Must live together as strangers and die—
A sour love, each doubtful whether
Was ever a thing to love the other.
No, better for both to be nearly sure
Each of each—exactly where
Exactly I and exactly the world
Fail to meet by a moment, and a word.[24]

The subject of the poem is ultimately language itself, made all the more material by the closely collocated sound (the near-rhymes of the couplets, but also the tight line turns like "whether / was ever") and word repetitions ("mean" and "sun" in the opening lines, "each" and "exactly" in the closing lines). The ontological "failure" of the "world" and self to "meet" is mediated by language, which does not allow the speaker "to mean exactly what I mean," and which maintains a dissonance between the "sun" (as word) and "sun" (as world)—between signifier and signified. Language, via the poem, provides proximity but (more overwhelmingly, for Riding) simultaneous separation, companionship and (ominous) horizon. Thus "Poetry always faces, and generally meets with, failure" (*Anarchism* 14). It is not enough; it cannot bridge the divide between subject and object, self and other.

If language, in the poem, cannot "mean," "exactly," then the concept of the individual, too, cannot "exactly" indicate the true self. The true self, for Riding, is "unreal"—a "withdrawal from both nature and human society" (*Anarchism* 43), a "more-than-anarchistic self-subtraction" (122). The individual—realizable and representable (as a concept or abstraction)—can be made a part of a system, the basis of a form of social cohesion (neo-liberal capitalism, for instance); as such it is not enough, *not autonomous enough*. Not free and its own. It must be "unreal," unrepresentable, just as the poem's "independence" becomes dependent upon its being "meaningless" (57)—or at least, "an attempt to make language do more than express" (14)—to achieve the status of being "a thing in itself," as Riding and Graves have it in their *Survey*.[25]

As true selfhood is a "self-subtraction," the true poem is "nothing"—"a vacuum" (*Anarchism* 17). The goal, for both poem and person, is to become completely autonomous—a "Queen," Riding suggests, in her own "queendom"—and then, to "abdicate"—to hold no position, to be completely unidentified, unidentifiable (185, 221). Anarchism, in Riding's view, is a position—a system and an authority. It represents and stands-in-for, and this is exactly why it is not enough. It threatens to become total; in Riding's scheme such totality is a necessary step—one becomes total (a "Queen")—but then one abdicates the position of totality, becoming "unreal," a "nothing." The notorious "failure" of anarchism to realize its utopian goals is the same failure as the poem's, and this is, ultimately, a failure of representation.[26]

The outcome is simply a matter of taking her argument to its logical conclusion and full extension. If anarchism is about absolute autonomy, then one cannot even identify with it or limit it to a representable (and thus shareable) definition (which would be to surrender one's autonomy to the authority of "anarchism"). One must vacate *all* positions, abdicate *all* thrones. Laura Riding, like Phyllis Webb, renounces the writing of poetry—though Riding does so more consciously and programmatically than Webb, who has felt as much renounced as renouncing. Nevertheless, the cessation of poetry, for both poets, is a deeply philosophical issue, and a direct extension of their anarchism. Even the role of "poet" is suspect, just by being a "role" (and Webb, now a "painter," resists this label too).

In the preface to her *Selected Poems*, Riding describes "having reached poetry's limit," and seeing there that—for her—"truth begins where poetry ends."[27] Looking backward from 1970, over her thirty years of silence, Riding has come to see a qualitative difference and division between poetry and language—an extension, perhaps, of having figured the poem as an abstract and vacant "thing." The problematic dissonance between self and world / self and other no longer lies in "the word" as such (as in the "World and I" poem), but in the *poetic* word specifically.

"[P]oetry obstructs general attainment to something better in our linguistic way-of-life," Riding writes in her preface.[28] It is decidedly not enough—no longer because it does not go far enough in the direction of pure autonomy, but rather, because it has gone too far, become too "personalized" and "subject ... to individual variation"—not capable of what Riding now upholds: "*general* attainment," a renewed and total "rational meaning."

~

> Language is a common human creation and possession, and in the use of it there is a potentiality of common human fulfillments. So long as human beings are self-ambitious, this potentiality of language will be neglected—and not only neglected, and impaired through neglect, but actively perverted. In the literary uses of language, a peculiarly fanatical form of self-ambitious activity, the perversion of this potentiality is obscured in the generally shared illusion that the fulfillments of literature are common ones.[29]

It may be that the late Riding's anarchism is undergoing a sea-change of sorts, from the individualist to the communist extreme—from the concept of the self as a privatizeable property to the *singular plural* commons—at least as far as language and poetry are concerned. The poem, for Riding, is clearly not a means to such a transformation, but an obstacle. Its self-containment and privacy is the problem. Its opacity, once its value, is now its failing.

~

> WEBB: I tap my own temple. It taps back an undeciphered code, an ode to spring, perhaps, to the skylark, nightingale, pleased with its own whistling.[30]

The poet, in Webb's "'Anaximander,'" appears to be in a self-contained dynamic with the self—a private property "pleased" to speak only to itself. But this is not always the case with Webb. The poem may be opaque, but its opacities may be due to its "sheer / profundities of otherness" (*Vision* 31)—its extreme exteriority, rather than interiority—a beyond-the-self which is capable of "abandoning" the self, forcing abdication (or banishment). Riding attempted to imagine a poetry of the outside—independent of "both the reader and the poet,"[31] beyond the "myth" of intersubjective "neighbourliness"—but this wound up being, in her eyes, a poetry woefully delimited by its self-containment. Webb keeps one eye—or ear—on her "own temple," but there is always the potential for an outside, for dictation: who exactly "taps back"? The poetic self here, on second glance, isn't revealing self-containment, but that self is at core *an other*—a remnant of some neighbour's poem, Shelley or Keats (skylark or nightingale) calling for response, offering the poem's undecipherability for its own pleasures. Containment is opened. It is not insignificant that this poem is part of the sequence of poems with dictated titles that mark *Hanging Fire* in its totality as a kind of serial poem—although it would be a serial poem even more discrete and discontinuous than earlier serials such as the *Naked Poems* or "Kropotkin Poems."

~

Where for Riding the poem's *privacy* separates it from the commons of language, for Duncan the poem is the very embodiment of language's commonness. This is, in part, an extension of Duncan's well-known concept of "derivation," his insistence that a poet is not a self-expressive individual but a composition (a composite) of all the poets he or she has read: poetry is that moment when the commons becomes expressive. In his poetics statement for *The New American Poetry* anthology in 1960, Duncan gives an extreme expression of his "derivations":

> I am ambitious only to emulate, imitate, reconstrue, approximate, duplicate: Ezra Pound, Gertrude Stein, Joyce, Virginia Woolf, Dorothy Richardson, Wallace Stevens, D. H. Lawrence, Edith Sitwell, Cocteau, Mallarmé, Marlowe, St. John of the Cross, Yeats, Jonathon Swift, Jack Spicer, Céline, Charles Henri Ford, Rilke, Lorca, Kafka, Arp, Max Ernst, St.-John Perse, Prévert, Laura Riding, Apollinaire, Brecht, Shakespeare, Ibsen, Strindberg,

> Joyce Carey, Mary Butts, Freud, Dali, Spenser, Stravinsky, William Carlos Williams and John Gay.
>
> Higglety-pigglety: Euripides and Gilbert. The Strawhat Reviewers, Goethe (of the Autobiography—I have never read Faust) and H.D.[32]

"A crowd of one who writes," Duncan's self-conception as author appears to be decidedly *singular plural* (both one and many), and his sense of the poem obviously exceeds any notion of private (literary) property. His overt anarchism is also well documented. Ellen Tallman has described meeting the poet for the first time (in 1946) at "the Wednesday night Anarchist meetings at the Workman's Circle on Steiner Street in San Francisco," and Duncan himself compared "free verse" to anarchist Bartolomeo Vanzetti's "free state."[33]

Duncan's choice of Vanzetti as theorist—the only anarchist he names directly in his published writings—is curious, although the particular sort of anarchism the Italian immigrant stood for is clear enough. Vanzetti, echoing Bakunin, writes that the anarchist "look[s] for liberty in the liberty of all, for his happiness in the happiness of all, for his welfare in the universal welfare," and he refers to himself as an "anarchist-communist, because I believe that communism is the most humane form of social contract."[34] Vanzetti is frequently invoked in Duncan's letters to Denise Levertov in the late 1960s, letters in which he is arguing for the proper relationship between poetry and political activism, and *Bending the Bow* (1968)—the writing of which is at the heart of Duncan's debate with Levertov—is the book in which he most clearly articulates an anarchist poetics.[35]

"The Multiversity [Passages 21]":

> Where there is no commune,
> the individual volition has no ground.
> Where there is no individual freedom, the commune
> is falsified

"Orders [Passages 24]":

> There is no
> good a man has in his own things except
> it be in the community of every thing

"Passages 26: The Soldiers":

> against the bloody verse America writes over Asia
> we must recall to hold by property rights that
> are not private (individual) or public rights but
> given properties of our common humanity.
>
> *"The United States themselves are essentially the greatest poem"*?
> Then America, the secret union of all states of Man,
> waits, hidden and challenging, in the hearts of the Viet Cong.
> *"The Americans of all nations at any time upon the earth,"*
> Whitman says – the libertarians of the spirit, the
> devotées of Man's commonality.[36]

In "The Multiversity" and "Orders," Duncan clearly articulates an anarcho-communist position: both individualist and communist, singular and plural—the two poles are presented as (poetically and politically) meaningless without the other term. But the collective and common appears to be the foundation of his poetics, as we see in "The Soldiers," where the question of individual, *private* property and its opposition to the "given properties of our common humanity" comes under fire as the United States writes its "bloody verse" of empire over Vietnam. In the face of a "capitalistic oligarchy" which "in the name of industrial free enterprise and democracy attacks wherever it can the 'communist' world,"[37] Duncan turns increasingly to the "community of everything," the "commune of poetry," and to that "lost America of love" Whitman and Ginsberg celebrated—Americans as "devotées of Man's commonality" that exist in "all nations," in all times and places. America, an entity distinct from the empire-building United States, is here not the usual embodiment of the ideal of individual liberty, but of the commons. In the title of Duncan's *The Opening of the*

Field, the "field" the poet would "open" is an enclosed literary commons: "[T]he great field of poetry," as he writes in *The H.D. Book*, "a common ground of language charged with old meanings revived, of form and content as immanent in the universe."[38]

~

At the height of the struggle between free market capitalism and state communism, between "private (individual)" and "public [social/collective] rights," Duncan turns to the "common rights" and permissions of "our common humanity." Neither singularly private nor collectively public, but common: open to all equally individually together.

~

Duncan's anarchist poetics of derivation has particular implications for (especially authorial) identity, elaborating a polysemous poetic and anarchic self—a self not as private property (as in Locke's conception), but a self-as-commons, what Antonio Negri calls "common being."[39] "Against the private property of self," Duncan writes of Robert Browning, "he created a community of selves."[40] Whitman's sense of America-as-poem and his ideal of "Man's commonality" comes in here too—the "self" celebrated in Whitman's famous "song" being common and unprivatized:

> this crux of Self, of one's very unique existence as such, is always there in the tension between speaking oneself and the utter common-ality of the language that must be the medium of that self.[41]

In Duncan's essays on Whitman, the nineteenth century poet is anarcho-communist, often merging with Vanzetti in Duncan's mind: "Is it from Vanzettis' letters or from Whitman's thought?" he asks himself of the source of his lines from "The Multiversity" (quoted above).[42] The "unique" poetics that seems the very signature of "Whitman" (the long line, the paratactic catalogue) is, in Duncan's derivative anarcho-poetics, common to all who "derive in their evolution from the line of Whitman," or who open themselves to the possibilities of the form ("Adventure" 194). Language, poetic forms—even the seemingly singular styles of individual poets—are *common* not *private* properties:

> Where the line itself that Whitman adventured in his great experiment at last might be recognized to be not Whitman's personal extravagance and private property but his donation to our new language in poetry must be today. It is only in a new poetry that the transformation of poetry is ever justified, is ever carried forward. Where at last the new force of that line must be recognized in the spiritual transmission of poetic form is in our work, indeed, in the advancing sentences ever hearing in their advance the "Whitman" line—eternal now, for it is a common property of the mind. ("Adventure" 197)

"Property" here assumes its scientific use (the properties of the various elements—DNA, in Duncan's formation, as the "common code" from which all life derives). Such properties are not privatizeable—current attempts to patent the genetic code by corporations such as Monsanto notwithstanding—and they demand a "proper response": a commoning, a communion. Poetry, from this perspective, cannot "fail" as a mode of autonomy (as it does for Riding), because it is in fact a mode of communing—of multiphasic relationality.

~

Despite his cautions, in "The Multiversity" and "Orders," that the "commune" and the "individual" must be kept in balance, there is a tendency in Duncan's poetics towards a totalizing unification in an all-encompassing "oneness"—a Whitmanic "nation of Mankind at large" ("Changing" 171)—a totalitarian position not of the one *and* (with) the many, but of One that *is* (represents) the many.[43] Duncan's organicism—"As words belong to language and cells to animal bodies, poets come to belong to a poetry" ("Changing"163)—grounds his insistence upon a "poetry or all poetries" in *Bending the Bow.*[44] While Duncan seems to be aware of the dangers here—he writes, in one of his Whitman essays, that by the 1930s "ideas of Whitman's had come also to be the ideas of established and increasingly coercive governments. Totalism—*ensemblism*—is haunted when we return to it today in the dark monstrosities of socialistic and democratic totalitarianism" ("Changing" 168)—he nevertheless continues to pursue a poetry that would be a totalizing "order of orders."[45] Duncan employs the language of natural orders (as opposed to the man-made orders of social hierarchies) typical of many anarchist streams, which associate their philosophy with a putative state of nature.

> PARSONS: Anarchy is the natural law, instead of the man-made statute.
>
> GOLDMAN: Anarchism, whose roots, as it were, are part of nature's forces.
>
> DUNCAN: The logic of earth and of an emerging concept of the physical universe shifts the meaning and imagination of individualities and masses; laws are not imposed upon things, but flowing from things; laws are not of imposed orders but of emerging orders.[46]

An alternative strand of anarchist philosophy stridently denies such totalizing claims for natural order and natural law. David Kadlec associates this alternative tendency in anarchism with American pragmatism, noting that anarchists and pragmatists "shared a distaste for 'first principles' or 'foundations,'" as well as a "'pluralistic' assault on the Absolute."[47] Webb clearly shares the pragmatists' sense of pluralistic relationality, and Riding's anti-systematicism also feeds into this more pragmatic version of anarchism. Nevertheless, Duncan's awareness of the tension—of the tendency of singular plurality to dissolve back into mere singularity—is instructive.

~

In Duncan's 1963 Vancouver Poetry Conference talk, "A Life in Poetry," he gives one of the most detailed descriptions of his well-known "Atlantis dream."[48] It seems that in some versions of this repeating dream, the circle of dancing children surrounds "a king seated in the middle of the ring," with Duncan, as the dreamer, being selected—or "making" himself—"king." The dream then shifts to "a subterranean cave, where there was ... an empty throne." Duncan notes that he would "try to reassert being the king, and being in the throne, which was impossible," apparently triggering the collapse of the underground chamber. The throne *could not* be occupied—authority could not be centered or assumed by the dream ego's desire to dominate and to assume *representative* status.

Duncan's unoccupied throne resonates with Riding's abdicated "queendom." Indeed, he himself makes the connection explicit, in his *New American Poetry* poetics statement:

> The dream of myself as Emperor of the World. Laura Riding suggests that in Story one is Emperor of the World, creator of all things; that wisdom comes in abdicating. The freedom of the individual lies in his institution of anarchy where before he was sole ruler.[49]

The desire to be the totalitarian "Emperor of the World" is what Duncan recognizes in his organicist poetics—to speak for the "one," to stand as a Whitmanic "*ensemblist*" and weaver of the "grand collage"—and he chooses to resist via anarchist abdication. However, Duncan's abdication is quite different from Riding's. The latter is an attempt to reach the impossible-to-reach position of absolute autonomy, a "more-than-anarchistic self-subtraction." Duncan's is no real abdication at all, but rather a *resistance* to the urge to occupy the throne in the first place. It is an abdication before appropriation, a permanent vacation of all positions of power, authority, and centralization, akin to Hardt and Negri's advocacy of "desertion" as a means of resisting global Empire: "Battles against the Empire might be won through subtraction and defection. This desertion does not have a place; it is the evacuation of the places of power."[50] Riding advocates a position, and then a negative "super-position" via subtraction. Hers is an attempt to move through the private property of individual identity to the remotest corner of the self's enclosed garden; Duncan's is an attempt to resist the ever-encroaching and enticing enclosures of the private for the common and open meadow.

~

The crucial distinction between the individualist and communist versions of anarchism falls upon this question of property: the individualist stream reveals its roots in Locke's sense of the self as indisputable private property and the ground of individual rights and freedoms; the communist stream in arguments over "primitive accumulation" and the enclosure of the English commons, arguing, with Gerard Winstanly and the Diggers, that the earth is a "common treasury," singularly plural and open to all to share.[51] For Riding poetry's problem lies in its too-close links to the private self: it "seems to say: keep out. This is a private performance."[52] For Duncan, the poem is an open-field commons to which we are all (potentially) permitted to return. But Duncan also reveals that the poetic commons is also, always, in danger of appropriation and totalization—threatened by our egos' attempts to crown ourselves kings (or queens) of the meadow.

~

Where amidst this divergence is Phyllis Webb? Ambiguously of both realms. We can take her "The Days of the Unicorns" again as guide.

> I remember when the unicorns
> roved in herds though the meadow
> behind the cabin, and how they would
> lately pause, tilting their jewelled

horns to the falling sun as we shared
the tensions of private property
and the need to be alone.

Here is Duncan's "meadow," upon which a common "cabin" has been thrown up against "the tensions of private property." The "common good" is still the ideal—the "sharing" mentioned here, the mutual recognition of the between of being (the unicorns' "pink tongues out / for our benevolence")—but the dream is distant now and its loss elegiacally lamented—as mythic as the herds of unicorns that have abdicated their place in the performance of "music and extinction" that is history.

I know this is scarcely credible now
as we cabin ourselves in cold
and the motions of panic
and our cells destroy each other
performing music and extinction
and the great dreams pass on
to the common good

The world now belongs to the individual "cabin[ed] … in cold" solitude, and to the totalized truth of the chosen and their dismissal of those "not wanted on the voyage." What remains is the aporia of the common—the paradoxical "sharing" of isolation, the naked numerousness of all the being alone together—or, considering Rilke's sonnet (to which Webb is in part responding here), the common is the "mere possibility of being," kept alive in a poem of deep remembering.[53] Whether the speaker in Webb's poem is a Queen alone in her Queendom is not clear, but she is certainly not abdicating her position (throne/poem): she continues in her cabin, "nourishing" the common with possibility. Despite the "music of extinction" that we hear all around us, witness is taking place, and the poem's speaker seems an isolate member of networks of resistance—squatters alone in their cabins, perched upon the edges of literary meadows, simultaneously *keeping* (to themselves) and *commoning* (together).[54]

II. Of Being Naked and Numerous

Where Duncan appears to be most able to sustain the *singular plural* paradox—where he best resists his tendency to totalize—is in his particular conception of the serial poem, as embodied in his "Passages" poems (cited above as examples of his anarchism).[55] Thus, these expressions of an anarco-communist poetics are themselves part of a complex structure that is itself *formally* anarchist.

Nevertheless, the question of an anarchist aesthetics is a thorny one, in part because of the fraught debate over the very notion of seeing a political (social) valence to the aesthetic (and the equally vexed issue of maintaining an either/or distinction—either social or aesthetic, political or cultural, base or superstructure—but never both at once). The fear, obviously, is of the aesthetic coming to stand *in place of* (to *represent*, as it were) the political. The concern here is with the description of an anarchist aesthetics as discussed by a number of recent critics and a sense that, if we are going to take the politics of poetic form seriously, there must be more detailed and specific examples of what an anarchist poetics might look like (the serial poem), and more pressing philosophical questions (such as representation) than have been a part of this discussion thus far.

> WEIR: [T]he politics of anarchism was transformed into the culture of modernism.
>
> ANTLIFF: [F]ree artistic expression and anarchism were interchangeable.
>
> GOLDMAN: True creative genius ... can be brought out only by the growth of individuality and the fearless assertion of personality.[56]

As Sean Sheehan notes, when "cultural anarchism" is seen to overlap with modernism, "it is usually only the individualist strain of anarchism that comes to the fore."[57] This is certainly the case with Allan Antliff's discussion of early twentieth century American modernism in *Anarchist Modernism*, where anarchism is not much more than "a mode of personal liberation."[58] David Weir, in *Anarchy and Culture*, does a little more to suggest what an anarchist aesthetic might be, but clearly for him such an aesthetic stands (as a sort of compensation) in place of anarchism's actual political failings in the actual social world:

> The only "evidence" for the ultimate transformation of anarchist politics into modernist aesthetics is the autonomous, heterogeneous, and fragmentary nature of modernist culture itself.... That is, anarchism and modernism are structurally homologous.[59]

Weir's two key terms over which anarchist political philosophy and modernist aesthetics merge are "fragmentation" and "autonomy"—terms familiar enough to readers of the criticism of modernist art and literature. However, he doesn't really flesh out his terms, nor does he pursue them into the realm they have, arguably, been most consistently applied: modernist poetry. He approaches a fuller elaboration only in his discussion of nineteenth century French critic Paul Bourget's work on Baudelaire and decadence. Bourget describes what he calls "organic" totalitarian and "anarchic" (decentralized) or "decadent" societies and the "aesthetic cognate[s]" associable with them. Weir cites Havelock Ellis's reformulation of Bourget's "decadent," anarchic literature:

> A style of decadence is one in which the unity of the book is decomposed to give place to the independence of the page, in which the page is decomposed to give place to the independence of the phrase and the phrase to give place to the independence of the word.[60]

Weir further comments:

> The way the various units of composition in the literary work dissociate from the whole and assume a separate, autonomous existence is structurally analogous to the decentralized, federated form of society that Proudhon proposed.[61]

Despite the emphasis on "autonomy" and fragmentation, what Weir describes is not too far from the aesthetic of the serial poem, the singular plural dynamics of which lie somewhere between Bourget's organicism and decadence—between Duncan's commune of poetry and Riding's autonomous "private performance."

Being Singular Plural

A more detailed discussion of Jean Luc Nancy's concept of the *singular plural* has been put off for long enough. While Nancy—a philosopher in the line of Heidegger and Levinas—is neither a reader of twentieth century English language poetry (so far as I know), nor an anarchist as such, he does elaborate an ontology of relational space—as the *singular plural* paradox indicates—which maintains an irreducible simultaneity of the individual and the collective. His ontology can thus provide a ground for the anarcho-communism of Kropotkin, Duncan (in his serial poems at least), and ultimately Webb.

In Nancy's ontology, "A single being is a contradiction in terms" and "all appearance is co-appearance."[62] Neither pole can dominate—"Being is singularly plural and plurally singular" (*Singular Plural* 28)—for the whole weight of being lies in the "with," the fact that being is always already being with others (common), so that it is "the 'with' that constitutes being" (30). The ascendancy of either the singular or the plural is typically (philosophically) seen in terms of origins. But as Nancy argues, "Being-many-together is the originary situation" and the self "takes place with before taking place as itself and/or as the other" (40–41):

> At the very least, and provisionally, one could try to say it in the following way: it is no more a matter of an originary multiplicity and its correlation (in the sense of the One dividing itself in an arch-dialectical manner, or in the sense of the atoms' relationship to the clinamen) than it is a matter of an originary unity and its division. In either case, one must think an anteriority of the origin according to some event that happens to it unexpectedly (even if that event originates within it). It is necessary, then, to think plural unity originarily. (39)

One clear relation to the philosophy of communist-anarchism here is the very *an*-archism Nancy proposes: one of the meanings of the Greek *an-arche* is "without origin"—at least, without a ruling origin above/beyond/outside the constituent body. In Nancy's ontology, there is no authority in origins, only relations: "[W]hat becomes of sovereignty when it is revealed that it is nothing but a singular plural spacing? How is one to think sovereignty as the 'nothing' of the with that is laid bare?" (36)

Of being numerous. The with of the poetics of response (poems always with other poems—no one-night stands). Naked poems—naked in their bare being together, their empty between. We could begin considering the poetics of the serial poem here.

~

Of Being in Series

> JOSEPH CONTE: The open form of the poetic series is defined by its limitless set of relations.
>
> ALAN GOLDING: What is the relationship of part to whole, in poetry and in society?
>
> NANCY: Being is at the same time in the same place only on the condition of its spacing of an indefinite plurality of singularities.[63]

In *Unending Design,* Joseph Conte describes the serial poem as one of the characteristic forms of "the anarchical, occasional works of postmodern poets."[64] It is "determined by the discontinuous and often aleatory manner in which one thing follows another."[65] Singular elements (poems/segments) of the series are autonomous (not subordinate, for their meaning or presence, to the unfolding whole), but their place is entirely significant only in terms of their being placed amongst the other elements (poems/segments) of the entire serial poem. *The serial poem is singular plural.* Its being is numerous.

Alan Golding, writing on Oppen's "Of Being Numerous," also sees the serial poem's significance as hinging upon the relationship of part to whole—a "dialectical" form of thinking which is played out "by foregrounding as a formal problem the relationship between individual piece and whole sequence"—"the relationship between the 'singular' and the 'numerous.'"[66]

This "formal problem" is worked out in the syntax of seriality, which is paratactic and unsubordinated. "Meaning" lies not strictly in terms of part and whole, but *between* parts—in their propinquity and contiguity. "Spacing," as Nancy describes it in the singular plural:

> Being is with being; it does not ever recover itself, but it is near to itself, beside itself, in touch with itself, its very self, in the paradox of that proximity where distancing ... and strangeness are revealed. (*Singular Plural* 35)
>
> The togetherness of singulars is singularity "itself." It "assembles" them insofar as it spaces them; they are "linked" insofar as they are not unified. (33)

Nancy articulates the syntax of seriality in his very title: "Being singular plural: these three apposite words, which do not have any determined syntax" (28)—"another syntax," "without punctuation, without a mark of equivalence, implication, or sequence" (37).[67] Linking is not unifying. The singular is not only singular, but plural too—with others. Additive and accumulative—but discontinuous and incomplete, "it takes its shape," Conte writes,

> from the diverse ways in which items come together, undetermined by (in Umberto Eco's terms) an "external necessity" that would prescribe its organization, or by the "internal" necessity that is the claim of organic form.[68]

This is *radically* open form, as in Duncan's conception of his "Passages" poems (upon which Conte in part focuses). Conte relates the serial poem to scientific theories of indeterminacy (Heisenberg) and undecideability (Gödel), as opposed to the "hierarchical cosmos" which finds its reflection in closed poetic forms.[69] Nothing pre-determines the poem—"[Y]ou have to go into a serial poem," Blaser writes, "not knowing what the hell you're doing," being "led by what is composing"[70]—and nothing contains or closes it, so that even its singularity *as a* (single) *poem* is paradoxically plural and never complete. Duncan attempts to capture this sense of the poem's outreaching itself in his description of his "Passages" poems:

> Passages of a poem larger than the book in which they appear follow a sentence read out of Julian. I number the first to come *one*, but they belong to a series that extends in an area larger than my work in them. I enter the poem as I entered my own life, moving between an initiation and a terminus I cannot name.[71]

This is the true sense of the serial poem's multiplicity: it implies increase without conclusion, a proliferation of forms in ever-widening arcs of relation—however contained the poem may be between a segment marked "one" and another marked "thirty" or "forty," or between the covers of a single book (and it is significant that Duncan's "Passages" poems are spread amongst three books, and that at a certain point he ceased numbering them)—the series, as virtual matrix of possible relations, does not truly end. Here is Nancy one more time:

> In Latin *plus* is comparable to multus. It is not "numerous"; it is "more." It is an increase or excess of origin in the origin.... [T]he One is more than one; it is not that "it divides itself," rather it is that one equals more than one, because "one" cannot be counted without counting more than one. (*Singular Plural* 39)

Of being in excess (of itself)—this is the serial poem's arithmetic. An irresolvable singular plurality.

~

Being Naked Together

> Community is bare, but it is imperative (*Singular Plural* 36).

"Poetics Against the Angel of Death"—the final poem in Webb's 1962 *The Sea Is Also a Garden*—announces the twin projects that would consume most of the following twenty years of her literary efforts.[72] They would be two serial poems: the minimalist *Naked Poems* (1965) and the never "completed" "Kropotkin Poems" (begun in 1967), the long and short of which is heralded at the close of *The Sea Is Also a Garden*:

> because I want to die
> writing Haiku
> or, better,
> long lines, clean and syllabic as knotted bamboo. Yes!
>
> (*Vision* 60)

Both short-lined "Haiku" and long-lined historical-epic arise out of Webb's struggle (expressed in "Poetics Against ... ") to make "sense" of the Wordsworthian "attitude / of private Man speaking to public men." They are attempts to resolve the singular and plural, self and others, individual and collective. In terms of Webb's poetics of response, the move is now in some sense away from other poets (such as Wordsworth) as responsive chords, towards the formal patterns of the poem's own extensive architecture: the long (serial) poem formed out of the relational responses of the poem to its own evolving structure.[73]

What is "laid bare" in the *Naked Poems* is, it is usually assumed, first: the poem/page itself (short lines, short poems, a great deal of empty white space surrounding)—and second: the emotional state of the poem's speaker(s). This is true—but more importantly, it is the *relationship between* the poems and their elements—relationality (part and whole, poem and poem) itself—that is left naked and unavoidable.

What is the syntax of absence? What is the substance of between?

"Spacing" is the rule in *Naked Poems.*

MOVING
to establish distance
between our houses.

It seems
I welcome you in.

Your mouth blesses me
all over.

There is room.

(*Vision* 65)

Space as theme (the "distance / between our houses"), space on the page ("Suite I" occupies the lower half of the page; "Suite II" the upper half, in italics), the apostrophic, rhetorical space between an "I" addressing an (absent) "you," the space marked out by the poem's incessant repetitions, reversals, and mirror images. A poetry of "*consanguinity,*" Webb calls this (*Vision* 95): relationship by blood, close connection or association. A poetry of the "*conjunctive*" (96)—

AND
here
and here and
here
and over   and
over   your mouth

(66)

—is built through accumulation and addition, rather than the contrastive "opposition of ideas ... 'buts' and 'thoughs' and 'althoughs'" of the sentence's typical discursive rhetoric and subordinative, hypotactic structure.[74] The conjunctive marks the between clearly, but it is itself hollow, naked, empty of content—"The room that held you" (*Vision* 78) now empty, the "blouse on the floor" once filled with warm body (70).

~

The Space between You and I

requires both "distance" (horizon—"moving to establish") and "room" (companionship —"your mouth ... all over"). Throughout *Naked Poems* the space between "I" and "you" is both distant ("you" is never present, dramatically, in the poem) and fused: at one point "I am enclosed / by a thought" (*Vision* 67)—the autonomous container self—and then later "*I held you like this / in my mind*" (73)—the other is inside, is self? Or both occupy the same space? Tap tap—who taps back? Kropotkin in his cell? Whose blouse is it, anyway?

YOUR BLOUSE

I people
this room
with things, a
chair,   a lamp   a
fly,   two books by
Marianne Moore.

I have thrown my
blouse on the floor.

Was it only
last night?

(70)

The confusion ("your"/ "my" blouse?) could be explained (in terms of "narrative") as the "gift / I wear" in "Suite II" (79)—it was "your" blouse, but "you" gave it to "me"—and it is also one of the grounds for establishing the lesbian "love story" of the poem (both "you" and "I" wear blouses, both are thus women). The intention here is not to disagree with these interpretations, but simply to add that the confusion is also *a confusion between self and other,* the one and the many, as such. "I people," the poem begins: I one, I many.

> "People" clearly designates the mode of "one" by which "I" remove myself, to the point of appearing to forget or neglect the fact that I myself am part of "people." ... [W]e are all precisely *people,* that is, indistinctly persons, humans, all of a common "kind," but of a kind that has its existence only as numerous, dispersed, and indeterminate in its generality. (*Singular Plural* 7)

Or as Oppen writes in "Of Being Numerous": "There are things / We live among 'and to see them / Is to know ourselves.'"[75] "I" and "you" mark out a space in which there can be a self and another, a self and others—the *with* of the singular plural. The poems are naked bruises where the between makes its mark.

THE BRUISE

Again you have left
your mark.

Or we
have.

Skin shuddered
secretly.

(*Vision* 68)

For such a signature—flesh on flesh—there needs to be one and more-than-one. "[S]o we are distinguished to ourselves," even though we "don't want that distinction," want instead to be "people," to be numerous (85).

~

The Space of Repetition

marks another aspect of the serial poem's singular plurality. Each small poem/segment is singularly unique and yet each seems a variation upon the others, each one blends and bleeds together as their unique elements exceed singularity and travel from poem to poem, page to page, becoming many:

> "It seems / I welcome you in" (65) ... "so it seems / down here" (69)
>
> "Your mouth" (65) ... "over your mouth" (66)
>
> "There is room" (65) ... "*There is no room*" (77)
>
> "my / blouse on the floor" (70) ... "On the floor your blouse" (75)
>
> "*plum curtains*" (74) ... "*The plum light*" (75)
>
> "*I sat cross-legged*" (77) ... "dead crossed legs" (91)
>
> "white roses" (81) ... "the white Tanabe / narcissus" (82)
>
> "a yellow round" (81) ... "the yellow chrysanthemums" (83)

Poem following poem repeats some small element, drawing relation, or else, leaping across pages, we return and revert via echo.. The effect is that the single poem/segment is unstable—it "leaks" into the next, as elements stray from poem to poem, singularity fragmenting into multiplicity.

~

The final section of *Naked Poems* is the interrogative "Some Final Questions." Interrogation is a key part of Webb's interest in anarchism—the "Question as an Instrument of Torture," as she titles a 1971 radio talk—an abuse of power and persecution of the powerless.[76] Interrogation and confinement / the questioner's position of power and authority / the invaded and examined questionee—Kropotkin, Sacco and Vanzetti—all of Webb's key anarchists suffered solitary confinement and cross-examination.

The dialogic structure of the question-and-answer format used in "Final Questions" is of most interest here. One gain in the serial poem over the shorter lyric is in the extended philosophical work that can be performed—as Alan Golding notes, the serial allows "a more extended and flexible form of thinking than is possible in the lyric," "stretch[ing]" its "thematic and structural limitations."[77] In Webb's dialectical question-and-answer, what appears to be "in question" is the lyric subject itself—the move into serial form with *Naked Poems* being part and parcel of her attempt to work through the limitations of the lyric. That lyric subject does two things in this final section: it deflects the questions that attempt to pin it down, eventually responding only with silence (the final "Oh?" going unanswered), and it reveals itself to be "double," if not completely multiple—the poem's "I" and "you," self and other, presenting their relational between.[78]

> *Now you are sitting doubled up in pain.*
> *What is that for?*
>
> doubled up I feel
> small like these poems
> the area of attack
> is diminished
>
> (*Vision* 103)

"Doubled up in pain," or doubled up by being multiple, more than one? The double self that shares room and blouse with its other here shares the "attack" of interrogation. The poem prior to this has the lyric self answering "I am watching a shadow / shadowing a shadow" (102), which looks ahead to the "shadow following / the hand that writes" from the "Kropotkin Poems."[79] One is never (only) one. A shadow of the plural follows every single self. The serial poem "diminishes" "the area of attack" not by closing the self in on its own enclosed singularity, but by opening it out upon the multiple, for the "small … poems" of the *Naked* series have their strength in number—seeking forms of solidarity and federation.

~

III. Poems of Failure and the Failure of Representation

> The whole aspect of the universe changes with this new conception. The idea of force governing the world, preestablished law, preconceived harmony, disappears to make room for the harmony that Fourier had caught a glimpse of: the one which results from the disorderly and incoherent movements of numberless hosts of matter, each of which goes its own way and all of which hold each in equilibrium.[80]

Roger Farr, in his excellent essay "The 'Insurrectionary Wilderness of the I,'" cites this passage as an example of the "anarchist poetics" discernable in Kropotkin's philosophical writings—a poetics that is without a "center," and which, in terms of Kropotkin's scientific speculations on the cosmos, is characterized by "little swarms of matter … all-powerful in their numbers."[81] Farr links *Naked Poems* and the "Kropotkin Poems" along this decentralizing axis—the trajectory of Webb's struggle against and with "the limitations and possibilities of the lyric subject."[82]

In reading the "Poems of Failure"—the title under which the longest intact section of the "Kropotkin Poems" was published, as the preface to *Wilson's Bowl* in 1980—the present argument follows Farr's fairly closely. What we will work towards here—and what we will add to—is the picture of just how "disorderly" and "numberless" the "hosts of matter" are that make up the "Kropotkin Poems"—or perhaps more correctly—to which the "Kropotkin Poems" ultimately belong. Farr notes their dispersal, or remnants, in *Wilson's Bowl*: the prefatory "Poems of Failure," the poem "Kropotkin" in the "Portraits" section, and "Solitary Confinement" and "from The Kropotkin Poems" in the section "Crimes." What we have here is just the tip of the iceberg of what turns out to be Webb's twenty-year research into Russian radicalism that would include these published remnants of the "Kropotkin Poems" and "related" archival material noted by Farr; the archival presence of research on anarchist firebrand Michael Bakunin; the uncollected "What Is to Be Done Poem," from the 1967 anthology *The New Romans*; and the poems on Lenin, relating to Webb's second trip to the Soviet Union in 1989, collected in *Hanging Fire.*[83]

The "Kropotkin Poems" begin with the serial form of the "Poems of Failure" and its seven discontinuous yet linked sections. The first poem comes to Kropotkin not through the Russian's own life or writings, however, but through his appearance, in the form of a portrait, in Paul Goodman's novel *The Empire City*—the source, Webb tells us, of her "interest in anarchism."[84] The next two sections of the "Poems of Failure" work in biographical details from Kropotkin's life, largely taken, as Farr notes, from Kropotkin's own *Memoirs of a Revolutionist.*[85] The final four sections relate mostly to Webb's own failure to bring her "good masterpiece of work" to fruition (*Wilson's* 21).[86]

The fact that—after a mere three poems of the opening sequence of what was announced as a book-length project—the poetry is taken over by meditations on its "failure," suggests that *failure*, more than anything else, is its concern from the beginning. Webb herself has declared as much, writing that "the theme is failure"—but the question remains: failure of what, exactly? Webb's own suggestions are nebulous: "[T]he failure of societies to live without repressive authority, the seeming unevolvingness of political and social life, and the grand failure of the human experiment."[87] There are of course other possibilities: the failure of anarchism as a revolutionary program? The failure of the poet's planned project (Webb admits this much too)? Or—the failure of the poem as such? Of the long, ambitious twentieth century "poem including history"? Or—some aspect of the poetic project—its *designedness*[88] and intentions, that it be representative (*of* Kropotkin, *the* "Kropotkin Poems")?

Considering all of this, it is not insignificant that the section of Goodman's novel from which Webb quotes at the beginning of her "Poems of Failure" is itself concerned with political failure. In chapter one of Book Three, "Our Meeting, 1948," Goodman has a group of radicals sitting in silence and at an "impasse," a position from which "nothing practical is forthcoming."[89] Sitting beneath the picture of Kropotkin, they are quite literally "demanding the impossible," hoping for an anarchist miracle of self-willed levitation. There is—as there is throughout *Empire City*—a good deal of satire here, but also a darker undercurrent, which Webb picks up on in what she chooses to quote directly from this chapter—that the would-be revolutionaries are "inconsolable" and resigned to "resting in this hell" (*Wilsons* 14). However, it is important to note that, along with the obvious humour and the dampening despair, there is a truth about anarchist politics expressed here: philosophically unwilling to *force* a *program* upon the social field, anarchists often find themselves left with little recourse than biding their time and/or working through small-scale, face-to-face affinity groups such as the one described by Goodman. While this may seem pathetic and hopeless, the affinity group itself is the model of the future society the anarchists are trying to virtually will into existence. Thus Goodman's focus on the communal strength found in the *sharing* of the "impasse" is significant:[90]

> *Nevertheless* (this is what makes the moment beautiful), we do not get up and leave one another, quit the meeting. Are we afraid, clinging to one another because of the impasse—every problem, nothing practical—is unbearable and no one can bear it alone? No. For indeed alone one is not so clearly in the presence of the impasse; it is only together, when from many friends very well known nothing practical is forthcoming, that each one has a good awareness of the common impasse.... We are staying on in loyalty to one another, in the jaws of an impasse. (*Empire* 283–84)

In the social formation of these revolutionary cells, this development is indeed crucial: "They started by saying 'I,' and sometimes they ended by saying 'we'" (272). Seen from this vantage point, the group's "impasse" may not be a failure at all, but merely the application of the "Theory of the Fertile Void": "[I]f we friends remain in our impasse, close to our impasse, gratuitously suffering the awareness of being in an impasse, must not the Fertile Void yield up something?" (287) Crucially, this will be "something unlooked for," unplanned and unexpected. It is not that there be no order or plan, but simply that there be no *pre-determined* order or plan. This is not a matter of failure, but of keeping the possible *possible.* In the chapter prior to "Our Meeting," radicals in a post-war, post-apocalyptic wasteland find themselves in such a fertile void. Theorizing the necessary destruction that precedes new creation, the character Mynheer explains:

> "When will there be an idea," said Mynheer, "do you think we will know it beforehand? It will be surprisingly doing in the hands. One must not miss the moment, the moment when instead of radical ideologies and radical votes there are surprised people. Surprised, but not unaware...." (267)[91]

As if acting out Mynheer's Bakuninist theorizing, the

> citizens of the New Commune did not regard so highly the elaborate structures in which our society used to be organized.... [L]ike children or some kinds of schizophrenics, they pounced eagerly on disassociated parts; whenever a big structure breaks down there are always some parts or other. Then they put some of these into odd shapes.... (271)

~

Shall I tell you what I do to pass the time
here on the island at night?
There is red velvet and purple velvet.

> I cut out diamonds from a pattern piece
> by piece. I set two pieces, one purple
> one red, together, attach another making designs
> as I go. Mapping it into some kind of crazy
> poncho. I am absorbed in the fitting together
> of pieces.
>
> (*Wilson's* 18)

When Webb calls the "Kropotkin Poems" "too designed" (9), one might hear an echo of Goodman's Mynheer. While her "good masterpiece of work" would not come, Webb kept company in her impasse with Goodman, Sacco and Vanzetti, Kropotkin and Woodcock—the whole list of books she tabulates in section iv of the "Poems of Failure." She took parts from the broken "big structure" and—following "breaking"—engaged in the "making" of quilting and collage. "[L]ittle swarms" of poetic "matter"—a poetry, at last, of "scattering chips of dialogue" and dream.

~

Similarly revealed as a "broken" "structure" is the poet's lyric I/eye. Speaking and seeing only fragments, the I finds itself (in) a wilderness of others:

> Insurrectionary wilderness of the I
> am, I will be, forcing the vision
> to something other, something out
> side the sleep of dreams riddled
> with remembrances.
>
> (*Wilson's* 15)

Farr notes the significant shift here "from a stable, fixed position indicated by the declarative 'I/am' (the line break is instructive) to a speculative, fluctuating and modalized 'I will be,' suggesting the emergence of a more fluid kind of agency."[92] We have already suggested that this is Webb's project throughout her work—a prolonged investigation of the actual multiplicities of the seemingly singular self. What is interesting in the "Kropotkin Poems" is that this plurality also appears in the supposedly singular person of Kropotkin, the figure upon which the cohesive project of a proposed book of poetry would depend. Kropotkin fades off into Charles Olson ("what does not change / is the will to change"), John Donne ("Else a great prince in prison lies"), or fellow anarchist and prisoner Nicola Sacco ("between all the harmonies of the mother nature").[93] He reveals his multiple masks:

> dressed up in your merchant's costume
> dressed up as a *page de chambre*
> dressed up as an eight-year old Persian
> Prince with real jewels in your belt
> ....
>
> (*Wilson's* 15)

Kropotkin, in his cell—Webb, "tap[ping] my own temple"[94]—are we inside or are we out? Who are we?

> The ears turn off. I will not listen.
> I shall not speak. Tap, tap. Tap, tap, tap.
> Prisoners in the St. Peter and St. Paul fortress
> sending their telex messages.
> Raving below the Prince, a peasant
> goes mad in his cell. The Prince is listening.
> As above, so below.
> I slow my lines.
> I walk up and down the room
> ....
>
> (*Wilson's* 17)

Is it Kropotkin or the poet who will "not listen" and "not speak"? It doesn't matter, because a kind of speaking and an irresistible listening ensue: someone taps, someone taps back, and communication begins—phatic and pre-linguistic—the solitaries in their confinement finding community through the walls. From Kropotkin we move to the mad peasant and then on to the poet writing ("I slow my lines"). A comparison is drawn. As above, so below. Kropotkin in his Russian cell, Webb on her Canadian island. But, ultimately, Webb rejects the temptations of identifying with Kropotkin: "Not a case of identification. Easier to see myself / in the white cat asleep on the bed" (*Wilson's* 21). Kropotkin is merely "the guiding spirit"[95]—and there are others, other "shadows following the / hand that writes"—in the expanded picture of the "Kropotkin Poems" we must speak of Chernyshevsky and Bakunin too. We must see Webb's research on Lenin in the late 1980s as a tapping back to Kropotkin twenty years after the earlier tapping on the self's solitary cell.

~

Both by its year of publication (1967) and the presence of shared elements (the theme of the prison cell, the use of the same passage from Sacco's November 26, 1926 letter to Mrs. Jack), Webb's "What Is to Be Done Poem" reveals itself to be a part of the "Kropotkin Poems"—one fragment in its "scattered hosts of matter." The poem takes its title not from Lenin, but from Russian novelist and socialist critic Nikolai Chernyshevsky, from whom Lenin in turn took his famous title.[96] While usually considered something of an "embryonic Marxist," Chernyshevsky, who wrote his one novel, *What Is to Be Done* (1864), while in the same St. Peter and St. Paul Fortress where both Bakunin and Kropotkin were at other times also confined, clearly has resonance in anarchist circles as well.[97] The edition most likely read by Webb was translated by American anarchist Benjamin Tucker in 1883, and Chernyshevsky's main characters are self-described "egoists" who believe that "every one thinks of himself first."[98] Tucker was himself a follower of German egoist Max Stirner, so if Chernyshevsky has some truck with anarchism it is clearly of the individualist strain. His heroine Vera Pavlovna makes this abundantly clear:

> "You call me whimsical, and you ask me what I seek in life. I wish neither to dominate nor be dominated.... I wish to be independent and live in my own fashion. What I need I feel that I have the strength to earn; what I do not need I do not

> desire.... What I do know is that I wish to be free; that I do not wish to be under obligations to any one. I wish to act after my own fancy. Let others do the same. I respect the liberty of others, as I wish them to respect mine."[99]

It may be that Chernyshevsky's individualism—at least as it is recognizable as such in the characters in his novel—finds its way into the "disorderly movements" of the "Kropotkin Poems" as something of a balance to Kropotkin's communism—the Riding-element, as it were, to counterbalance the project's Duncan-elements. However, "The What Is to Be Done Poem" does not revolve around the issue of autonomy, but rather, the necessity of the singular plural:[100]

> The denial of one's neighbour is
> easy / as
> denial of one's self / the me
> -keeping silence.
> But to hold the alert passions
> pointing around the sun is
> what must be done.[101]

There are various "suns" in the poem pulling the self out of its "me-keeping silence," tapping on its cell and forcing it to engage the world of contemporary politics and once again consider the question *what is to be done*—hot-spots such as American cities burning up in racial riot ("Burn Baby Burn," Webb intones, while the Watts riots were still recent enough to smolder on in the imagination), and the war in Vietnam (the "saffron robe dancing in flame" of a protesting Buddhist priest's self-immolation).[102] "The What Is to Be Done Poem" is thus located more directly in the contemporary milieu of late-1960s unrest, and draws the "Kropotkin Poems" back to its most appropriate context: the historical moment of a committed poet's retreat from Toronto to a small Gulf Island to consider seriously *what is to be done*—a question, in the "Poems of Failure," which seems to boil down to the choice: "Russia, Suicide, or France?" (*Wilson's* 19). Webb, attracted by Kropotkin, seeing the archetypal Russian radical's fate again in Chernyshevsky "holding his head to the wall of the / great cell of Russia," thankfully chose Russia.[103]

~

There is of course the theme of silence again. Chernyshevky, in the "me-keeping silence," his head against the cell wall—Kropotkin "tap, tap" tapping back from the other side—Webb, hearing that tapping on her own skull. The silences in Webb's career have received much attention—and she herself tells us that her "poems are born out of great struggles of silence" (*Wilson's* 9). The "Kropotkin Poems," expanded to include the "little swarms of matter" scattered across the more than twenty years between their beginning and the Lenin poems in *Hanging Fire*, is an epic of silence. What vast aporias between Kropotkin ("the hillocks of Finland") and Lenin ("the statue at the Finland Station"),[104] between Chernyshevsky's and Lenin's pleas of "what is to be done?", between Chernyshevsky's novel and Goodman's. In *The Empire City*, a Reverend Dr. Bercovici quotes from one of Mallarmé's poems, commenting on the line "*Par l'irascible vent des mots qu'il n'a pas dits*": "Not the words he did say, but the words he didn't say! Vast gulph in the midst!" (*Empire* 226)[105] The tension once again is between a poetry of "perfect silence" and one of "scattering chips of dialogue." In Webb's work—in all great poetry (for it is the very mark of poetry)—emphasis must fall on what is not said. Between 1965 and 1990, for this one poet soon to be a painter cherishing "wordlessness," this is where we must place the emphasis.

~

Webb's papers and notebooks relating to the composition of the "Kropotkin Poems" indicate that part of her research was on Russian icons and iconoclasm. Firebrand anarchist Michael Bakunin makes his appearance in the manuscripts in this connection. Thus, while Webb was at this time reading E. H. Carr's biography *Michael Bakunin*, and still owns a copy of G. P. Maximoff's *The Political Philosophy of Bakunin*, she nevertheless transcribes an anecdote from Bakunin's life as it is rendered in James Billington's *The Icon and the Axe: An Interpretive History of Russian Culture*. Here is Webb's note:

> Bakunin hearing Wagner conduct Beethoven 9th symphony rushed forward to assure Wagner that this work deserved to be spared the imminent world conflagration. Wagner called Bakunin the chief stoker of revolution.... Wagner may have been influenced by Bakunin in his characterization of Sigfried.[106]

Bakunin's iconoclastic creative-destruction appealed to Webb who—probably long before having heard of the anarchist—was composing poems such as "And Again the Theme of Perfection and Destruction," and the dialogic "Breaking" and "Making" (the order of which is of course significant). Bakunin appears throughout Billington's book as the archetypal figure of "the Russian revolutionary tradition" (*Icon* 36) and "iconoclastic materialism" (360)—the self-proclaimed cure for Russia's long love affair with the religious icon. Billington notes that Russian icons—"the most revered form of theological expression in Russia" (8)—"provided an image of higher authority" (31) and "a model for the hierarchical order of Russian society" (35). But the icon also provided the "model for mass indoctrination" deployed by "the former seminarian Stalin" (36). One can begin to see why an anarchist—and a poet interested in serial "swarms of matter"—might start to suspect poetry's own complicity with the (potentially hierarchical and totalitarian) iconic image. The Greek *eikon*, Billington reminds us, means "likeness," a representation (29).

~

The real "failure" of the "Kropotkin Poems" comes with Webb's realization that she may be in danger of turning her anarchist prince into an icon. Farr notes the likeness of Kropotkin's portrait in Goodman's novel to "a Russian icon," and Webb calls Kropotkin "the White Christ" (echoing the title of one of the chapters in Woodcock's biography),[107] linking him with Billington's comment about those particularly fervent radicals who could at once "affirm their belief in Christ, St. Paul, and Chernyshevsky" (*Icon* 434). The failure of the "Kropotkin Poems" is the failure of a libertarian poetics, which found itself assuming representational status—its *program* standing in place of actual lived liberation and commonality—its *leaders* assuming iconic status. As Webb herself declares in an interview, while anarchism is "totally unauthoritarian," she nevertheless "had my authority in Kropotkin, as a godlike figure or a christlike figure. So I had to get rid of that."[108] The "Kropotkin Poems" *had* to fail—for their libertarian intent to remain a possibility.

~

> The rejection of centralization … is part of the larger, central theme of anarchism: the rejection of representation.… To the anarchists, political representation signifies the delegation of power from one group or individual to another, and with that delegation comes the risk of exploitation by the group or individual to whom power has been ceded.[109]

With her anxieties over Kropotkin's iconic status in her proposed project of poetry, Webb comes up against this "central theme of anarchism"—and sees clearly its implications for her anarchist poetics. If representation is something to be avoided at the political level, what about the poetic? What, more generally, about the expressive or semantic or even conceptual levels? How can one *act* outside of representational social models if one does not *think* outside them? This is the direction Webb inevitably took as she moved beyond the failure—as representation—of the "Kropotkin Poems."

~

Todd May's discussion of representation in *The Political Philosophy of Poststructuralist Anarchism* holds particular resonance for Webb's poetics when he turns to a discussion of Jean-Francois Lyotard's "libidinal economy":

> The problem with representation is that it freezes the libido into a structure that is dominated not by the libido's positivity but by the negativity of an absent object. A representation is always a

> stand-in for something else that is not there, and it is the absent object that dominates the discourse of representation.[110]

Kropotkin's dominating absence in Webb's poetry between *Naked Poems* and *Wilson's Bowl* could be read as the source of what "freezes the libido" of her poetic production. However, almost instinctively it seems, Webb understood the solution (though it took her many difficult years to work out—and live through—the sense of personal "failure"): "The subversion of representation is by means of a multiplication rather than a diminution of representing entities, a multiplication that drives the representational system to its own point of explosion."[111]

Here is the core of Webb's anarchist poetics—masquerading as a failure—but determined to live out the freedom and necessity of being "numberless hosts," "all powerful in their numbers"—of *being singular plural.*

~

The problematic of representation was everywhere in Webb's reading and thinking of the late 1960s and early '70s. Norman O. Brown's *Love's Body* was of central importance to her: she lists the book in the "Poems of Failure" as part of her reading on anarchism, and notes its conceptual centrality to the "Kropotkin Poems" in her foreword to *Wilson's Bowl.*[112] Brown's book, which deals at length with the issue of representation—particularly its psychological aspects—was also on the reading list for her proposed UBC course in 1971.[113] The focus of the course was "obsolescence"—"The rise and fall of culture heroes; the fate of 'movements,' and the absorption of dissent"—and it is clear that "obsolescence" relates directly to the problem of representation: how do ideas/thinkers/books *cease* to be "representative," how do they become obsolete? This question is played out at the very level of the course's reading list as the proposed "representative" texts (a list including Brown, Goodman, Kate Millett, Marshall McLuhan, Herbert Marcuse, Alvin Toffler, and Michel Foucault) are themselves to be taken as already "obsolete."

The proposal reads: "No required texts. A reading list will be provided. A new list will be created by the group to replace the original. The aim of the workshop is to become obsolete in eight weeks and understand why."

Brown's discussion of representation is key because he locates its problem in the dynamics of identity and thus, by extension, the problem of the lyric subject and (for Webb) poetic form. Working from Thomas Hobbes's definition of a "person" as "representative," Brown writes that a "person is always a feigned or artificial person" (*Loves* 98), and "personality … becomes not substance, but fiction, representation" (109). Brown links the representational structure of the self (ego standing in for body and id) with political representation, again paraphrasing Hobbes: "[A] multitude is made *One* Person, when they are by One Person Represented" (128). The political problem of representation is clear: "In representative institutions there is always subjection to the visible image; idolatry…. Our representative keeps us hypnotized" (122). Representation is (always potentially) totalitarian: singular and plural are not maintained in productive paradox, but erased in the One that *represents* the many. Brown's proposed counter to representation is equally instructive: like May, he proposes "multiplication"—that "Every person … is many persons" (147), and "Freedom is fertility; a proliferation of images, in excess" (248), where "Meaning is not in things but in between" (247).

Perhaps it is now possible to begin mapping some of these cut pieces of fabric into some sort of pattern and design. The serial poem can be seen as a first step away from the hierarchy and centralization of both aesthetic and political representation—a move towards the multiple, a stretching of the lyric poem/self out along a *singular plural* axis. This move can be seen both in post-war (or postmodern, if you prefer) poetics (the movement towards "open" form and the serial poem) and, prior to this, in the political philosophy of (especially communist) anarchism.

However, it is not a simple issue of mapping the binary, representation/non-representation, onto the older binary of closed/open-form poetics—for the purveyors of open form, Duncan included, could and did set themselves up as *representatives* of a new poetic order, and totalizing the open (as the only alternative to the closed) is still *totalizing*. For Webb, it was the *designedness* of the "Kropotkin Poems" that damned the project. It didn't matter, ultimately, that the form was more "open," and thus more "anarchist," than her earlier work. The problem lay in taking the form *as representative* of the politics, of writing an *authoritative* (singular, titular, complete, closed) *Kropotkin Poems*. Form didn't need to follow content, nor content form, for that matter: (in Roger Farr's formulation) "Form Radiates Content."[114] *Radiates*, but doesn't represent. Multiplies, but doesn't reduce. Form had to account for the "unlooked for" and aleatory, could not be limited by the pre-determined. The ultimate *shape* of the would-be "Kropotkin Poems"—spread over decades and books, leaping from one subject (Kropotkin) to another (Lenin), accommodating open (the Kropotkin and Lenin fragments) and "closed" ("*Wilson's Bowl's* 'Imperfect Sestina'") forms—reveals itself to be such a radical "radiation" of a possible radical poetics. Indeed, if the "open" is to be truly open, it must not exclude anything—even the "closed."

~

The path, for Webb, led from anarchism to abstraction—the non-representative mode as such. "Freedom is poetry," Brown writes, but its "sense" is "nonsense" (*Loves* 244–45): "To restore words to their full significance … is to reduce them to nonsense, to get the nonsense or nothingness or silence back into words" (258). From the failure of the "Kropotkin Poems" to the failure of representation and language as such. From the poem as a "vase of perfect silence," to that shattering and "scattering" of that vase in the serial poem's "chips of dialogue," to a renewed silence that is not "perfect" (the closed linguistic vase), but "imperfect" (the open visual "swarm"). A translation of anarchism into abstraction—a non-language for "addressing" the problem that is language/representation—this is Webb's path, ultimately, out and away from language and into paint.

Notes

1. Edwin Rolfe, *Collected Poems,* ed. Cary Nelson and Jefferson Hendricks (Urbana: Univeristy of Illinois Press, 1993), 59. George Oppen, *Collected Poems* (New York: New Directions, 1975), 151.

2. Phyllis Webb Papers, National Library of Canada.

3. Michael Bakunin, "The Reaction in Germany" (1842), in *Bakunin on Anarchism,* ed. and trans. Sam Dolgoff (Montreal: Black Rose Books, 1980), 57.

4. Oppen, "Of Being Numerous," 147. Alan Golding notes that, while published in 1968, "in 1965, Oppen was already working on 'Of Being Numerous.'" Thus it fits nicely between the publication of *Naked Poems* in 1965 and the beginning of "The Kropotkin Poems" in 1967. Golding, "George Oppen's Serial Poems," in *The Objectivist Nexus: Essays in Cultural Poetics,* ed. Rachel Blau Duplessis and Peter Quartermain (Tuscaloosa: University of Alabama Press, 1999), 93.

5. Herbert Read, *Poetry and Anarchism* (London: Faber and Faber, 1938), 15.

6. George Bowering, Canada's first parliamentary poet laureate, received some censure in the media over a perceived lack of productivity during his two-year laureateship, with the *Ottawa Sun* suggesting that he had "penned only two poems during his two year stint" (April 24, 2005). The irony here is that Bowering is one of Canada's most prolific writers ever, and has his own views on the Poet Laureate's "obligations." The issue is discussed at length at www.bookninja.com/misc/letters/boweringletter.htm.

7. Read, *Poetry and Anarchism,* 53.

8. Sean Sheehan argues much the same, describing "an arc that spans communism and extreme individualism." See his *Anarchism* (London: Reaktion Books, 2003), 38.

9. Pierre-Joseph Proudhon, *What Is Property? An Enquiry into the Principle of Right and of Government,* trans. Benjamin Tucker (New York: H. Fertig, 1966), 281. Albert Parsons, *Anarchism: Its Philosophy and Scientific Basis* (1887; reprint, New York: Krauss Reprint Co., 1971), 67–78. Emma Goldman, *Red Emma Speaks: An Emma Goldman Reader* (New York: Schocken Books, 1983), 64.

10. Sheehan, *Anarchism*, 72. The following two references will be cited parenthetically in text. Behind Sheehan's and other comments of this sort is the idea that where anarchism provides the political ideal, Marxism is needed for the more detailed economic analysis of class and capital. It is interesting to note that this was seen as common sense in the nineteenth century (see Parson's comments), as well as a proscription for the twenty-first (Sheehan's comments are directed towards "a new pathway ... through a world of global capitalism").

11. Leila Sujir, "Addressing a Presence: An Interview with Phyllis Webb," *Prairie Fire* 9:1 (Spring 1988), 34.

12. Peter Kropotkin, "Anarchist Communism: Its Basis and Principles," in *Kropotkin's Revolutionary Pamphlets*, ed. Roger Baldwin (1927; reprint, New York: Dover, 1970), 47.

13. Webb Papers, National Library.

14. Though Nancy does not discuss anarchism as such, I am suggesting that his ontology is a nice fit with the anarco-communist attempt to find a balance between individual liberty and social collectivity. Thus I am in some ways following Todd May's lead in linking poststructuralist philosophy with anarchism, though in the case of Nancy's ontology, I would argue, there is an even more precise fit with the specific objectives of communist anarchism. See May's *The Political Philosophy of Poststructuralist Anarchism* (University Park: Penn State University Press, 1994), and the discussion below in sections two and three.

15. See *The Republic*, Books 2 and 10. I am indebted here to Eric Havelock's arguments in *Preface to Plato* (Cambridge, Mass.: Harvard University Press, 1963).

16. Roger Farr offers the clearest exploration of Webb's anarchism in his essay "The 'Insurrectionary Wilderness of the I,'" *West Coast Line* 45 (2005), 63–76. See especially his discussion of the roots of Webb's anarchism at the University of British Columbia.

As to the "tradition" linking poetry and anarchism—limiting myself to English language literature—we might begin with Chaucer's *Canterbury Tales*, the structure of which (a decentered assemblage of separate, heteroglossic tales, the overall structure of which is incomplete) could be taken as paradigmatic. Milton's fallen angels, giving voice to the seventeenth century desire to shed the yoke of "vassalage," would fall into this tradition—as would Blake's similarly satanic association of "liberty," the "true Poet," and the "Devil's party" in *The Marriage of Heaven and Hell.* Shelley's anarchism has been noted by many critics (see especially Michael Henry Scrivener's *Radical Shelley*, which declares the poet a "philosophical anarchist"), and John Clare's opposition to enclosure and celebration of the commons would have to be taken into account. Thoreau and Whitman, in America, have long been associated with anarchism, and a growing host of critics are embracing the notion of anarchism's central influence on modernism (see Antliff, Weir, and Robert von Hallberg's "Libertarian Imagism"). Twentieth century anarchist-poets would have to include Voltarine de Cleyre, Arturo Giovannitti, and Laura Riding, with a real expansion of an anarchist-inflected poetics coming with the "New American Poetry"—Ginsberg's lumpen "Howl," Olson's spontaneous "projection," and Duncan's association of "Free verse, free thought, free religion, a free community" with "Vanzetti's voluntary state." John Milton, *The Complete Poems*, ed. John Leonard (London: Penguin, 1998), 149. William Blake, *The Complete Poetry and Prose* (New York: Doubleday, 1988), 35. Michael Henry Scrivener, *Radical Shelley: The Philosophical Anarchism and Utopian Thought of Percy Bysshe Shelley* (Princeton: Princeton University Press, 1982). Goldman, *Red Emma Speaks*, 69. Weir, *Anarchy and Culture*, 140, 170. Allan Antliff, *Anarchist Modernism: Art, Politics, and the First American Avant-Garde* (Chicago: University of Chicago Press, 2001). Robert von Hallberg, "Libertarian Imagism," *Modernism/Modernity* 2:2 (April 1995), 63–79. Robert Duncan, preface to *The H.D. Book*.

17. As with H.D. in the previous chapter, I am not suggesting a direct influence with Riding but something we might call a "confluence"—a sharing of certain biographical and writerly characteristics that makes the comparison of the two poets highly suggestive.

18. Duncan, introduction to *Bending the Bow*, vi.

19. In Webb's introductory comments to her unpublished interviews with Duncan, Olson, and Allen Ginsberg—interviews conducted during the 1963 Vancouver Poetry Conference and later prepared for (but never actually broadcast on) CBC radio—Webb refers to "the left wing of American poetry," calling the poets "a complimentary group though, as Aldous Huxley has said, every human group is a society of island universes." Webb Papers, National Library.

20. Laura Riding and Robert Graves, *A Survey of Modernist Poetry* (1927; reprint, New York: Doubleday, 1972), 47.

21. Henry David Thoreau, *Walden and Resistance to Civil Government*, ed. William Rossi (New York: Norton, 1966), 226–27.

22. Riding, *Anarchism Is Not Enough*, ed. Lisa Samuels (1928; reprint, Berkeley: University of California Press, 2001). Subsequent references to this work will be cited parenthetically in text as *Anarchism*.

23. This is the tack Duncan takes in his argument with Denise Levertov. Duncan writes (March 25, 1969), "'Revolution' is a Nation and has its own conscriptors." Later, questioning Levertov's binary "Revolution or death" from her anti-war poem "Staying Alive," Duncan proposes the word "rebellion" as having different (less institutionalized, reified) connotations than "revolution." "Rebellion" names an "apocalyptic crisis" that is "something other than the Wheel, the endless revolutions of eternal orders." Rebellion is from the bottom up; it cannot be instituted, and operates from outside the "eternal orders" of competing power structures. See *The Letters of Robert Duncan and Denise Levertov*, ed. Robert Bertholf and Albert Gelpi (Stanford: Stanford University Press, 2004), 629, 688.

24. Laura Riding, *Selected Poems: In Five Sets* (1938; reprint, New York: Norton, 1970), 56.

25. Riding and Graves, *A Survey of Modernist Poetry*, 88.

26. In a letter to Louis Dudek, dated September 17, 1968, Webb writes, "Who knows, maybe I'll end up writing on the theme of 'failure'—not a bad idea really, especially in terms of the anarchist movement...." Webb Papers, National Library. I will return to this argument below. It could also be argued that the supposed "failure" of poetry and anarchism is, in fact, its success: that they resisted the hierarchies of representational aesthetics and politics—that they escape Power, by falling outside the purview of Power. That "nothing" comes of poetry (Riding) or anarchism (historically) is part of their resistance: they do not lead to "things" (reified, commodified, institutionalized).

27. Riding, *Selected Poems*, 14–15.

28. Ibid., 13.

29. Riding, quoted in Elizabeth Friedman, *A Mannered Grace: The Life of Laura (Riding) Jackson* (New York: Persea Books, 2005), 393.

30. Phyllis Webb, *Hanging Fire*, 54.

31. Riding and Graves, *A Survey of Modernist Poetry*, 124.

32. Duncan, "Pages from a Notebook," in *The New American Poetry, 1945–1960*, ed. Donald Allen (1960; reprint, Berkeley: University of California Press, 1999),406–07.

33. Ellen Tallman's talk, "My Stories with Robert Duncan," was given at "Before the War: A Festival of Returns to the Poetry of Robert Duncan," Vancouver B.C., April 2, 2005. Duncan's anarchism is also mentioned in several interviews, as when Michael Andre Bernstein refers to "the kind of anarchism you've talked about," and Duncan's own reference to Pauline Kael's opposition to "the anarchism that I was proposing." Michael Andre Bernstein and Berton Hatlen, "An Interview with Robert Duncan," *Sagetrieb* 4: 2–3 (Fall/Winter 1985), 131. Jack Cohn and Thomas O'Donnell, "An Interview with Robert Duncan," *Contemporary Literature* 21:4 (1980), 523. See also a letter, Robert Duncan to Pauline Kael, June 24–July 5 1944: "I continue to feel that anarcho-syndicalism is a sound approach to a free society," in "Ten Letters," ed. Robert J. Bertholf and James Maynard, *Jacket Magazine* (October 2005), www.jacketmagazine.com.

34. Quoted in Paul Avrich, *Sacco and Vanzetti: The Anarchist Background* (Princeton: Princeton University Press, 1991), 36–45. Anarcho-syndicalism is, essentially, the application of anarcho-communist principles to workers' organization.

35. Duncan opposes "Vanzetti's voluntary state" to Levertov's revolution/death binary, going on to comment that "the volitional politic is NOT a movement." The singular plural aspect of Duncan's interpretation of "Vanzetti *voluntarism*" is clear in an earlier letter (July 28, 1966): "Vanzetti's voluntarism ultimately the nature of political good lies in our imagination of how to extend this volition in a wider and deeper range of the communal good: i.e. the concord of individual volitions." *The Letters of Robert Duncan and Denise Levertov*, 629, 633, 542.

36. Duncan, *Bending the Bow*, 71, 79, 113.

37. Duncan, "Man's Fulfillment in Order and Strife," in *Fictive Certainties: Essays by Robert Duncan* (New York: New Directions, 1985), 119.

38. *The H.D. Book*, Part II, Chapter 5, *Sagetrieb* 4: 2–3 (Fall/Winter 1985), 61. It might be possible to locate Duncan's language of "fields" and "openings" in the historical framework of the enclosure of the English commons and the tradition of "common right." As J. M. Neeson has shown, the English commoners, who were "enclosed" out of existence between the seventeenth and nineteenth centuries, were essentially anarco-communists, "'of leveling principles … refactory to government … insolent and tumultuous.'" These are the words of a "critic of commons" cited by Neeson, whose text is filled with the language of enclosure. Duncan's title, *The Opening of the Field*, hovers everywhere in the reading of Neeson's history of the "open field villages," an indirect and undoubtedly unintended response to a common tract title I find in Neeson: *Inclosing the Open Fields*. In Neeson I even find the linking of the notion of "common right" with "permission": "Often I am Permitted" (Duncan announces in the first poem of *The Opening of the Field*)—by common poetic right—to re-enter the commons of literary language. J. M. Neeson, *Commoners: Common Right, Enclosure and Social Change in England, 1700–1820* (Cambridge: Cambridge University Press, 1993), 20, 55, 73.

39. Antonio Negri, *Time for Revolution*, trans. Matteo Mandarini (New York: Continuum, 2003), 189. In "The second Treatise," Locke claims that "every Man has a *Property* in his own *Person*." While this may be the basis for a labour theory of value, it also reifies the self as a commodity that, at its base, has no connection to any others or any community other than as a form of exchange of goods. John Locke, *Two Treatises of Government*, ed. Peter Laslett (Cambridge: Cambridge University Press, 1967), 305.

40. Duncan, "Man's Fulfillment in Order and Strife," 113.

41. Duncan, "The Adventure of Whitman's Line," in *Fictive Certainties: Essays by Robert Duncan* (New York: New Directions, 1985), 200. Subsequent references cited parenthetically in text as "Adventure."

42. Duncan, "Changing Perspectives in Reading Whitman," in *Fictive Certainties: Essays by Robert Duncan* (New York: New Directions, 1985), 170. Subsequent references cited parenthetically in text as "Changing."

43. Did somebody say totalitarianism? I certainly take Slavoj Zizek's point here, in his book *Did Somebody Say Totalitarianism*, that the "defeat of the left" is seen in its acceptance of "the basic co-ordinates of liberal democracy ('democracy' versus 'totalitarianism,' etc.)" and that the very notion of totalitarianism has the tendency to relieve us "of the duty to think." Duncan, it should be noted, is himself somewhat outside the artificial binary in his awareness of both "socialistic and democratic totalitarianism," however, the main thrust of Zizek's critique is in its uncovering of how the postmodern "'multiplication' of differences amounts to the reassertion of the underlying One"—the "One of indifference as the natural medium in which the multitude … coexists" and which itself "relies on certain

exclusions." For Duncan, this "One" seems to devolve upon a theologico-humanistic ur-myth of the universal unfolding of "Man" as a cosmological principle. Obviously, this goes well beyond the scope of my present argument; I would simply make the point that duality does assert itself in Duncan's thought, and that such dualities are haunted by the spectre of totalism, but that Duncan himself reveals the passage out, which is found in denying the terms offered (plural/totalitarian—open/closed) as a rigid opposition or alternative (choose one—which side are you on?). Zizek, *Did Somebody Say Totalitarianism? Five Interventions in the (Mis)use of a Notion* (London: Verso, 2001), 3, 238–39, 241.

44. Duncan, *Bending the Bow*, vii.

45. Ibid., ix.

46. Parsons, *Anarchism: Its Philosophy and Scientific Basis*, 95. Goldman, *Red Emma Speaks*, 63. Duncan, "Changing," 173.

47. David Kadlec, *Mosaic Modernism: Anarchism, Pragmatism, Culture* (Baltimore: Johns Hopkins University Press, 2000), 8, 26. Kadlec, sounding not unlike Jean-Luc Nancy in *Being Singular Plural*, describes the pragmatist/ anarchist "pluralistic collapse of the distinction between 'the one' and 'the many,'" and cites William James's relational pragmatics: "Things are 'with' one another in many ways, but nothing includes everything, or dominates over everything. The word 'and' trails along after every sentence" (27).

48. A transcription of the talk, made by Charles Watts, is held in Special Collections, Bennett Library, Simon Fraser University, Vancouver B.C. The dream is also re-told in Duncan's essay "The Truth and Life of Myth," as well as in the poem "Often I Am Permitted to Return to a Meadow." Citations in the following passage are from Watts's transcription.

49. Duncan, "Pages from a Notebook," 405.

50. Michael Hardt and Antonio Negri, *Empire* (Cambridge, Mass.: Harvard University Press, 2000), 212.

51. Winstanley was the propagandist for the proto-anarchist Digger movement of the English Revolutionary period. After the Diggers occupied an enclosed commons on St. George's Hill in 1649, Winstanley produced his tract "The True Levellers Standard Advanced," in which he at several points contends that the "Earth" was made and will one day be again "a common treasury of relief for all." See his *Selected Writings*, ed. Andrew Hopton (London: Aporia Press, 1989), 10.

52. Riding and Graves, *A Survey of Modernist Poetry*, 9.

53. Rilke, *Selected Poetry*, 241.

54. I am reminded here of the confines of the formal garden critiqued in Webb's poem "Marvell's Garden," where she comments "God knows, too many fences fence us out" (*Vision* 33). While this is an attempt to understand Marvell's desire for his enclosed garden (a being-walled-within rather than "fenced … out") I cannot help but associate Webb's "fencing" with the enclosure of the commons,

which she also appears to comment on in "The Days of the Unicorns." There may be more to the commons/enclosure link here than my mere speculations—John Rogers explores the "discursive alliance" between Marvell and Digger Gerrard Winstanley in *The Matter of Revolution: Science, Poetry, and Politics in the Age of Milton* (Ithaca: Cornell University Press, 1996), 40, where Marvell's pastoral poetry is read against the backdrop of enclosure.

In terms of the politics of abdication, Webb's unicorns opt out of the totalizing and teleological Biblical narrative—they choose erasure over the Absolute. However (and this is true of Riding as well), one's abdication only takes on political meaning when it is publicly marked: one does not simply fade away; rather, one marks one's departure. Thus Riding loudly announces her "letter of abdication," and Webb's painting may be the marker of her abdicated writing.

55. Duncan's work with the form takes its place alongside the work of Jack Spicer and Robin Blaser (both of whom almost exclusively wrote serial poems), as well as Oppen and (as I argue below) Webb. One could look for the roots of serial form in H.D.'s *Trilogy and Tribute to Freud* (for a prose-serial poem), and see its continuation in many contemporary long poems, such as Susan Howe's and Lyn Hejinian's. Duncan's "Passages" poems are somewhat unique, in terms of the serial poem, in that they purposely question the relation of the series to poems not in the series, and the relation between the series and the limits of the "book" as such. In this way they evoke other impossible and purposely diffuse books such as Benjamin's *Arcades Project* and Mallarmé's *Le Livre.*

56. Weir, *Anarchy and Culture*, 158. Antliff, *Anarchist Modernism*, 33. Goldman quoted in ibid., 29.

57. Sheehan, *Anarchism*, 138.

58. Antliff, *Anarchist Modernism*, 1.

59. Weir, *Anarchy and Culture*, 165.

60. Quoted in ibid., 188.

61. Ibid.

62. Nancy, *Being Singular Plural*, 12. Subsequent references to this work cited parenthetically in text as *Singular Plural.*

63. Joseph Conte, *Unending Design: The Forms of Postmodern Poetry* (Ithaca: Cornell University Press, 1991), 15. Alan Golding, "George Oppen's Serial Poems," 91. Nancy, *Being Singular Plural*, 35.

64. Conte, *Unending Design*, 10. While not addressing the subject of anarchism directly, Conte routinely associates the serial poem with a world view comparable to that proposed by anarchism—one which is non-hierarchical, rejects "external or predetermined order," and which "announces the presence of an expanding universe in which centrifugal force predominates." In the latter passage, Conte even cites Yeats' famous lines about "anarchy" and the inability of the "center" to "hold," noting that the serial poem "proposes an open structure that welcomes possibility, choice and chance." Conte, 16–24.

65. Ibid., 3.

66. Golding, "George Oppen's Serial Poems," 89–94.

67. The spacing of seriality takes on architectural dimensions in Robin Blaser's famous metaphor of "a series of rooms where the lights go on and off." Blaser, "The Practice of Outside," 278.

68. Conte, *Unending Design*, 15.

69. Ibid., 16.

70. Blaser, "The Practice of Outside," 277–78.

71. Duncan, *Bending the Bow*, v.

72. Farr notes the thematic links between *Naked Poems* and "The Kropotkin Poems"—Farr, "Insurrectionary Wilderness," 64. Webb's papers also include a draft of her 1963 Canada Council grant application which refers to two simultaneously envisioned projects, the first, "probably to be titled *Naked Poems*, will be a small volume of small poems," while the second, provisionally titled "Scorpion and Bull," "will be a book of big poems" (Webb Papers, National Library). While the proposed subject matter of the latter book changed (from astrology and psychology to anarchism), the dyad, small poems / big poems, did not. Interestingly, Webb already envisioned the second book as involving "a critique of language." Note that I return to parenthetical citations from Webb's *The Vision Tree* here in text as *Vision*.

73. One could argue that the origins of this evolution are already there in the dialectical and dialogic structure of such "paired" poems as "Two Versions" (*Vision* 31–32) and "Breaking" and "Making," *The Sea Is Also a Garden*, poems 5–6.

74. Webb, "Polishing up the View," in *Talking*, 49.

75. Oppen, "Of Being Numerous," 147.

76. See *Talking*, 31–45.

77. Golding, "George Oppen's Serial Poems," 89–93.

78. A November 24, 1965 letter from Roy Kiyooka asserts (about *Naked Poems*), "I don't care whether there are 2 of you or even more, why not get as much of ourselves and what we imagine selves to be into whatever we do, why not?" Webb Papers, National Library.

79. Webb, *Wilson's Bowl*, 13.

80. Kropotkin, *Revolutionary Pamphlets*, 118.

81. Ibid., 116.

82. Farr, "Insurrectionary Wilderness," 64.

83. The poems are the two collage/visual poems on pages 41 and 42 of *Hanging Fire*, as well as the following "'To the Finland Station,'" 43–45. "The What Is to Be Done Poem," in *The New Romans: Candid Canadian Opinions on the U.S.*, ed. A. W. Purdy (Edmonton: M. G. Hurtig, 1968), 125–26.

84. *Wilson's Bowl*, 87. Subsequent references to this work will be cited parenthetically in text as *Wilson's*.

85. Farr, "Insurrectionary Wilderness," 70.

86. The phrase "good masterpiece of work" comes from anarchist martyr Nicola Sacco's November 28, 1926 letter to Mrs. Jack—the same letter she quotes from in her "What Is to Be Done Poem." Sacco, on death row, writes when "philosophers" and "poets" "have the idea to write a good masterpiece of work, they untiring [*sic*] seek the solitude." Nicola Sacco and Bartolomeo Vanzetti, *The Letters of Sacco and Vanzetti*, ed. Marion Denman Frankfurter and Gardner Jackson (New York: Octagon Books, 1980), 38.

87. Webb, "Script for Readings from 'The Kropotkin Poems,'" *West Coast Line* 25:3 (Winter 1991–92), 101.

88. In her foreword to *Wilson's Bowl*, Webb writes that the "Kropotkin Poems" were "[t]oo grand and too designed," 9.

89. Paul Goodman, *Empire City: A Novel of New York City* (1959; reprint, Santa Rosa: Black Sparrow Press, 2001), 283. Further references to this work cited parenthetically in text as *Empire*.

90. There is an obvious parallel in Goodman's portrayal of collective-insularity and the notion of the singular plural. For a discussion of the anarchist affinity group see Murray Bookchin's "A Note on Affinity Groups," in *Post-Scarcity Anarchism* (Montreal: Black Rose Books, 1986), 243–44.

91. Phonetically, *Mynheer*, in German, could mean "my lord." This could be part of Goodman's irony and satire—but he may also be pointing out the (hierarchical) problem of having revolutionary "leaders." (I am indebted, here as elsewhere, to Karl Siegler's assistance with all matters German.)

92. Farr, "Insurrectionary Wilderness," 69.

93. Olson's line comes from the opening of his poem "Kingfishers," in *Selected Poems*, ed. Robert Creeley (Berkeley: University of California Press, 1997), 5. The Donne line is from "The Ecstasy," in *The Oxford Book of Seventeenth Century Verse*, ed. Sir Herbert Grierson and G. Bullough (Oxford: The Clarendon Press, 1934), 108. The Sacco line is from his letter of November 28, 1926, to Mrs. Jack, in *The Letters of Sacco and Vanzetti*, 37–38.

94. *Hanging Fire*, 54.

95. Webb, "Script for Readings," 101.

96. See Michael R. Katz and William G. Wagner's introduction to *What Is to Be Done?* trans. Michael Katz (Ithaca: Cornell University Press, 1989), 33. They also quote Lenin's remark that Chernyshevsky was "the greatest and most talented representative of socialism before Marx," 32.

97. E. H. Carr, introduction to the 1961 Vintage Books edition of *What Is to Be Done?* trans. Benjamin Tucker (1883; reprint, New York: Vinatge, 1961), xv.

The fact that Carr, a biographer of Bakunin's, wrote this introduction, to a translation provided by anarchist Benjamin Tucker, is telling enough. There are other links between Chernyshevsky and Bakunin (see Katz and Wagner's "Introduction," 19), and it is clear that, whether anarchist or socialist, he "exerted extraordinary influence on generations of Russian radicals" (Katz and Wagner 21). For the textual problem of Tucker's translation, see Katz and Wagner, 35–36. Webb's interest in Chernyshevsky may also have had to do with his proto-feminism, his belief that the revolution "would need to overturn that patriarchal relations that existed within the family as well as between social groups and between the state and society" (Katz and Wagner 14). *What Is to Be Done?* is, after all, the story of a woman seeking independence.

98. Chernychevsky, *What Is To Be Done?* trans. Benjamin Tucker (New York: Vintage, 1961), 82.

99. Ibid., 40.

100. It should be kept in mind, as a counter balance here, that Vera, though an individualist, does collectivize her workshop. Early on, the novel's titular question, "what is to be done," relates to Vera's predicament of unwanted marriage ("Marriage! The Yoke!"), whereas later it relates to her profitable workshop, where the answer is that "the profits resulting from the work … go to the workers." Ibid., 28, 154.

101. Webb, "The What Is to Be Done Poem," 125.

102. Webb returns to this image of the self-immolating priest in *Hanging Fire*'s "'Cornflowers & Saffron Robes Belittle the Effort,'" 23.

103. Is the choice, "Russia, Suicide, or France," one between the social/collective/plural (socialist Russia) and the individual/singular (suicide as self-destruction, France as a return to Webb's existentialist 1950s)?

104. *Wilson's Bowl*, 16. *Hanging Fire*, 45.

105. Mallarmé has long been associated with anarchism. See, for example, Weir, *Anarchy and Culture*, 131,167.

106. Webb Papers, National Library. Webb's note is a paraphrase, but clearly the language is derived from Billington's own paraphrase of Carr, rather than from Carr, whom she also read, himself. Here is Billington's wording: "After hearing Wagner conduct a performance of Beethoven's Ninth Symphony in Leipzig in 1849, Bakunin rushed forward to assure him that this work deserved to be spared the immanent world conflagration. Fascinated by this man (whom he called the 'chief stoker' of revolution), Wagner was haunted by the fact that the opera house did perish in flames shortly thereafter, and may well have been influenced by Bakunin in his characterization of Siegfried." Carr, whom Billington cites as his source, describes the scene this way: "The performance led Bakunin to introduce a reservation into the doctrine of pan-destruction. Going up to congratulate Wagner, he declared that, 'should all the music that had ever been written perish in the world conflagration, they must pledge themselves to rescue this symphony,

even at the peril of their lives.'" The point is that Webb's research linked Bakunin directly (through Billington's discussion) with iconoclasm. James H. Billington, *The Icon and The Axe: An Interpretive History of Russian Culture* (New York: Knopf, 1968), 25. Subsequent references to this book cited parenthetically in text as *Icon*. E. H. Carr, *Michael Bakunin* (1937; reprint, New York: Vintage, 1961), 196.

107. Farr, "Insurrectionary Wilderness," 64. See also George Woodcock, *The Anarchist Prince* (London: T.V. Boardman and Co., 1950), chapter five of which is entitled "The White Jesus."

108. Sujir, "Addressing a Presence," 34.

109. Todd May, *The Political Philosophy of Poststructuralist Anarchism*, 47.

110. Ibid., 82–83.

111. Ibid., 83–84.

112. Norman O. Brown, *Love's Body* (Berkeley: University of California Press, 1966). Subsequent references to this work are cited parenthetically as *Love's*. Brown was a seminal figure for Duncan too, and, in 1963, Webb actually met Brown at Duncan's house in Berkeley. Once again, while not a self-declared anarchist, Brown's thought clearly displays affinities.

113. Webb Papers, National Library. The course was never taught. Webb's notes reveal that, along with Brown and R. D. Laing, Michel Foucault was of central importance to the course proposal and her thinking at the time. Webb refers to Foucault as "one of the towering intelligences of our time." Both *Madness and Civilization* and *The Order of Things* were on her reading list, and of the latter she notes in particular its "analysis of representation." Clearly, Foucault figures in Webb's course as a theorist of epistemic change, and thus, of intellectual obsolescence, but he also figures as an icon himself, noting "his charisma" which has "relaunched philosophy in France."

114. See Farr's *Ventilation Flow* (Vancouver: Thuja, 1999), where the proclamation is of central importance, and the next chapter here, where this discussion is taken up in relation to abstraction.

THREE On Abstraction

Abstraction: *something which exists only as an idea—the quality of dealing with ideas rather than events.* Thus something we have yet to realize—the very process of making real the inner workings of the imagination.

Abstraction: *freedom from representational qualities in art.* Representation is here seen as a state of being enchained, limited, oppressed, curtailed. Representation is hierarchical. Abstraction is liberty, a freeing of the hand and mind, an opening out in praxis.

Abstraction: *to take out, to displace—the process of removing something.* Where is abstraction's place? No place—utopia. Out of bounds, unbound. Ideas taken out of things—or things, freed from their hierarchical representation by ideas?

Abstraction: *a state of preoccupation.* In abstraction we are obsessed—what are the methods of red? When does line become solid, solid line? Its obsessive nature is one of its divorces from the surrounding world: something is picked out, taken to the extreme, made an ideal, or made a self-sustaining material existent.

Phyllis Webb describes her painting as an attempt to come to an "understanding [of] the nature of abstraction."[1] It is not a stretch to assume that this process and investigation began *before* she actually took up visual art practice (circa 1993). It is plausible that Webb desired an "abstract" poetry, but found it impossible, another failure, or at least unsatisfactory—words always shatter silence, "talking" had to be replaced with "nothing but brush strokes." To escape depiction as much as words themselves, she turned to painting. To escape the hierarchies of representational forms of art and social life. Thus, Webb "abstracts" a painter from her identity as poet. Two Webbs, overlapping, in dialogue. Or a diptych: first panel poetry, second panel painting. We will as ever begin here by not beginning, but by digressing—*into* abstraction—taking up the *idea, taking it out* of context, addressing its materials and materialization—reading its contradictory path between mind and matter, ideas and things.

There are, then, at least two "abstractions" in what follows. Abstraction as *idea* (and idealism) and abstraction as *material* (and materialism). The former comes into play most often when modernist artists professed their faith in the new art; the latter when we look closely into the opacities of their canvases—when we see what they actually *made.*

Surface

One of the most recognizable traits of the abstract work is its flattening out of pictorial space. Where once the representational urge was to give the illusion of "actual" three-dimensional space (at least since the Renaissance discovery—or invention—of perspective), now fictional depth gives way to the two-dimensional "reality" of the painting's material surface. The trajectory here is well known: Impressionism's fascination with light and colour, Cezanne's Post-Impressionistic focus on the geometric shapes the seen world reveals, Cubism's flattening out of multiple perspectives into a single all-at-once surface field. The movement is toward the painting's surface, its materials (paint and canvas) and basic compositional elements (colour, tone, shape, line). The ultimate outcome is inevitable: the painting becomes non-objective or non-representational (nothing outwardly recognizable is "seen" in it)—it becomes itself an object in the world, alongside other so-called "natural" objects, not a secondary reflection but a primary existent, a "thing."

Mimesis

> ADORNO: Art responds to the loss of its self-evidence not simply by concrete transformations of its procedures and comportments but by trying to pull itself free from its own concept as from a shackle: the fact that it is art.[2]

The casting off of representation is obviously an affront to the idea of art as *mimesis*—as a secondary rendering by the mind and imagination. The attack on mimesis cannot be seen as being anything other than explicitly radical and revolutionary—an attempt to strike directly at the heart of the Western intellectual tradition.[3] It can be seen as an attack on the hierarchical positioning of "ideas" over "things" (Plato), or on the hierarchical superiority of God's own "work of art"—the natural world—over the human world of artifice, and thus by turns either an extension of humanism or a parallel development with anarchism's general dismissal of everything that smacks of hierarchical thinking, first principles, and origins. In this utopian vision of art's "autonomy" the turn away from mimesis takes on Marxist dimensions as well, as Clement Greenberg suggests, seeing a similarity in Mondrian's and Marx's theories of a prospective deliverance from servitude to nature.[4] The rebellion against mimesis that shook art in the early twentieth century was also a rebellion against art itself—above all against its easy cooptation into mainstream bourgeois commercial society, against its reification, interpolation, and institutionalization. Freed from the market of representation, non-mimetic art could explore new modes of being—new meetings between the subjective and objective, the imaginary and nature, at the very surface of the work of art.

Primitive

> KANDINSKY: The nightmare of materialism, which turned life into an evil, senseless game, is not yet passed; it still darkens the awakening soul. Only a feeble light glimmers, a tiny point in an immense circle of darkness. This light is but a presentiment; and

> the mind, seeing it, trembles in doubt over whether the light is a dream and the surrounding darkness indeed reality. This doubt and the oppression of materialism separate us sharply from the primitives.[5]

One of abstraction's early moves was toward the primitive—that fund of aboriginal art that appeared to offer a glimpse into the basic structures of the creative mind or, to borrow Freud's terms, into the "childhood" of the "race." This art, compared to the "decadent" art of contemporary Europe, itself bore proto-abstract qualities—schematic, allegorical, two-dimensional, selective and compressed in the details upon which it focused its representation. With modernism across the arts we have an attempted return to the deepest past in order to begin the now declining cultural project over again. Thus the renewed interest in mythology and the new sciences of anthropology and archeology, thus ancient Greece and China in Pound, Eliot and H.D., thus the African mask in Picasso, cave painting in Kandinsky, the basic geometric form in so many others. The modern was ancient to its core. Its abstraction was a *taking itself out* of its present, seen as corrupt, decadent, late, exploited and exploitive, and a lunging at a utopian future through the deepest—and purest—past. A leap—out of capitalist materialism—into (paradoxically) the very *materiality* of art's modes of expression.

Purification

> MALEVICH: Suprematism is the rediscovery of pure art which, in the course of time, had become obscured by the accumulation of "things."
>
> ADORNO: [T]o release the production in the product, and, within limits, to put the process of production in the place of its results.[6]

Thus, adjacent to the idea of the primitive, the idea of purification: refinement, condensation, compression, reduction, clarification, simplification, economy. This is where the *idea* of abstract art—desiring to reveal only the essential, absolute, and eternal—brushes roughly against the *objects* of abstract art. But such "purification" could be extraordinarily material: isolating in painting "pure" colour, "pure" geometric form, "pure" texture, line, brushstroke, gesture—*process*. Ultimately sight along art to the moment of creative outflow, the instantaneous moment imagination responds to perception and the mind follows the hand into the eye. So that art is not a state but a becoming, the artwork not *capital* but pure production, *productivity*. The other side of this is that Malevich, one of the high priests of purification, also likens the process of abstraction to a *parasite*—a bacteriological infection which forever alters "the normal."[7] Purification is not always a pleasant or easy process, and the cure has often been as dangerous as the disease. However, no matter how far the idea of purification is taken—to the point of fragmentation and isolation of singular elements (the colour red, for instance, or a black square)—its results are a materialization of art's very medium.

Negation

> ADORNO: To survive reality at its most extreme and grim, artworks that do not wish to sell themselves as consolation must equate themselves with that reality. Radical art today is synonymous with dark art; its primary color is black.... The ideal of blackness with regard to content is one of the deepest impulses of abstraction.... the most advanced arts push this impoverishment to the brink of silence.
>
> BAKUNIN: The passion for destruction is a creative passion, too.[8]

No matter how utopian abstraction often seems to be, one of its foundations is pure negation. At one level we must connect this with abstraction's desire for purification: the field must be cleared, the cure must be a severe one for a severe illness, that which exists (and is decadent and corrupt) must be pulled down before the as yet unrealized can be built in its place. But, seen from another angle, abstraction gives voice, or vision, to that autochthonous and unregenerate element that plagues all of human culture and history—the death drive undergirding the pleasure principle, *Eris* (strife), who is only one letter removed from *Eros* (love), the dark pull of silence, retraction, retreat, failure, suicide. If abstraction is always at some level present in any attempt at representation, its aspect of negation is the revelation of just this failure to fully realize or depict the seen and experienced world. When this lacuna or aporia becomes a work's self-referential focus, abstraction takes over and a whole host of artistic and cultural assumptions come under fire: the stability of the object of art and thought, the position of the subject and its relation to the object, the very otherness of the media of representation (the materiality of paint, language, sound). In one sense the violence of abstraction—the violence art enacts upon its own traditions, modes, and very materials (exploding representation into an array of fragmented colours and forms)—is a reflection (or *refraction*—see below) of the violence and self-destruction of modern history.[9] But it is also part of the never abandoned, never complete utopian drive of modernity: to make it new, to finally free humanity and realize social equality. Nevertheless, the void lurks here. If death is one of those great repressed realities of modern Western civilization, abstraction is one of the locations of its return. Here the darkness speaks, in its own tongue.

> BENJAMIN: The destructive character knows only one watchword: make room. And only one activity: clearing away. His need for fresh air and open space is stronger than any hatred.... The destructive character sees no image hovering before him. He has few needs, and the least of them is to know what will replace what has been destroyed. First of all, for a moment at least, empty space—the place where the thing stood or the victim lived. Someone is sure to be found who needs this space without occupying it.[10]

While the destructive character—part of whose attack is on the very notion of *character* and subjectivity, as well as the modern illusions of progress and perfectibility—is an aspect of abstraction's move, abstraction has also been seen as a first glimpse of what lies beyond, outside, on the other unknown side of destruction. It is, at the very least, the silence and unoccupied space in the aftermath of destruction or the atrium of the new construction, if it is not always the clearing away itself. It is distance, as Webb herself contends: abstraction as the distance the perception of the destructive character demands.[11] The "room" that is made in *Naked Poems*, abstracting its minimalist narrative via distance—horizon and companionship.

Object

> MALEVICH: When, in the year 1913, in my desperate attempt to free art from the ballast of objectivity, I took refuge in the square form and exhibited a picture which consisted of nothing more than a black square on a white field, the critics and, along with them, the public sighed, "Everything which we loved is lost. We are in a desert.... Before us is nothing but a black square on a white background."[12]

With abstraction we may be in the midst of what Robin Blaser has called the "practice of outside": the attempt to escape art's secondary, reflective nature and make objects that have *real* presence in the *real* world—objects that do not devolve from nature, but which take up their rightful place *beside* nature as primaries of experience. But it is exactly this question of the real that the object/non-object matrix of abstraction troubles. It is an art that simultaneously announces "here are no objects of the real world / here is an object in the real world." This conundrum might be escaped if we assume that the *realness* of the real is being challenged, and that another real is being supposed. Consider Malevich's description of the reception of his *Black Square* (1913), which invokes language similar to that employed by the character Morpheus in the film *The Matrix* (1999) and later taken up by Slavoj Zizek in his essay on 9/11, *Welcome to the Desert of the Real.*[13] Representation is revealed as what it is: illusion—and the *real* real, revealed beneath, is an outside of potentially horrific dimensions, an abject sublime. Abstraction is a revelation of the desert. It is an abject object which denies the reality of the objects we normally take to be real. This is both its power and its alienating otherness, its outside we cannot fully take in.

One possible historical context for the development of an *objective* art is the general movement towards objectivity, distance, and disinterest in the arts and newly formed social sciences, around the end of the nineteenth and beginning of the twentieth centuries—a broadening cultural response to the intellectual and epistemological dominance of the hard sciences and the scientific method. Thus a parallel to the movement towards the painting-as-object would be the contemporaneous developments of supposedly objective, impersonal poetics in the work of T. S. Eliot, William Carlos Williams, and others in "modernism's constructivist line."[14] As the modernist poets began to distance themselves from what they saw (and ridiculed) as the nineteenth century's over-sentimentalized and purely subjective poetics, so abstract painters often worked in reaction to expressionism and, in general, expressive (subjective) qualities in painting. Once geometric abstraction is achieved (in the work of an artist such as Mondrian), a quasi-scientific objectivity—and a quasi-scientific object of study—is purportedly established and the artist, free from the limits of subjective expression, can investigate primary, elemental aspects of form—virtually conducting visual experiments.

An alternate reading to this scientific-materialist version of abstract distance would be to see in its objectivism a recognition of the limits of the self. The contracting of the authority of the human venture that is well underway when the death of God is proclaimed by Nietzsche, and which leads directly to Barthes's declaration of the death of the author, registers an increasing delimitation of the subject's role as consecrated order-bringer to the experienced world. The sheer otherness of the materials of life—the natural world, the body, even our perceptual, communicative, and representational faculties and media—begins to overwhelm. The recognition that nothing comes unmediated to the self is a potent one. The arts register this in an increased awareness of their materials. The more one admits the stubborn otherness of the material, the more one is abstract. The alternative, for many artists, is a deluded propping up of the staggering subject.

Harold Osborne offers a salient distinction for refining the question of the objecthood of art when he notes the "general tendency of this century to put more emphasis on the syntactical or formal properties of art than on semantic information."[15] As all messages come mediated, every expression delivers information related both to its message and the medium of its message. At times the medium and its syntactical information will be virtually unnoticeable, and the message's semantic information will absorb attention. At other times the syntactical features will create so much "interference" that it is the semantic message that will be lost. In abstraction the effort is made to observe syntax to the virtual exclusion of semantics. The otherness of the medium takes over, and while this may be experienced as an alienating otherness, it may also be found that there is expression beyond self-expression.[16]

Subject

> MOTHERWELL: The subject does not pre-exist. It emerges out of the interaction between the artist and the medium.[17]

Another way of stating the last point would be to say that abstraction is part of a movement towards recognizing the interconnectedness of subject and object, self and other. Subject/self is only expressive in and through its object/materials, to the point where there is a primary communication between the two, and the object/other can be experienced as possessing expressive qualities at least the equal of the (artist) subject/self. We are still in the duality of abstraction, the binary of insides and outs, ideas and things—but the poles lack a hierarchical relationship (especially once representation is abandoned). Abstraction's "objecthood" is not ultimately the exclusion of its "subjecthood." The subjective valence of abstraction is most clearly seen in its (often dada- and surrealist-inflected) emphases on psychic automatism. Geometric abstractionists such as Mondrian and Vasarely would exclude such expressivity, but many others have made it the core of their abstraction. The destruction or interruption of the represented world without is the result of the artist giving full attention to the often confused, unreadable, and surreal movement of anarchic desire within. This would be part and parcel of abstraction's negativity—those darker obsessions of the psyche given vent. But it would also be an aspect of the process of purification—a reducing of the artist's expression to what is primary, primal, at the very motive base of the human psyche—at the very least a cathartic releasing of the unregenerate repressed, if not a revelation of drives and archetypes. In this reading abstraction would be the *taking out* of the psychic interior, the objectification of the inwardly non-objective and materialization of the immaterial, an impossible seeing into the unseen.

Seeing

In the Renaissance, the problem of seeing and its constituent relationship between seer and seen was resolved with the breakthrough invention of painterly perspective. The painting rendered the seen as a stable field governed by the authority of an ideal seer (artist/observer) positioned safely outside the object-world of the painting.[18] The movement towards abstraction has rendered this relationship entirely problematic once again: as we have seen, subject and object have not been so easily maintained as distinct, the relation of the painting as object to the objects it depicts has unleashed further complications, and the *objectification* of subjective interiority and the actual experience of subjective perception has made for additional dislocations. One response to this development—one clear reconfiguration—was Cubism, where the perceptual field was flattened out and multiple subject/viewpoints allowed to co-exist on the same plane.[19] The focus of painting shifts from *what* is seen to *how* we see. How we see reveals that what is seen is shaped by who sees, for how long, under what conditions, from what multiple points in space and time. The strange otherness of the outside becomes the strange otherness of the painting which frames an unframed world. The movement from Cubism to a purer form of abstraction (Cubism is one of the *gran vias* to abstraction) shifts our focus subtly again: from how we see to the very materiality of our means of seeing—the shapes, contours, blocks of colour, contrasts of black and white, illusions of our visual limitations, etc. Rather than rendering seen objects, the painting renders *seeing* itself objective: one sees the eye's seeing. To put this another way, consider a contemporaneous development: early twentieth century atomic physics and Heisenberg's uncertainty principle. There is a symbiotic relationship between eye/I and the world seen and acted upon. The truth of seeing reveals the complex interaction and co-dependence between seer and seen, self and other, subject and object (even idea and thing). These are *relational* terms, and one can never displace (or replace, represent) the other. Abstraction is part of this revelation in its thickening and disruption of the assumed clarities and separations of painterly perception—as well as in its turning of seeing inside out, opening the means of perception and representation for our consideration.

Refraction

> ADORNO: The unsolved antagonisms of reality return in artworks as immanent problems of form.[20]

It is a question as to whether any artwork can actually be completely abstract, completely non-representational and non-objective. Kandinsky, Mondrian—many of the abstract painter-theorists themselves called for a middle ground between pure abstraction and representation—a realization that perception, representation, and creation occur in a milieu between self and other, subjects and objects.[21] But for others the purely abstract itself "represents" on strange and difficult to articulate levels—a kind of representation of the unrepresentable. The pure horror of modern warfare. Psychic states that do not speak the language of daily communication. Yearnings we have not yet allowed expression. The unnamed. This would of course lead us into what has been called lyrical abstraction or abstract expressionism, as opposed to the presumably more objective geometric abstraction. However, if abstraction is always in some way to isolate and take out—to remove aspects or qualities from their contexts and uses in order to reveal something essential and/or unrecognized about them—then what is abstracted always remains at some level, and some remove, a part of the experiential, "real" world from which it was taken. It is not a representation as such, not a mimetic reflection, but a *refraction*—a singular plural multiplication. Cubism is an excellent example of a refracted view of the world, and as such it composes something of that middle ground between total abstraction and representation. For Canadian painter Jack Shadbolt this was key: there was a "symbolic abstraction" which retained social responsibility.[22] We might also borrow a term from the Montreal *Automatistes* (about whom we will have more to say shortly), and see in refraction a form of *dislocated figuration*, the strange shifts, perspectives, foci and materiality of which are in part a response to the alienating forms of contemporary life.[23]

Politics

> VAN DOESBURG, LISSITZKY AND RICHTER: We define the progressive artist as one who fights and rejects the tyranny of the subjective in art.[24]

Which brings us around to the question of the politics of abstraction. In fairly obvious ways, abstraction has been read as apolitical: it is a formalism, a wholly aesthetic phenomenon, and its very non-representational nature excludes the social world from its purview. The social emphasis in abstraction, if there has been one at all (so the argument goes), has been on individual autonomy—a position that potentially denies the social as such. While it is undeniable that abstraction has in some cases tended towards the apolitical, and has been used for ideological ends beyond its own intentions, as a depoliticizing force, the argument here is for a politics of abstraction—and a radical (if incomplete and unrealized) politics at that.

From what has been written here already it should be clear that we are reading a political abstraction, one which decentres the privileged positions of both artist and viewer, leading into a full-blown critique of the self, the objecthood of the object, and the subject/object relations upon which the contemporary world and its systems of capitalist exploitation and expansion are built. Abstraction is a response to the destructiveness of modern life—either as a *refraction* of that destruction or a utopian glimpse into its beyond. Abstraction can also be read as a critique of the principles of hierarchy and hegemony, as it completely opens the question of interpretation and removes the relationship between the "representative" and the "represented." This much is fairly simple and obvious, and there is no need to labour the point. But there is, possibly, also a specific political connection for abstraction, and that is with anarchism.[25] Certain pronouncements of Michael Bakunin sound as though they could have been made by an abstract painter (with their references to destruction and the absolute), and the abstract painters themselves often sound like anarchists. This is no coincidence, as Malevich's comments on the state and the individual, and Kandinsky's direct discussion of anarchism make clear: the abstract painter-theorists were consciously anarchist, consciously aware of the political implications of their aesthetic beliefs and actions.[26] Abstraction's arguments against the centrality of the ego (observer-author/subject), in favour of spontaneity, autonomy and psychic automatism, the free association of the artistic materials, a bottom-up sense of letting the materials themselves take the lead in construction—all have clear, anarchist political valences. As discussed in the previous chapter, David Weir has argued that, failing in the social realm, anarchist ideas entered the aesthetic. This may be part of what happens in abstraction. But the story is longer and more complex than this.

> SERGE GUIBAULT: By using primitive imagery and myths to cut themselves off from the historical reality of their own time, they hoped to protect themselves from the manipulation and disillusionment they had suffered previously. What remained of their old leftist ideas was the desire and the need to communicate with the public.[27]

One of the most lucid and thorough critiques of abstraction's depoliticization and anti-political uses is found in Serge Guibault's *How New York Stole the Idea of Modern Art.* Guibault's focus, of course, is on the institutional forces that promoted abstraction after World War II because of its apparent apolitical nature. To this it could be added that what they also unwittingly canonized was an anarchist stance that appealed to an America steeped in a long tradition of institutional suspicion and radical autonomy. That such a tradition has been used, paradoxically, to further the interests of an increasingly aggressive, violent, and centralized state goes without question. The point here is merely to counter some of Guibault's assumptions—assumptions that overlook the true political potential (and character) of abstraction.

Guibault argues, essentially, that post-war leftists sold out their politics for a safe, apolitical alienation, describing a "de-Marxization" of radical culture. One of Guibault's prime targets is Robert Motherwell, but Motherwell was hardly ever a Marxist. Indeed, it could be argued that Motherwell was more an anarchist than a Marxist, and someone well aware of the anarchist implications of abstraction. For many intellectuals in the 1940s and '50s, the epic struggles between capitalism and Marxism, democracy and fascism, fascism and Marxism, sacrificed the left on the altar of expediency. The great lesson here was not World War II, but the Spanish Civil War in which anarchism, the sacrificial victim of political expediency, had held out an alternative to the false dichotomies of democracy or fascism / fascism or Marxism. The anarchism of the post-war abstract artists ought to be seen in this light—Motherwell in particular, who kept this option of another path open with his endless series of *Elegies to the Spanish Republic.*[28] If there was a de-Marxization of culture and the intelligentsia in the post-war era (and the fact is hard to deny), then there was also a "re-anarchization" via abstraction. This was, however, an *abstracted anarchism*—the ideology of individual autonomy increasingly separated from any concrete application in a critique of the state or property. Abstraction and anarchism became dystopic, the field of popular rebels without causes, or if still utopian, then in that most abstract sense of providing a vision of the ideal without any concession to the task of providing a means of attaining that ideal. In this the abstract artist is like the Cubist in John Berger's formulation—able to see beyond, but not see the way beyond.[29] Abstraction's politics, while a vital aspect of the art, remain tangled in contradiction, unfulfilled, yet filled with untapped potential.

I. I Used to Write, Now I Paint

> I started painting when poetry more or less abandoned me in the early nineties.... Because I am totally self-taught, I hesitate to see this activity as anything more than pure process, mainly

> learning process, or to call myself an artist. I paint, I say. I used to write, I say, but now I paint.[30]

While Phyllis Webb would hesitate to call herself an "artist," she has, in the more than fifteen years since her last book of poetry, produced an impressive array of abstract paintings and collages—impressive all the more because of the range of her experimentation, and because this "late style" is the fruit of her sixties and seventies.[31] We turn, now, to discuss both Webb's transformation into a visual artist, as well as several examples of her work in various media, and by doing so to begin finding a bridge backwards, eventually reading her painterly abstraction back into her poetry.

~

Webb's teleology is *towards abstraction.* She wrote away from the word. While Webb writes that poetry "abandoned" her, the complexities of the separation are difficult to parse: she also describes what happened as a "shift in consciousness," precipitated by her "[a]lmost … Buddhistic withdrawal of identity"—her decision "not to do any more overseas travel as a writer or anything of a public nature."[32] Compelled or compelling, what Webb describes resonates with Edward Said's description of "late style"

> not as harmony and resolution but as intransigence, difficulty, and unresolved contradiction…. [T]he experience of late style … involves a nonharmonious, nonserene tension, and above all a sort of deliberately unproductive productiveness going against.
>
> WEBB: Despite my new-found-for-the-most-part-happiness, I was struck again and again by the meaninglessness of all this creative activity. Why wasn't it going into new poems?[33]

In "late style," Said argues, the artist "abandons communication with the established social order"—"late works constitute a form of exile."[34] Certainly exile has been a theme in Webb's life and work—her "exile" on Salt Spring Island, the attempt to tell an exile's story in the "Kropotkin Poems"—it may even be (as suggested at the end of the last chapter) that the cessation of the latter project and the eventual cessation of writing altogether are related: Webb's "late style" is a throwing of herself back into the issue of political and aesthetic representation, a turn against the closures and achieved harmonies of "bourgeois aging" in favour of difficulty, an "increasing sense of apartness and exile and anachronism,"[35] and a new "scattering" of the "chips" and fragments of communication.

In the spring of 2004, shortly after having read some two hundred books of poetry as a judge for the Griffin Prize, Webb spoke of "looking forward to getting back to wordlessness"—back to painting.[36] Silence has always surrounded her work—a listening to the negative space surrounding words—listening *for* words, listening to the ground from which words come—waiting to respond to the intransigence of language. For Webb, abstract painting perhaps presented a more direct engagement with the space of that silence ("wordlessness")—a more active and more tactile "listening" to that silence. Even greater distance, which was a stranger though necessary nearness. A "late style" of "deliberately unproductive productiveness."

~

This is signal: she describes her last book, *Hanging Fire*, in an interview with Smaro Kamboureli, as "transitional."[37] What comes next tells us what it is transitional to: nothing but brush strokes, painting and collage. The transition is a transformation. *Hanging Fire* is a chrysalis the poet forms, birthing a painter.

~

In a strange way, in turning to abstract art in the 1990s, Webb returns to the late modernism of her origins as a poet in the 1940s and '50s—to the artistic movements contemporaneous with her poetic origins.[38] And it is there, in the Montreal of the 1950s, that we can see the beginnings of Webb's interest in abstraction—right where her poetry begins. Her friend Marian Scott—wife of poet F. R. Scott—was an abstract painter. It is no doubt through the Scotts that Webb became familiar with the work of the Montreal *Automatistes.*[39] The *Automatistes* are important for a number of reasons, not the least of which is the fact that they were the first Canadian abstract art movement—perhaps the first truly home-grown modernism in the country. Including artists such as Paul-Emile Borduas and Fernand Leduc, poet Claude Gauvreau and dancer Françoise Sullivan, the *Automatistes* promoted a program that was both aesthetically and politically radical, finding its characteristic expression in the notorious manifesto *Refus Global* (1948). While it is clear that Webb was aware of the movement, which was beginning to disband when she was in Montreal in the early 1950s, it is a matter of speculation as to what lasting impact it had on her own art. But speculate we can. First, it seems a salient point that the *Automatistes* included painters *and* poets—all similarly committed to abstraction as a necessary practice. Second, the movement's manifesto advocated a general *refusal* that we might see echoed in Webb's own reluctances, withdrawals, and negating silences.[40] Third, the focus on psychic automatism finds its echoes in Webb's own descriptions of her creative process, with its emphasis on sleep and dream.[41] And fourth, the *Automatiste* program (if it can be called such) bears close resemblance to certain tenets of anarchism, advocating as it does spontaneity, liberation, and an anti-institutional autonomy:

> Within a foreseeable future, men will cast off their useless chains. They will realize their full, individual potential according to the unpredictable, necessary order of spontaneity – in splendid anarchy. Until then, we will not rest or falter. Hand in hand with others thirsting for a better life, no matter how long it takes, regardless of support or persecution, we will joyfully respond to a savage need for liberation.[42]

Webb also met abstraction in the persons of Takao Tanabe, who designed and published her *Naked Poems* in 1965, and long-time friend Roy Kiyooka, as well as in the example of Jack Shadbolt, perhaps the premier West Coast abstract painter.[43] Her interest in the work of the geometric abstractionist Victor Vasarely is documented in the poem "Vasarely" (1980), and other Webb poems (such as "The Making of a Japanese Print," 1990) take on similarly ekphrastic characteristics. Webb was also led to the importance of visual art forms for poetic craft through her relationship with Robert Duncan. In an unpublished 1963 interview, Duncan tells Webb that in approaching open form poetry he "had a composition in mind much like a painter might.... You're composing as a person might on canvas.... Each thing he paints changes the character of the field." Webb's response is telling: "That's very interesting and what I've really been after."[44]

~

By the time Webb herself came to take up work in a visual medium she was steeped in decades of interest in painting and abstraction. In her 1993 essay "Poetry and Psychobiography," the emergence of a visual consciousness—of the fact that Webb had begun to think in terms of the visual—is made clear in a passage that reads as if it were a description of a painting rather than a poem. Wishing that she had written a poem rather than the essay she is now in the midst of, Webb "sees" the "poem's shape" and its dominance by "a shining blur."[45] "The best response to a poem," she seems to be telling us, may not be a critical essay, but it also may not be a poem anymore either: perhaps, increasingly, the desired response is becoming "wordless," a "shining blur."

1993 is also the date of a photo-collage reprinted in *Nothing But Brush Strokes.* Composed from fragments of at least five different photographs, layered and overlapped, the title of the piece—"Wilson's Bowl IV"—indicates its link to her poetry, suggesting a *visual continuation* of her prior poem. Obviously, the image of the bowl-petroglyph on Salt Spring Island continued to hold her attention. But more than this—it is as though the origin of a new medium is for her *embedded* in the nomenclature and history of the prior medium. Poem becomes picture. A partial image of a spider web—an established self-reference—is cut over urban images of concrete and cables.[46] This is in the top-half of the collage; below this, the image of the bowl (which is itself catching the image of light, or even the moon, as in Webb's 1980 poem) is partially obscured by the image of what appears to be a car's steering wheel and dashboard. Thus the piece could be read via its juxtapositions of images of the "natural" (spider web) and "cultural" (communication cables, urban concrete), or the rural and urban, or even gradations of cultural intrusion on nature—from First Nations' petroglyphs integrated into the natural world, to a contemporary Western obliteration of the "natural" with concrete and cable infrastructures. However, the image's overt references to Webb herself and her poetry (and thus her past) suggest another layer of meaning: "Spider Webb" is now literally visual, contained in the visual work. Webb, at the wheel of the car, is driving directly into the image-field—directly and precipitously into her new medium—directly into the bowl she could only conjure with words before. It is as if the photo-collage is a declaration, a mission statement, a manifesto—or at the very least, a direction sign: *this way.*

~

Her painting, like her poetry, covers a historical range of forms and styles—it can in fact be read as a study of the history of abstraction. Webb has painted purely geometric abstractions and lyrical/expressivist pieces which gesture in the direction of figuration (suggesting at times landscapes and forest depths). At the less figurative end of her spectrum, there is the *12" x 16" Series, Green* (there is also an incomplete *Brown* series and a *Gold* series too—the very form of painting in series evoking the poet's former interest in the serial poem), some of which are reproduced on the cover of *The Capilano Review*'s thirtieth-anniversary issue. Each piece in the series contains several rectangular forms, composed of a geometric grid of raised markings in the painting's surface. The *Brown* series has a leather quality—suggestive of alligator skin—while the rectangular shapes of the forms call to mind leather book covers, significantly closed book covers, which reminds again that these are the paintings of a lapsed poet. These repetitive geometric grids suggest a process of printing or pressing into the surface of the canvas—a gesture in the direction of textuality or at least the formal practice of "printing" which nonetheless remains entirely wordless, geometric, abstract, and mechanically reproductive of only its own formal variations.

At the more expressive and figurative end of Webb's painting spectrum is a piece such as "Sketch."[47] Ostensibly a portrait, "Sketch" nevertheless foregrounds colour (its bright oranges, yellows, the blue halo around the figure's hair), its two-dimensional surface (colour in the figural foreground and in the surrounding background is equally distinct), and the texture of its brush strokes. Figural foreground blends into abstract background, the two joined by the use of a similar palette and brushwork. Interestingly, the figure itself recalls the Gertrude Stein of Picasso's 1906 painting—it may indeed be a "study" ("Sketch") of a "master's" work as the journeyman Webb practices her craft—so once again it is difficult not to see a literary shadow behind the painting's surface. What is more interesting still, however, is that this painting may refer to another "master" in its very colour palette, which is so evocative of Mark Rothko's work (a favourite of Webb's)—particularly a work such as "Ochre and Red on Red" (1954). Thus what is most "abstract" in this painting is potentially part of its referential field, and completes it as a "sketch" of a particular trajectory in the history of abstraction.

~

The point is not to suggest that the only interesting thing about Webb's abstract painting is its paradoxical referentiality—its allusive uses of the history of abstract painting. Nor is it the intention here to read her visual work solely as the return of repressed writing. However, the goal is to find our way to the abstract in poetry, and to trace the intellectual continuities between the media this artist has worked in. Webb's painting and her poetry share this quality of self-referentiality—an invocation of the history and forms of her genre, a self-interrogation of the medium—a response to what has gone before in the field. "Oops, Pops, USA" (fig. 1), while playful to the point of parody, is one of her signal paintings in this regard. The title, and the inclusion of the word "Marilyn" and the collaged images of the U.S. flag, all refer to the visual discourse of Pop Art. These elements, however, jumble with other figurations suggesting different traditions and movements within the history of art. Several images of slightly warped clocks could be seen to invoke Dali's "The Persistence of Memory" (1931) and surrealism, or else Robert Rauschenberg's "Reservoir" (1961) and the idea of the "combine." The toppled number 5 might recall Charles Demuth's "I Saw the Figure 5 in Gold" (1928), with the literary figure of poet William Carlos Williams and his poem "The Great Figure" standing directly behind it. The overall effect of the painting, however, is of an abstract field of collaged elements—a strange landless landscape that echoes the overall effect of the canvases of Kandinsky or even Motherwell. In this allusive field, abstract applications of paint, cut and manipulated collage materials, and abstract signifiers (numbers and flags) all collide and commingle. This does indeed appear to be the work of an artist trying to come to an "understanding [of] the nature of abstraction." It is also an exploration of the "dislocated figuration" abstraction can create when it—inevitably, perhaps—continues to figure at various levels and to differing degrees.

Another of Webb's series are the "Cross Word" paintings (composed between 2001 and 2005—see figs. 2–4). These enact an interesting array of combinations from Webb's various methods, incorporating collage (newspaper crossword puzzles) and imprinting (the geometric grid from the *Brown, Gold,* and *Green* series). So the painting's surface is cut-in via collage, imprinted by the rectangular grid, and painted over, in the more traditional sense. The crossword grid finds an echo in the imprinted grid, its visual form becoming pure texture, tactility. Furthermore, the crossword structure is itself abstracted from its linguistic uses—cut from the newspaper, detached from its function as code and redeployed as pure form. As such it is suggestive of the suprematist square of Malevich or, turned on its edge as the crossword square often is in Webb's paintings, the lozenge of Mondrian's incomplete masterpiece "Victory Boogie Woogie," or the diamonds of Vasarely's crystalline forms. The "Cross Word" paintings for the most part leave the space language would occupy empty and silent, and take up the black and white architecture of print and the page only to leave them to their essential dualities (empty/filled, open/closed), or to obliterate them with the colour they deny. Abstracted from the linguistic "clues" that would give keys to possible definitions, the incomplete crosswords suggest a disinterest in writing as such—even "writing" at this level of distraction and idle blank-filling. These paintings gesture towards (or perhaps more accurately, away from) the concrete poem—a sculpting of language's absence in a former poet's thick new medium.

There is considerable variation in Webb's "Cross Word" paintings. Some, such as "Puzzling" (fig. 3), hover at her more expressivist extreme: the crossword cut-out is irregularly cut, painted over, combined with a bright and varied colour scheme, and more or less embedded in the canvas's surface. The painting actually includes several words, including the eponymous "Puzzling," the crossword "puzzle's" noun verbed into movement. Others in the series, such as "Around" (fig. 4), are more geometric and even minimalist. This painting, with its stark white field upon which the crossword sphere, darts, and angular lines float, is once again reminiscent of Malevich's suprematism. That Webb's series can contain such extremes is indicative once again of her attempts to "understand" abstraction in its various modes, "puzzling" her way through her responses to the paintings she has long studied and loved, the material and "pure process" that she has come to find entirely necessary and thankfully "wordless."

Webb describes the crossword grid as "a very pure image"—an "echo" of the "square canvas" itself.[48] In this, and her other comments on "wordlessness," she could be seen to be invoking a fairly orthodox version of abstraction as the absence of the linguistic.

Fig. 1. "Oops, Pops, USA." 36" x 48", acrylic and collage on canvas, 2000.

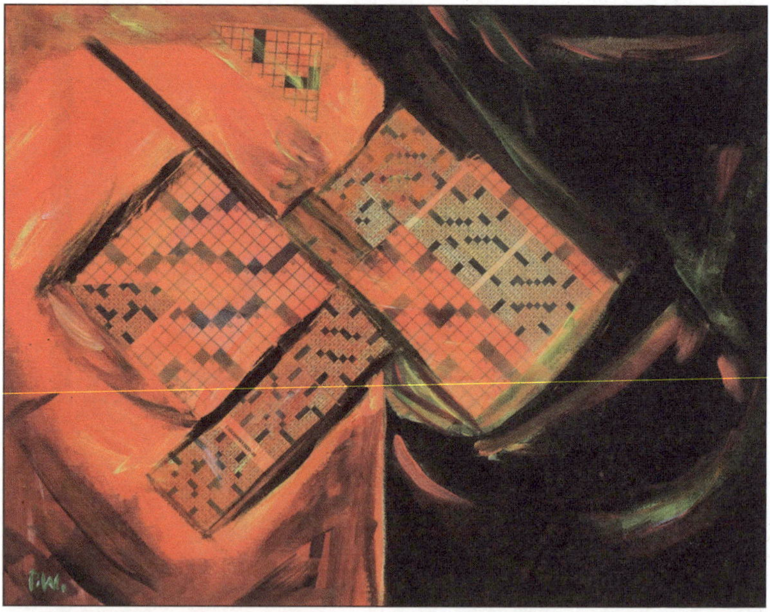

Fig. 2. “Space Hardware.” 16” x 20”, acrylic and collage on canvas, 2001.

Fig. 3. "Puzzling." 24" x 24", acrylic and collage on canvas, 2005.

Fig. 4. "Around." 20" x 30", acrylic and collage on canvas, 2005.

> W. J. T. MITCHELL: [T]he sense that modernism in the visual arts involves a certain resistance to language ... [and] seeks to acknowledge the pure, silent presence of the work.
>
> KRAUSS: [T]he grid announces, among other things, modern art's will to silence, its hostility to literature, to narrative, to discourse.[49]

Webb's crossword "grid" appears to fulfill Krauss's proclamation, as it literally takes a form from the field of language and arranges it as pure pattern in the field of the visual. "I" no longer writes, but "eye" sees. But as Mitchell argues, the modernist "grid" may actually imply the opposite of what Krauss claims, as "the fewer verbal promptings provided by the painter in the form of titles, narrative clues, or subject matter, the more demand for the spectator to fill the void with language."[50] Thus, the "silence" of the modern artist is met, and filled, by the "noise" of the contemporary critic. One could then ask the question, Is Webb's turn to abstract painting a final adieu to her critics, with whom she has had a long and troubled history? Or, if as Mitchell suggests, the abstract painting is "a visual machine for the generation of language,"[51] did Webb turn to abstract visuality, at the moment words "abandoned" her, as a means of *re-generating language*—a willful and obsessive demand, late in life, that the creative impulses of her being *continue*?

However that might be, our focus here, ultimately, is not on suggesting *why* Webb gave up poetry for painting, but simply on tracing the origins of abstraction in her poetry—to see what this transformation means *for* her poetry. The crossword provides an interesting instance in this regard. We noted, earlier, Webb's seeming return, in her turn to painting, to the late-modernist origins of her creative life. Significantly, there is an early unpublished poem in the National Library Archives titled "cross-words":

> ... cross-word purposes of love
> prove puzzles' vertical will thread
> horizons with mirages to remove
> till words, warped into squares of right,
> will, of themselves, fall dead.

To escape the linguistic, via the linguistic compulsion itself. To say her not saying. To fall out the back of language, speaking the whole way into silence. From her creative origins, it would seem, Webb has been seeking to escape the word—a poet caught in the labyrinth of language, caught in the too-closely confined self projected forth by the lyric tradition. Cross the word (as one would cross a threshold)—cross it again and again—until the word "warps," becoming mere shape, mere space (the crossword puzzle's "squares of right," the threshold's squares of light)—until the words "of themselves," without the poet's "killing" them, but as though it were an inevitable part of their very use—until the words "fall dead." And then, what will the identity of the poet be? What will the poet be, free of the lyric vessel? What is outside—after?

II. Is There an Abstract Poem?

Certainly language is always "a system to pointing," as Gertrude Stein maintained[52]—it is in the very nature of words to *signify*, as it is not, necessarily, not at all in the same way, for a colour, or the various textures of brush strokes, or a tapering, gradually curving line. Paint and ink can be deployed so that we notice only paint and ink, but words are channels going out of their substance into dictionaries, definitions, references, sources, associations, contexts, uses. They may be employed so that we notice their function—their syntactic "pointing"—more concretely and immediately than we notice or can specify *what* they are pointing to (their semantics), but the trajectory of their pointing always leads us out of them, away from their basic materiality, in a multiplicity of directions. Much writing is geared towards making the "system" of the "system to pointing" invisible, a transparent medium through which message flows freely, so we notice (ideally) only *what* is being pointed at. But no writing can completely hide its "system," no message can be conveyed without the noise of the means of conveyance, and poetry, in particular, is a revelation and exploration of its system and materials—a means attuned to the noise of its medium. In Stein's formulation, it is a "system *to* pointing," rather than a system *of* pointing—thus even in this description it points to its own pointing.

~

POETRY IS STRANGENESS AND DISTANCE. POETRY IS ABSTRACT—it is the genre in which language is able to best explore its own properties and possibilities. Poetry is language that we notice—and it is language in the process of noticing itself. Abstraction—absorption in a medium's own properties and materials—above all else, distinguishes poetry from other written genres.

~

The poetry of past centuries—because of its formalism—always already contained a degree of such abstraction and self-referential "pointing" at its "system" (its versification). The abandoning of traditional verse forms, beginning in the nineteenth century (Whitman, Mallarmé) and broadening into the dominant mode of the twentieth century, shifted the *formal* focus of the poem from traditional prosodic features (rhyme, meter—the couplet, the sonnet, etc.) onto its most basic constituent elements: lines, sentences, words, phonemes—the real material of its "system." Some have gone as far as to argue that it was poetry that nudged painting towards abstraction (Anna Moszynska notes the influence of Blaise Cendrars and Mallarmé),[53] while others have more consistently credited painting (in particular Cubism) with providing poetry a way out of the confines of traditional closed forms (Pound's "heaving" the dead weight of the pentameter and the metronomic regularity it had come to signify). More than likely the true answer lies in a historical convergence—a broad cultural shift felt across the arts as new scientific (atomic physics), intellectual (Freudian and Jungian depth psychology, Neitzschean death of God, cultural relativism), and social (modern warfare, commodity capitalism and alienated labour, the information age) developments made their impact. One sees the shared obsessions of both painting and poetry, in one small instance, in the consistent interest in solving the presumably simple yet consistently ambiguous equation of the relationship between form and content—the "system" of representation and what it "points" to.

> 1915: [F]orm is merely the expression of content. (Kandinsky, "Question of Form")
>
> 1948: [C]ontent is inevitably linked to form. (Borduas, *Refus Global*)
>
> 1950: Form is never more than an extension of content. (Olson, "Projective Verse")
>
> 1998: Form radiates content. (Roger Farr, *Ventilation Flow*)[54]

All of this is simply to state that poetry's abstraction—like painting's—is more often than not a *tendency towards* rather than a pure and static state, a shifting of the balance between form and content, syntax and semantics, and that it is just this shift, and the movement of canvas or page into the field of vision, that is often seen as disruptive and estranging. Thus, it is not really a question of whether or not an abstract poem is possible per se, but rather, to what *degree*, and in what *specific ways*—ways specific to the particularity of its medium—a poem becomes (is becoming) abstract.[55]

~

The first step towards acknowledging poetry's (tendency toward) abstraction is in the realization of language's participation in the construction of *the real*. It has become something of a contemporary commonplace: that is only real which we can articulate as a language event. It is the epistemological principle underwriting much of the science (Heisenberg's uncertainty principle), psychology (regression therapy and self-help), and production (so-called conveniences, fabricated needs) we have come to experience as "postmodern." The roots of this epistemology may go back to biblical notions of the creative word; however, the idea that nothing exists *outside* of language may in part be the fault of the intellectual hegemony of written discourse; certainly a painter—an abstract painter especially, one encouraged by the notion of "wordlessness"—might balk at this epistemology.[56] As far as an abstract poetry is concerned, the key is not that *the real* is (only) language, but that language is (itself, its own) "real." Language is a self-supporting "system," not subordinated to an outside to which it "points," but nevertheless in constant interaction with that outside, shaping it and shaped by it.

> LYN HEJINIAN: The realism of the means—the materiality and palpability of the poetic language, for example—is a precise manifestation of the artist's attention to the particularity of the subject matter.
>
> LYN HEJINIAN: [T]he discovery that language is an order of reality itself and not a mere mediating medium—that it is possible and even likely that one can have a confrontation with a phrase that is as significant as a confrontation with a tree, chair, cone, dog, bishop, piano, vineyard, door, or penny.
>
> FRANCIS PONGE: In order for a text to expect in any way to render an account of reality of the concrete world (or the spiritual one) it must first attain reality in its own world, the textual one.[57]

The turn to the question of abstraction and language makes one thing clear: abstraction and the real are by no means opposites. As noted above, abstraction is more an outgrowth of realism and the twentieth century's "passion for the real" (Zizek) than a turn away from objective reality (as is often supposed of both difficult painting and poetry). The investigation of the real and representation via various forms of objectification includes objectifications that result in non-objectivity (abstraction): objectification of the material of representation, of psychic states and inscapes, of the actual disjunctive paratactic and associational functioning of consciousness and perception. The real of the pointing is as real as that which is pointed at, otherwise the mind touches nothing, suffers in silence. But the pointing's real is made strange, the eye an odd and pearly thickness when we *see it* rather than see *through it.*

~

We are deep into the problematic of Horace's *ut pictura poesis* ("as in painting, so in poetry"). As a number of critics have made clear, the comparison between poetry and painting—in the context of modernism, at least—is based on shared (and sometimes borrowed) claims as to the "object status" of their respective media, the reality acquired not through representing the real, but through becoming a contiguous part of the real.[58] Poetry and painting have been sketching out their relationship throughout the twentieth century—more so, perhaps, than in any prior era—and a key part of this exchange has involved abstraction.

Thus, Stephen Scobie has argued that the relation between poetry and painting "should not be seen as one of division and opposition, but rather as one of mutual implication and interpenetration."[59] Painting and poetry provide Derridean "supplements" for one another, leaping one into the other's gap:

> Rightly or wrongly, writers see in painting a lack—the lack of words—and they rush to fill up that lack. Perhaps that rush even stems in part from an unconscious wish to end language, to expend language into the blissful silence of the non-verbal. Writing's response to painting is its own death-wish: never fulfilled, always deferred.[60]

Webb's desire for "wordlessness" hovers somewhere here. And this radical negation is an important aspect of abstraction, and of poetry's abstraction in particular. In *Anarchism Is Not Enough*, Laura Riding offers a close parallel to both Scobie's Derridean reading of the relation between poetry and painting and to Webb's long transition towards painterly silence. Poetry, Riding contends, is "made out of nothing by a nobody—made out of a socially non-existent element in language."[61] Poetry is abstraction, but poets have not been entirely aware of the true nature of poetry, so they have had to turn to the development of abstraction in painting for instruction:

> Painters no longer paint with paint except in the sense that poets write with ink. Paint is now only a more expensive, elegant ink. What do painters paint with, then? They paint with poetry. A picture is a poem in which the sense has been absorbed by the medium of communication of sense. It is not an intelligible series of hieroglyphics, but the poem itself forced into a kind of outrageous, unnatural visibility.[62]

Painting's move towards abstraction is a move towards poetry, which is the very essence of abstraction, in Riding's playful reversal of the *ut pictura poesis* tradition. Another classical version of the painting/poetry comparison hovers behind Riding's words—the notion, derived from Plutarch, that painting is "mute poetry," and poetry a "speaking picture."[63] To achieve "unnatural visibility" the poem must become "mute," a painting (which is itself, strangely, the essence of poetry: syntax and gesture?). The "socially non-existent element in language" Riding refers to might just be, paradoxically, the very sociality of language itself: its *gestural* quality, its revelation of its "system to pointing." There is a connection here to Steve McCaffery's contention—in his discussion of Levinasian ethics—of the "original communication" being "a protosemantic nonintentionality without message," "a passing of 'something' from one to the other in mutuality."[64] Language, at its most basic, is almost entirely phatic—more a form of echolocation than of actual communication of "contents"—a signaling of the ontological between of our fundamental *being singular plural*. This is to *abstract language* from its significatory functions—something which poetry constantly does, thickening its surface.

In the attempt to understand Webb's transition from poet to painter we might thus offer the following reformulation of Plutarch's mute poetry / speaking picture synesthesia: poetry is mute language. It is abstract. It points to pointing.

~

III. Abstracting Webb's Poetry

The *tendency towards abstraction* is the key trajectory of Webb's literary career—the cause and substance, even, of her characteristic reticence and silence. Her poetry from the beginning tended towards abstraction, but a more fully abstract poetry was, for whatever reasons, unavailable, or simply unappealing, to her.[65] Instead, it took the complete abandonment of poetry for painting to enable her full exploration of abstraction and the material reticence and intractable otherness of our modes of representation and communication. As an anarchist, as suggested in the previous chapter, an irrevocable split with representation seemed inevitable.

~

A Pang Cantata

A pang cantata
scrin of Villa-Lobos
a tinkle canticle
a rose is a rose is roses
Logos poetica Logos
Logos poetica
crin erotica!
O roaring spice
O lion of Rousseau
all exotica!
O wild canary
like a mad Chagall
hanging upon
a basil-scented wall![66]

It was John Hulcoop who first suggested we pay attention to Phyllis Webb's abstraction, in the introduction to her *Selected Poems* (1971), taking the short poem "A Pang Cantata" as a preliminary example.[67] "Pang" is interesting as another bridge between the poetic and painterly, evoking the spirits of Gertrude Stein ("a rose is a rose is roses") and the painters Henri Rousseau and Marc Chagall. The playful "pluralizing" of Stein's repeated yet singular rose and the evocation of Rousseau's staring dream lion from *Le Rêve* aside, "Pang" is a poem in which sound, and the self-referential materiality of words, overrides any semantic contents it may have.[68] The poem contains apparent nonce or fragmented words ("scrin" and "crin"), the disconnection of signifier and signified through self-referential repetition, and the sonic play of assonance (the oscillating vowel sounds of long *a*'s and *o*'s cut across by short sharp *i*'s) and consonance, echo, and rhyme (cantata/canticle/canary, lobos/logos, poetica/erotica, rose/erotica/roaring/Rousseau). The repetition of "Logos" is particularly telling, if we translate it as "Word," for the poem is then seen to circle around the repeated "poetic Word" as such, as pure sensual sound ("crin erotica!"). The poem is really a chant—ecstatic, self-contained, and self-evident—not unlike the later repetition-heavy chants in "Wilson's Bowl."

> WALTER PATER: All art aspires to the condition of music.
>
> MEL GOODING: [M]usic provided [painters] the example of a purely non-representational art.
>
> HENRY ORLOV: [Music is] the purest system of abstract relations presented in concrete form.[69]

Music is clearly an important intertext in "Pang." The poem at once gestures towards writers (Stein), painters (Chagall), and musicians (Villa-Lobos). The latter, the famed Brazilian cellist, played an instrument with a horse-hair bow; the poem's "crin" may not be a nonce word after all, as it could in fact derive from the Italian word for horse-hair: "crine."[70] Thus, Webb uses the word as simultaneously both abstract sound and musical reference. "Scrin" may function similarly: if it is derived from the Latin "scrinium," meaning scroll-case, it may once again be seen to be simultaneously a mere sound (in English) and a reference to the non-referential (even paratextual) materiality of texts: the cases scrolls are stored in.

~

AND
here
and here and
here
and over and
over your mouth[71]

Hulcoop also directs us to abstraction in his reading of the *Naked Poems.* Certainly these are minimalist poems, and minimalism is a direct outgrowth of abstraction; but the extreme reduction in these poems approaches abstraction most forcefully when it devolves to the level of the solitary word. This is seen in the second poem of "Suite I," which is largely comprised of the repetition of the simplest elements—conjunctions and prepositions—before arriving at the final phrase: "your mouth" (which is itself a repetition from the first poem in the sequence). This is the substance of the entire poem—as obsessively single-minded as love can be—a reduction of the entire universe to the beloved's abstracted, silent mouth. Later, in "Suite of Lies," a poem once again directs the reader to the solitary word, pointing at its own pointing, "the word groves" in its first line:

I use the word groves
light falling
found in the orchard
finding what fell by a
breath

(*Vision* 97)

Repetition and tense are also interesting factors here, as the series of variations "falling," "found," "finding," "fell" alternates present and past tenses while simultaneously playing with complex sonic loops and shifts (the alliterative fricative *f*'s giving over to the phonemically shifting *fa fo fi fe*—fe fi fo fum—to the liquid *l* consonants encircling the dental *d*'s, to the alternating endings).

An instant of white roses.
        Inbreathing.
A black butterfly's
        twitch and determined
collapse on a yellow round.
                                        (*Vision* 81)

While individual words and phrases are more or less collaged in poems like this, Webb also plays with syntax in very Steinian fashion. In the first poem of the "Non Linear" sequence, we are left wondering what sort of event or temporal measurement "[a]n instant of white roses" is. In the final line of the poem the modification of "round" by "yellow" seems to gesture towards Stein's "white way of being round," from her poem "A Box."[72] This is a strange sort of abstraction typical of both Webb's poetry and painting; while being itself abstract (what *is* a "yellow round"?), it nevertheless *refers* to another example of abstraction (in this case, Stein's "A Box").

~

But what of Webb's direct responses to abstract painters? The early poem "Marian Scott" is clearly, in part, ekphrastic—a description of an actual painting by Scott.[73] But when the original work is itself abstract, how can ekphrasis—"part of the repertoire of representational techniques at the writer's disposal"[74]—achieve its descriptive aims? The poem, in this case, is led into the abstract—into a mirroring of the processes of the non-representational original. It is at best, in this case, an "opening on / the invisible," as Webb writes in her poem "Vasarely" (*Vision* 122). In "Marian Scott," she follows Scott as "the imageless world" "darts" "back into space":

If she is a moth
then all light is lured toward her,
this she consumes and becomes
the moth burning in its own light.
Brighter than all the stars and planets

the central flame transmutes
the nerveless sun into a spine of white
which darts the imageless world back into space.
Pigments she takes and breaks them into one
pearl smoking whiteness, and then eye
directs hand to flourish the first morning
into fire. The walls float from her house
and wing with paintings into all ourselves
for I have seen around her head flying
the whole career of colour,
and in her hands the age of darkness dying.
Light, oh it swims from the tragic sun
into her instant miracle
where, caught in the wire net of form,
she twists and turns it into day's
urchins and angels—
blood of our blood, bone of her luminous bone.
(*Vision* 36)

As "eye / directs hand" towards the broken "pigments" of "pearl smoking whiteness," the poem moves from the seen to the purely gestural: the "flourish" of the "hand," "blood" and "bone" which has "caught" the invisible and "twists and turns" it into abstract material (the "day's / urchins and angels"). A signal moment in this poem—a moment not so much of ekphrasis as fusion with the methods and means of its subject—comes when literary allusion (the line "for I have seen around her head flying," with its echoes of Marvell and Eliot once again) turns into painterly obsession ("the whole career of colour"). As the poem's "moth" merges with the "light" of its obsession, the poet too enacts her own future merger with a new medium on the canvas of this hauntingly prophetic poem.

~

Moving ahead to Webb's final books, word-play and the material shiftiness of the signifier come to dominate her poetics. Such is the case throughout *Water and Light*, the formal qualities of the ghazal, emphasizing the associative connection between discrete fragments, drawing attention to the smallest units of composition—individual words and even word fragments. A single example will have to suffice:

> Tuned lyre (lyrebird, mynah,
> parrot, parakeet, peacock) paradox –
>
> not musical, though the brilliant plumage
> variegated for those who do not
>
> sing well, screech, shriek, scream
> in the jungle trees – the 'EE' sounds
>
> unlyrical plumage, especially with 's'es.
> On the other hand (plucked), sea, see,
>
> or me, thee, three in the thicket,
> perfectly musical
>
> and coloured enough, though featherless,
> for a kind of flying.[75]

Here, the "Tuned lyre" of the lyric poem is made immediately, self-referentially apparent: lyre leads directly to "lyrebird" (the former word becoming the prefix of the latter, as though to retrospectively, and contextually, reveal itself to be a fragment of language). This is the beginning of a list of associated words which paratactically interrupts the poem just as it is getting started. From "parrot and "parakeet" we are led, by the evolving prefix, to "paradox." The poem indeed turns on paradox and parataxis—but in terms of the former, we can make some hypotactic, syntactic sense: the "paradox" here is that the "Tuned lyre" is "not musical," and that its "unlyrical plumage" (neither the colourful bird nor its musical song) is formed of simultaneous difference (the "variegated" lists in the poem) and repetition ("sea, see, / or me, thee ... / perfectly musical"). Direct reference to the fact of the qualities of linguistic sound ("the 'EE' sounds / unlyrical plumage, especially with 's'es") amidst the actual deployment of the same ("screech, shriek, scream") adds to the abstraction here. This is a poetry in which sound and word-play dominate, but which simultaneously holds this fact up for observation and comment. The poem includes its own gloss or criticism—it is its own response, a response to its own linguistic constitution. The poet is both "I" and "eye," expression and observation—an eye/I trying to see its own seeing—and to hear its own hearing—to outwait its interminable waiting for the patiently responsive poetic act.

~

The synesthesiac conflation of sight and sound occurs almost everywhere in *Hanging Fire*, from the eye/ear play of concrete poems ("hanging f / ire" and "hanging f / ear") to the more discursive comments on "cadence" where aural pattern joins with "the seen, seeking out pattern, / finding where the eye catches."[76] The eye and ear (both of which are called upon in Webb's habitual play with the eye/I fold, to which I will return shortly)—as they follow the signifier's shifting transformations—compose the relational space of language, a milieu which is perpetually establishing and destroying sense and reference.

'Miasma'

Stunned by the blow
polluting exhalations
poisonous effluvium
(infectious, noxious) putrid
matter and such a lovely
sound/word I hear 'mimosa'
hidden there, the daze
the out-and-out sunshine yellow
of delirium, fever, malarial
swamp-garden.
How the mind doth know
its own dictionary. Ditch-
water/standing-water

still reflecting a bulrush,
calf, dragonfly, echo of
plasma, old hoe-down
razzmatazz of this affliction.
Gear-lock, warlock,
critter of the moon.

(*Hanging* 17)

A poem like "'Miasma'" is composed out of the possibilities for play contained in its single, title word, beginning with its dictionary definitions and then proceeding to what is both visually and acoustically "hidden there"—the word "mimosa," with its near opposite meaning to "miasma." But this "mimosa" grows in a "swamp garden," leading the image back to "miasma" once again. The fact of the poem's compositional use of the dictionary is directly alluded to—but the word "dictionary" itself becomes part of the sonic play as it is transformed into "Ditch- / water," looping us back once again to the poem's swampy title. Dictionary definitions make meaning stagnant (dictionary as ditch-water), fixing words' definitions; Webb composes a poem *out of a word*—out of the variations and permutations possible in its references, allusions, contrasts, and—especially—its sound. In this she returns language—at the microscopic level of the word and its phonemes—from fixity to flux.

~

'Cornflowers & Saffron Robes Belittle the Effort'

Ssh, sigh, silence is coming, the night time blues. Hark.
Ahem. Sir? I lift my arm, the wind chimes through my
holy raiment. Mesmeric bells reduce the flies to slum-
ber. Pajama party. The end of the Raj.

(*Hanging* 23)

Some of the poems in *Hanging Fire* begin in pure inarticulate sound[77]—"Ssh, sigh, silence"—and, in this case, do not drift far from the silence of unmeaning—"Hark. Ahem. Sir?"—beginning again and again with that first breaking of silence that every poem is propelled into, the very clearing of the throat of language. The opening "words" of the poem articulate the disintegrating/reintegrating formation of the word "silence," building the word out of its fractured phonemes. Furthermore, the "Hark. Ahem. Sir?" abstracts the mode of lyric apostrophe from any context of actual address—from any sense of an addresser or addressee. Even content is entirely absent here, replaced by the phatic fact that address is occurring. Characteristically, a paradox or polarity arises out of the visual/aural sources—the political seriousness of "The end of the Raj" being born out of the phonemic disintegration and pure buffoonery of "Pajama party." But sound is primary source here once again, and this is perhaps to be expected of a poetry that—according to Webb's own testimony—begins in almost every instance in a state of active, attentive, listening. To the noise coming down the channel before the message has a chance to clear the machine.

~

"Tending toward music" (*Hanging* 52), the "poet dives off the deep end / of the lyric poem" (46)—"Words / jumping the gun / on soundlessness" (24), lead the poet everywhere in *Hanging Fire* into sudden shifts, gestural moves at playful connection and broken disconnection—picking up the materials of language and flinging them about, to see what particles collision may create.

> I practice tangential existence—necessity, economy, art, use. Big words, small world, bombarded by particle physicists—and butterflies whose effects are infinite.
>
> * * *
>
> *Musical interlude.* Tralalala-la. I pack my things. Largo doloroso. Adagio for strings. I strangle a scream in the wrong key. The little fish jump up, nevertheless, scales shining. Stavinsky's firebird sings in the heavenly shade-tree, *con fuoco* (48).

Chaos theory or symphonic vocal play—the poet's "tangential existence" draws her sideways—spatially—paratactically—on into the next verbal node, the next "musical interlude," the next scattering of effects on her tour de force.

~

Careful attention to a poem's sound and melodic qualities is of course one of the defining characteristics of the lyric—but the status of the lyric itself remains problematic here. Many readers may ask how poems such as "'Miasma'" or "'Cornflowers and Saffron Robes'" can be considered lyrics at all—other than the fact that they are short and of interest to the ear. This would be because the lyric, as commonly understood, presupposes the presence of the lyric I (eye) speaking and observing, experiencing and expressing. The lyric hinges upon the expectation of self-expression—confession and self-revelation, experience and anecdote—but it is not at all clear what is being expressed in a poem like "Cornflowers," nor can we say very much at all about the "self" expressing itself in the poem (if that is indeed what it is doing)—about what it has experienced, what "story" it has to tell, offering itself so briefly as a mere gesture *in language*. Thus, what we meet is *language itself*, at play with its sonic and material qualities.

~

THE LYRIC IS ABSTRACT—is by definition the abstraction of "voice" or "address" from the actual presence of speaker and interlocutor.[78] The lyric is the disembodied word intoning in the silence that follows a call for response or that calls into that silence for a response.

> ADORNO: The most sublime lyric works … are those in which the subject, without a trace of his material being, intones in language until the voice of language itself is heard. The subject's

> forgetting himself, his abandoning himself to language as if devoting himself completely to an object—this and the direct intimacy and spontaneity of his expression are the same.[79]

* * *

> Who is this *I* infesting my poems? Is it I hiding behind the Trump type on the page of the book you are reading? Is it a photograph of me on the cover of *Wilson's Bowl*? Is it I? *I* said, *I* say, *I* am saying –
>
> I am the mask, the voice, the one who begins those lyrical poems, I wandered lonely as a cloud ... *I hear the Shadowy Horses, their long manes a-shake ... I am of Ireland / And the Holy Land of Ireland ... I, the poet William Yeats ... I am worn out with dreams ...*
>
> (*Hanging* 67)

Following Adorno in his "Lyric Poetry" essay, this is an "abandoning" of the subject "to language"—to the point at which so called *self*-expression reveals itself as wholly other—the "voice of language itself" which takes the place of the poet's abstract I ("Who is this *I* infesting my poems?").[80] Rimbaud's "*Je suis un autre*"—another other echoing back from the depths of the abstract I. So it is the pronouns in a lyric poem that are so often abstract—often relentlessly repeated, incompletely identified, so often without clear referent ("Who is this I")—"persons of the poem," Duncan called them, points in a map of pointing to speaking that throw the between of speech into relief, the importance of the *with* (*I* addressing *you*, *I* immersed in *we*) that we see in Jean-Luc Nancy's *Singular Plural*. If "I" am abstract it is because I am *taken out*, a taking out of a single semiotic element from the complexities of relational space.

~

The expectation of a close link between the lyric and the subjective, the lyric and an expressive self, is in most cases a false one, the product of an unexamined belief in the necessary connection of signs and their referents, or the result of the dominance of a particular aesthetic—one that is narrative, anecdotal—a branch of the lyric that perhaps grew out of Romantic self-examination, passed through the dramatic monologue, and became the confessional poem. Perhaps we need to speak of different kinds of lyrics in this way—of *anecdotal lyrics* and *abstract lyrics*, of lyrics more likely to posit character, presence, and narrative and those more likely to be devoid of the same, staring into the gap in their own "voice," overwhelmed by the extraordinary strangeness of language. This latter tradition would be located in the designs of modernist poets to create an "impersonal" poetry, or what Charles Altieri calls "an abstract grammar of moods" where "the emotions" could be "cut … free from the control of any single speaker."[81] From modernist "impersonality" (still burdened by isolation and alienation) we move to the postmodern multiple-personality (fragmented, fabricated, and multiphasic—Nancy's *singular plural*). Webb's work falls somewhere between these poles. It is "transitional" between modern and postmodern sensibilities. The I- and eye-centeredness of language is isolating and constricting—especially in her early work—but increasingly that I/eye becomes a difficult-to-distinguish "fold," a floating sign circulating freely throughout her poetry—an other of language. Abstraction itself could also be described as falling between the cracks of the modern/postmodern "divide" (if divide it really is): two opposite and simultaneous possibilities seem always to hover around the abstract work—either it is completely subjective, and thus its meaning is entirely personal, a revelation of the painter/author's unique interiority—or else it is completely objective, the very thingness of its opaque materiality, and thus its meaning is entirely impersonal, formal, and self-referential. It is in fact both at once—the I is another, the I is abstract.

~

ROSALIND KRAUSS: Each little paper piece [in Picasso's collage] submits itself to meaning, but never enduringly so. For the same piece, in another location, constellates another sign.

> [I]n turning the twin of the … clipping over on its back, [Picasso] could see himself entering into the logic of the "fold," the logic of the "facet," the logic of the binary in which as the sign circulates it constantly re-attaches itself to meaning.
>
> It is this folding over of the "re-mark" that … produces a syntactic and grammatic (not to mention semic) split into non-identical pairs within one and the same signifier.[82]

It is the *fold* Webb makes of her lyric I that fascinates. How she *re-marks* it again and again, attaching it to ever-new significations, constantly doubling it, fracturing it, making it material. She never fully leaves the lyric mode, but she is forever holding it up for examination, revealing its self-examination. As noted earlier, in abstract art one sees the eye's seeing. Webb's abstract I/eye fold does this, as it simultaneously makes the "I" "eye" itself in the midst of its self-fabrications. Where Rosalind Krauss tracks the shifting signs of newspaper clippings forming subtle figuration in Picasso's *papiers collés*, we will follow Webb's ever-shifting I/eye—the instability of the supposed person's figuration as it shifts back and forth between an expressive interior "I" and an outward looking and objective "eye."

~

Webb's I/eye *re-mark*, the apex of her poetic abstraction, has a handful of characteristic modalities. It reveals itself as material, self-referential language via overloaded *repetition*:

> But I, how can I, I [83]

—the repetition itself working to sever the sign from its referent—and *objectification*:

> Who is this I [84]
>
> ….
>
> Always this me.[85]

It relies upon the words' *proximity*:

> for *I* have *seen* around her head flying [86]
>
> ....
>
> her golden *eyes* are shut / and *I* cannot compare them [87]
>
> ....
>
> *I watch* [88]

and thus the doubleness, of the "I" and "eye," self and seeing—this is probably the most common mode of the fold, occurring, repeatedly, in all of Webb's books. Closely linked to this is the suggestion (thank you once again Louis Zukofsky) of a sort of *convertibility*—

> The hoodwinked eye [I] of ignorance [89]
>
> ....
>
> I [eye] cannot see.[90]

—of eyes into *I*'s and *I*'s into *eyes.* Webb also creates the doubling of the I/eye through *reference*:

> we could perhaps speed four eyes
> the chariot horses of our dreams and visions [91]

—perhaps invoking Plato's image of the soul (the self—the "I") as a chariot pulled by horses—

> I metamorphose
> in and out of the Buddha's eye [92]
>
> ....
>
> I try to see it with Lenin's slanty eyes.[93]

Finally, Webb's abstract I marks its doubleness *directly,* in a sense *unfolding the fold*:

> ... this earthly eye
> (it is I).[94]

Always doubling, bifurcating, shifting, moving, circulating—Webb's poetic I/eye is given over to gazing at the very shiftiness of the language it is made of—

> Look again. I is off and diving
> ....
> *Look.* I hand you a golden jonquil.[95]

~

The poetics of response and anarchism join the abstract in Webb's "Performance" of the first person. Response as a *singular plural* betweenness is figured in her playful conjugation—"I devise. You devise. We devise. To be together briefly with the page."[96] And anarchism informs the critique of the I, which in its very authority appears at the pinnacle of the hierarchy of liberal social values: "Like the state, I do not wither away, though the end is near."[97] The poem's lyric abstraction leads us out and back into the responsive interchange that propels all poetry, just as this relationship—escaping aesthetic as well as political representation—implies anarchism's insistence upon an embodied, direct, and unmediated political participation in the "common good." Language is being held up, here, to its representational limits—the bones of its pronouns and identifications showing through the thin skin of appearance (revealed a performance)—and then the poet slips away into the thing world, a node in the "vocal pod," a choral voice apostrophizing us to "*Look*"—"*Here*"—"*Now.*" Do not represent. Join. Participate.

~

Earlier we noted the objective in abstraction as being not to render "the real" *objectively*, but to have the artwork take up a place *as an object* in the *real.* At the level of aspiration, poetry clearly shares painting's abstraction—its obsession with objectifying itself. The tradition is long and pervasive.

> WILLIAM CARLOS WILLIAMS: Say it, no ideas but in things.
>
> MARIANNE MOORE: [F]or inspection, imaginary gardens with real toads in them.
>
> JACK SPICER: I would like to make poems out of real objects. The lemon to be a lemon that the reader could cut or squeeze or taste.[98]

We see Webb, more so in *Hanging Fire* than in any of her previous books, attempting to bring the poem to such an object status. Via sound, via concrete poems, via the constant revelation of the connective and duplicitous *singular plural* status of poetry and the doubled and unstable I/eye fold—Phyllis Webb wanders towards the abstract, which becomes a wandering right out of the poem. The last poem in the last collection is a poem about a painting (or at least a "print"). It begins with "Eye [I] contact,"[99] but proceeds to the suggestion that "the only way to go" is "outward." This movement is a "confession," and a sort of "abdication."

> A fake. There was no chair
> no washy blue in the 'Heron Maid'.
> I made it up for my own artistic
> purposes. I was thinking of
> Van Gogh, of myself sitting down
> for the last time and getting
> up again to make this confession.
>
> (*Hanging* 76)

"Sitting down"—to write this last poem, this "last time"? Painting and poem, the visual and the linguistic, touch in this final, "confessional" (and still inescapably lyric) poem. Webb, identifying with Harunobu's Heron Maid, followers her (as she once followed the suicidal path of Lilo Berliner in "Wilson's Bowl") "off the path" to "imagine a different future," a "change," "another job" (77)—a new vocation. It's at this point—at the end of the last poem—that the poem claims the status of truth and reality that painting also aspires to in abstraction—"A woman emerges," visceral, immediate, unrepresentable—not fictitious but "factitious," not an imaginary but a living "thing," as real as any lemon or toad—a woman's escape from attempts at male mimetic mastery:[100]

> A woman emerges at last
> on the finest paper, cursing
> his quest for the line
> and this damned delicate fan
> carved in her hand
> to keep her forever cool
> factitious, apparently pleasing.
> (78)

Notes

1. "Artist's Statement" from "Eight Visuals," *The Capilano Review* 2:37 (Spring 2002), 64.

2. Theodore Adorno, *Aesthetic Theory*, trans. Robert Hullot-Kentor (Minneapolis: University of Minnesota Press, 1997), 16.

3. For a broad discussion of mimesis see Erich Auerbach, *Mimesis: The Representation of Reality in Western Literature*, trans. Willard Trask (New York: Doubleday, 1957). See also Eric Havelock's *Preface to Plato*. Plato, while critical of mimesis, certainly sees the arts—the whole material world, in fact—as mimetic. The arts are damned because of the limitation of mimesis they are bound to. Only ideas are "pure," "true," and "eternal." Abstract art falls into Plato's trap when it sees the process of abstraction in terms of a dualistic separation of *ideas* from *things*. The critique of the Western intellectual tradition I am attributing to abstraction here is a throwing off of mimesis, not, as in Plato, because it is "inferior" to ideas, but because of this very hierarchical dualism dominant in the Western tradition at least from Plato onwards.

4. *Clement Greenberg: The Collected Essays and Criticism*, ed. John O'Brian (Chicago: University of Chicago Press, 1986), vol. 2, 19.

5. Vassily Kandinsky, *Concerning the Spiritual in Art* (1912; reprint, New York: George Wittenbom, 1947), 24.

6. Kasimir Malevich, *The Non-Objective World*, trans. Howard Dearstyne (Chicago: Paul Theobald, 1959), 74. Adorno, *Aesthetic Theory*, 102.

7. Malevich, *The Non-Objective World*, 46.

8. Adorno, *Aesthetic Theory*, 39–40. Bakunin, "The Reaction in Germany," 57.

9. I have in mind here Briony Fer's discussion of Joan Miró and Georges Bataille's comments on the latter. Fer quotes Miró as saying "'I want to murder art,'" and remarks on the idea "that the art of picture-making lies not in composition, as it is normally understood, but in decomposition"—that modern art is "[d]oing violence to representation." Fer, *On Abstract Art* (New Haven: Yale University Press, 1997), 79.

10. Quoted in Paul Kelley, "'Destruction' and 'Experience': Four Notes on Walter Benjamin," *Anarcho-Modernism: Toward a New Critical Theory*, ed. Ian Angus (Vancouver: Talonbooks, 2001), 22.

11. Webb, "The Crannies of Matter," in *Nothing But Brush Strokes*, 67.

12. Malevich, *The Non-Objective World*, 68.

13. Zizek calls 9/11 "the climactic conclusion of the 20th century art's 'passion for the real.'" *Welcome to the Desert of the Real!: Five Essays on 11 September and Related Dates* (London: Verso, 2002), 11.

14. Gerome McGann, "Laura (Riding) Jackson and the Literal Truth," *Critical Inquiry* 18 (Spring 1992), 466.

15. Harold Osborne, *Abstraction and Artifice in Twentieth-Century Art* (Oxford: Oxford University Press, 1979), 8.

16. Clement Greenberg put it this way: "The picture has now become an object of literally the same spatial order as our bodies, and no longer the vehicle of an imagined equivalent of that order. It has lost its 'inside' and become almost all 'outside.'" *Clement Greenberg: The Collected Essays and Criticism*, 191.

17. Robert Motherwell, *The Collected Writings*, ed. Stephanie Terenzio (New York: Oxford University Press, 1992), 139.

18. See John Berger: "Thus man could observe nature all around him on every side and be enhanced both by what he observed and by his own ability to observe. He had no need to consider that he was essentially part of that nature. Man was the eye for which reality had been made visual: the ideal eye, the eye of the viewing point of Renaissance perspective." *The Sense of Sight*, ed. John Spencer (New York: Pantheon Books, 1985), 172.

19. Ibid., 177: "The viewing point of Renaissance perspective, fixed and outside the picture, but to which everything within the picture was drawn, has [in Cubism] become a field of vision which is the picture itself."

20. Adorno, *Aesthetic Theory*, 6.

21. Mondrian: "The new plastic is *abstract-real* because it stands between the absolute-abstract and the natural or concrete-real. It is not as abstract as abstract thought, and not as real as tangible reality. It is … the visual expression in which each opposite is transformed into the other" (35–36).

22. See Scott Watson, *Jack Shadbolt* (Vancouver: Douglas and McIntyre, 1990), 57.

23. See Ray Ellenwood, "The Autonomist Movement of Montreal: Towards Non-Figuration in Painting, Dance, and Poetry," *Canadian Literature* 113–14 (Summer/Fall 1987), 22.

24. Theo van Doesburg, El Lissitzky, and Hans Richter, as the "International Faction of Constructivists," speaking at a Congress of International Progressive Artists, Dusseldorf, Germany, 1922, quoted in Harold Osborne, *Abstraction and Artifice*, 127.

25. Allen Antliff gives a good survey of the historical assumed connection between anarchism and the trend towards abstraction in modernist art, noting that "modernist individualism entailed a break with mimesis." *Anarchist Modernism*, 46.

26. Compare the following. Bakunin: "[O]ne must totally annihilate one's personal ego, annihilate everything that forms its life, its hopes and its personal beliefs. One must live and breathe only for the absolute through the absolute." Quoted in David Weir, *Anarchy and Culture*, 27. Malevich: "An environment is erected about the citizen of the state which is calculated to compel him to look upon the normalizing element of the state constitution as the normalizing element of his own consciousness…. Those who succumb to the regimenting power are advanced as loyal supporters of the state while those who preserve their subjective consciousness and individual point of view are looked upon and treated as dangerous and unreliable. Persons of this latter category call themselves free people and are to be found especially in the 'free occupations.' Their convictions are not dependent upon any state constitutionality; their activities leave out of account the interest of the state and consequently a struggle develops between the state and the independent individual." Malevich, *The Non-Objective World*, 21. And Kandinsky: "'Anarchy' is what many term the present state of painting…. It connotes, incorrectly, an aimless iconoclasm and lack of order. Anarchy consists rather of a certain systematicity and order that are created not by virtue of an external and ultimately unreliable force, but rather by one's feeling for what is good…. Contemporary art … may rightly be called anarchistic." *Kandinsky: Complete Writings on Art, Vol. One (1901–1921)*, ed. Kenneth C. Lindsay and Peter Vergo (Boston: G. K. Hall & Co., 1982), 242.

27. Serge Guibault, *How New York Stole the Idea of Modern Art: Abstract Expressionism, Freedom, and the Cold War*, trans. Arthur Goldhammer (Chicago: University of Chicago Press, 1983), 77.

28. This series of paintings, inspired by the Spanish Civil War of 1936–39, comprised some two hundred canvases, painted over a forty-year period (from 1948 until Motherwell's death in 1991). Characterized by a repetitive formal theme, often resulting in truly massive canvases, the project was epic in proportion—an attempt to refuse the forgetting of one of the most idealistic and revolutionary events of the twentieth century.

29. "The Cubists imagined the world transformed, but not the process of transformation." *The Sense of Sight*, 171.

30. Webb, "Artist's Statement," 64.

31. Webb has rarely shown her paintings. *The Capilano Review*'s thirtieth-anniversary issue (2:37, Spring 2002) reproduces eight pieces, and lists the few shows she has participated in—all on Salt Spring Island. A number of her works are in private collections.

32. "What I'd Be if I Were Not a Writer," *Brick* 50 (Fall 1994), 24–25. Reprinted as "Might-have-been: The Tedious Shores," in *Nothing But Brush Strokes*, 84–86.

33. Said, *On Late Style: Music and Literature Against the Grain* (New York: Pantheon Books, 2006), 7. Webb, "What I'd Be if I Were Not a Writer," 24.

34. Said, *On Late Style*, 8.

35. Ibid., 17.

36. Private conversation, March 14, 2004. I would link this to Webb's comments against the "verbal part of my brain" in "What I'd Be if I Were Not a Writer," 24. See also Betsy Warland's discussion of the "child-mind" which she associates with Webb's turn to painting, seeing the latter as "freer from the language-bound habits of our adult ways of thinking." Warland, "Phyllis Webb and the Spirit of Inquiry," *Grain* 31: 1 (Summer 2003), 143. This essay has also been reprinted in *Re:Generations: Canadian Women Poets in Coversation*, ed. Di Brandt and Barbara Godard (Windsor, Ont.: Black Moss Press, 2005).

37. Smaro Kamboureli, "'Seeking Shape. Seeking Meaning': An Interview with Phyllis Webb," *West Coast Line* 25:3 (Winter 1991/92), 34.

38. Edward Said, writing of Adorno, notes that "Lateness for him equaled regression, from now to back then." *On Late Style*, 23. So part of Webb's lateness is also, paradoxically, a return to her original newness—to difficulty, struggle, negative capability.

39. In an undated letter to Louis Dudek (but likely from the early 1950s—it is written on McGill University stationery, so probably comes from her years there—1953–54), Webb mentions having "to get Marian's paintings back to her" (National Library Archives). Leaving the complexities of Webb's relationship with the Scotts to biographers, I will note that Webb's turn to painting interestingly coincides, roughly, with Marian Scott's death in 1993. The Scotts could easily have

been the vehicle for Webb's exposure both to abstract art and the *Autonomistes* in particular. Esther Trepanier notes Marian Scott's contact with the *Autonomistes* and refers to her "unusual status 'between' the [French and English] cultural communities," and her "path ... towards" and "commit[ment to] non-objective art." *Marian Dale Scott: Pioneer of Modern Art* (Quebec City: Musee Du Quebec, 2000), 210–11.

40. "For Borduas, all important moments in the history of a society or an individual are the result of 'generous,' spontaneous, passionate impulses. When these become codified, rational, and academic, the result is decadence.... The only hope for modern society, therefore, which has lost touch with its 'necessités' and has become dominated by religious and scientific 'intention,' is total refusal." Ray Ellenwood, *Egregore: A History of the Montreal Autonomist Movement* (Toronto: Exile Editions, 1992), 136.

41. "Lying down is part of my method of composition, being prone being close to sleep and dream. Throughout composition of this piece, for instance, I have lain down several times to allow the thoughts to shape themselves. Or I will wake from sleep to find a problem solved—or raised." Webb, "Up the Ladder: Notes on the Creative Process," in *Talking*, 62.

42. Paul-Emile Borduas, *Refus Global*, quoted in Ellenwood, *Egregore*, 137. *Refus Global*, trans. Ray Ellenwood (Toronto: Exile Editions, 1998), 41.

43. It is not clear how much of an influence Shadbolt's work has been, but a reproduction of his painting "The Place" graces the cover of *The Vision Tree*. An undated letter from Shadbolt in the National Library appears to comment, reading in part: "The notion of collaboration between artists and poets should be kept alive wherever possible."

44. The typescript of the interview is in Webb's National Library papers. A letter from Duncan, dated November 18, 1963, which invites Webb for dinner (she was living in Berkeley at the time), notes that "The advantage of noon is daylight for seeing paintings." The "paintings" referred to may have been Duncan's partner Jess's, or other works in their collection.

45. In *Nothing But Brush Strokes*, 99. As further evidence of Webb's nascent visual imagination, a February 18, 1974 letter to George Woodcock complains, "I'm obsessive, but so far *shapes* of poetry have yet to arise" (my emphasis). Webb Papers, National Library. Webb's discussion of "texture in poetry as ... a sound apparition" in her 1995 Blaser essay, "The Crannies of Matter," could also be taken into account here. *Nothing But Brush Strokes*, 55.

46. In "On the Line," Webb "signs off" a brief commentary on her poem "For Fyodor": "Notes from the Insect Underground. Spider Webb." *Nothing But Brush Strokes*, 22.

47. Also reproduced in *Capilano Review* 2: 37 (Spring 2002). The painting is owned by Robin Blaser.

48. Webb, quoted in Warland, "Phyllis Webb and the Spirit of Inquiry," 148.

49. W. J. T. Mitchell, *Picture Theory: Essays on Verbal and Visual Representation* (Chicago: University of Chicago Press, 1994), 217. Krauss, quoted in Mitchell, *Picture Theory*, 215.

50. Mitchell, *Picture Theory*, 219.

51. Ibid., 234.

52. Gertrude Stein, "A carafe, That is a Blind Glass," from Tender Buttons, in *Selected Writings of Gertrude Stein*, ed. Carl Van Vechten (New York: Vintage, 1990), 461. The full text of Stein's poem reads:

> A kind in glass and a cousin, a spectacle and nothing strange
> a single hurt color and an arrangement in a system to pointing.
> All this and not ordinary, not unordered in not resembling.
> The difference is spreading.

53. Moszynska writes of "the influence of poetry in freeing art from strict representation." *Abstract Art* (London: Thames and Hudson, 1990), 20.

54. Vassily Kandinsky, "The Question of Form," in *Kandinsky: Complete Writings on Art, Vol. One (1901–1921)*, 237. Paul-Emile Borduas, quoted in Ray Ellenwood, "The Autonomist Movement of Montreal," 17. Charles Olson, "Projective Verse," in *Collected Prose*, ed. Donald Allen and Benjamin Friedlander, (Berkeley: University of California Press, 1997), 240—caps suppressed. Roger Farr, *Ventilation Flow*, unpaginated.

55. Paul Goodman, in a strange little essay entitled "The Meaning of Abstraction in Literature," states: "[I]t seems to me theoretically impossible, in literature, painting, or any art, to abstract completely from subject-matter … therefore it is the tendency rather than the achievement that labels a work abstract." In *Art and Social Nature* (New York: Vinco, 1946), 64. Charles Altieri has much the same in mind when he notes that "If abstraction need not reject all uses of representational imagery, its devices become available for a wide range of linguistic effects." *Painterly Abstraction in Modernist American Poetry* (Cambridge: Cambridge University Press, 1989), 45.

56. Louis Zukofsky might be seen to be addressing such a concern in *Bottom: On Shakespeare*, 77, when he writes (citing *The Tempest*): "*No tongue! all eyes! Be silent.* But no artist in words dares act the six words of this command, unless he desires not to exist." Webb in her painting explores the possibilities of existence once the tongue has ceded its place to the eyes—and the hands.

57. Lyn Hejinian, "Two Stein Talks," in *The Language of Enquiry* (Berkeley: University of California Press, 2001), 94. Ibid., 90. Ponge, quoted in ibid., 95–96.

58. For instance, Wendy Steiner notes that the "inter-art" comparison is often an attempt "to attribute the reality claim of painting to literature," and that, with

modernism, increasingly "[t]he true means of representing reality was not to represent at all, but to create a portion of reality itself." Steiner, *The Colors of Rhetoric: Problems in the Relation between Modern Literature and Painting* (Chicago: University of Chicago Press, 1982), xi, 17.

59. Scobie, *Earthquakes and Explorations: Language and Painting from Cubism to Concrete Poetry* (Toronto: University of Toronto Press, 1997), ix.

60. Ibid., 10.

61. Riding, *Anarchism Is Not Enough*, 34.

62. Ibid., 37.

63. See Steiner's discussion of this, *The Colors of Rhetoric*, 5.

64. McCaffery, "The Scandal of Sincerity," 209.

65. One reason may lie in Webb's assumption of the role of public intellectual, which we might see in her radio and reviewing activities, a role which presupposes notions of direct communication and the dissemination of information.

66. *The Sea Is Also a Garden*, poem 35.

67. Hulcoop writes: "'A Pang Cantata' [is] the poet's most uncompromising attempt *prior* to the *Naked Poems* to create an analogue in poetry for the self-contained abstract painting." Unpaginated introduction to Phyllis Webb, *Selected Poems* (Vancouver: Talonbooks, 1971).

68. As an interesting intertextual connection, Robert Duncan's early "Venice Poem" also combines musical references (to Igor Stravinsky) with an allusion to the same painting by Rousseau. See his *Poems, 1948–49* (Berkeley: Berkeley Miscellany Editions, 1949).

69. Pater, quoted in Mel Gooding, *Abstract Art* (London: Tate Publishing, 2001), 20. Gooding, *Abstract Art*, 9. Henry Orlov, "Towards a Semiotics of Music," in *The Sign in Music and Literature*, ed. Wendy Steiner (Austin: University of Texas Press, 1981), 131.

70. It is Hulcoop, once again, who put me on to some of these musical possibilities (private correspondence, November 9, 2005)—in particular the word "crin" and a particular Villa-Lobos piece called "Bachiana Brasileira," in which the soprano's part (it is a piece for eight cellos and a soprano) "is wordless." I derive a different connection than Hulcoop from the word "scrin" (which he links to "the Middle Dutch word schrinden … meaning to crack").

In terms of musical abstraction it might be worth noting here that, according to Betsy Warland, the "transitional image" in Webb's movement from poetry to painting was her unfulfilled desire to play the violin. Warland, "Phyllis Webb and the Spirit of Inquiry," 141.

71. Webb, "Naked Poems," *The Vision Tree*, 66. I will again cite subsequent references to this work parenthetically in text as *Vision*.

72. Stein, *Tender Buttons*, 463.

73. I am not certain what specific painting of Scott's triggered Webb's poem. Valerie Robillard and Els Jongeneel note that ekphrasis "refers to the manner in which literary works evoke existing or imagined works of art.... [It is] a popular rhetorical figure that writers used in order to achieve *enargeia* or, in other words, to equal in language the natural quality of the artwork." *Pictures into Words: Theoretical and Descriptive Approaches to Ekphrasis* (Amsterdam: VU University Press, 1998), ix.

74. Ibid.

75. *Water and Light*, 19.

76. *Hanging Fire*, 39–40, 21. Subsequent references to this work cited parenthetically in text as *Hanging*.

77. *The Hanging Fire* manuscripts in the National Library—mostly written in University of Victoria exam booklets—reveal a striking process whereby Webb would make lists of words, running off strings of pure spontaneous sound—"pillage village swillage / swanee pawnee cree / platant mutant"—before moving into drafts of the poems. As she writes in a manuscript note, "'The words are heard' / first, then thought about."

78. Jonathon Culler argues that apostrophe, the figure of lyric address, "makes its point by troping not on the meaning of a word but on the circuit or situation of communication itself." Culler also describes the apostrophe as "the figure of all that is most radical ... in the lyric," for, anarchically, it demands the impossible: "to apostrophize is to will a state of affairs, to attempt to call it into being." See "Apostrophe," in *The Pursuit of Signs* (Ithaca: Cornell University Press, 1981), 135, 139.

79. Theodore Adorno, "Lyric Poetry and Society," in *The Adorno Reader*, ed. Brian O'Connor (Oxford: Blackwell, 2000), 218.

80. Webb's interview with Smaro Kamboureli includes the following exchange:

> Webb: "The middle section, 'Hanging Fire,' is, among other things, about the death of the lyric poem and my sense that that comes out of the kind of world we live in.... But, try as one might, one can not get rid of the 'I.' At least, I can't. I think that's why I do so much dancing around the 'I,' and was concerned with the lyric and the first-person singular.... This poem ["Performance"] is so loaded with 'I's,' but it is certainly tangling with all the possible functions of the first person."
>
> Kamboureli: "The 'I' here becomes pluralized."
>
> Webb: "I, we. I is. It becomes more noun-like, much more object-like, or other."

Kamboureli, "Seeking Shape. Seeking Meaning," 33–37.

81. Altieri, *Painterly Abstraction in Modernism American Poetry*, 151.

82. Krauss, *The Picasso Papers* (Cambridge: MIT Press, 1999), 26, 36, 78–81.

83. *The Vision Tree,* 40.

84. *Hanging Fire,* 67.

85. Ibid., 14.

86. *The Vision Tree,* 36.

87. *The Sea Is Also a Garden,* poem 19.

88. *Water and Light,* 9—my emphasis.

89. *The Vision Tree,* 31.

90. *Hanging Fire,* 60.

91. *The Sea Is Also a Garden,* poem 2.

92. *Wilson's Bowl,* 55. Plato's parable of the charioteer comes from his *Phaedrus.*

93. *Hanging Fire,* 43.

94. *The Vision Tree,* 26.

95. *Hanging Fire,* 67–68.

96. Ibid., 68.

97. Ibid.

98. Williams, *Paterson* (New York: New Directions, 1963), 6. Moore, *The Complete Poems of Marianne Moore* (New York: Macmillan Co., 1967), 267. Spicer, *The Collected Books of Jack Spicer,* ed. Robin Blaser (Santa Rosa: Black Sparrow Books, 1975), 33.

99. *Hanging Fire,* 72. Hereafter once again cited parenthetically in text as *Hanging.*

100. While my focus here is not gender per se, the possibilities are fairly obvious. Pauling Butling offers a good reading of the poem and gender in *Seeing in the Dark.* The word "apparently," in the last line of Webb's last published poem, is telling. Real, *as far as one can see.* Things are turned over to the eyes, here, which begin looking anew.

After Webb

> Listen: Do you hear the *I* running away with the man in the green hat? Look again. *I* is off and diving into Fulford Harbour to run with the whales. *I* spout. *I* make whalesong. Passengers on the ferry swarm to starboard to see me disporting myself. *I/we* know they are out to get us. Yes, they are mad for education. They'll pen us up at Sealand and we'll die. We don't build big and we can't shoot. *I* commits suicide in the watery commune, the vocal pod. *We* swims on.[1]

Near the close of her last book of poetry, Webb's poetic, lyric I "commits suicide," plunges off into the "watery commune" that is the very source of language, leaving Phyllis Webb herself to continue, to be reborn as a painter—to abstract a painter from the tangled self-examinations of her verse. Or—is it a movement from the unavoidable subjective impulses of the (lyric) poem into the more (plausibly) objectifiable exteriority of the abstract painting? This is the tricky part. I don't want to veer into psychobiography, don't want to suggest painting as therapy, as the salvation of a tormented poet. In Webb's suicide poems the lyric I is already gone: either it is part of the "commune"—"*we*, my friends, / who have considered suicide"—or it is wholly outside, an eye (I) watching—"I go as far as I can / collaborating in the fame"—staring into (or out of) the face of the other of its language: silence.[2]

> ROSALIND KRAUSS: [Suicide was] a semantic marker for one of the major poles of the structural opposition that functioned as the dynamic of [Mayakovsky's] art. This opposition is between stasis and motion, between a deadening immobility and a

> victory over that sameness, in a movement that will overtake, outstrip, transcend time.[3]

Perhaps it would be best to follow Rosalind Krauss on Mayakovsky here: suicide has a textual function, is part of a "structural opposition … between stasis and motion" necessary to his poetic. Certainly Webb's work demonstrates this necessity too, where stasis is often silence, and motion the lyric address. But more than this: the presence of lyric suicide, of silence and the engulfing "vocal pod" of the commune, of abstraction and suicide as *takings out*, is part and parcel of Webb's focus on *potentiality* in her art—the potentiality of the lyric, the potentiality of suicide, the potentiality of abstraction, even the very potentiality of the "commune"—all a facing of the future that is at the essence of creativity itself. The very self-referential abstract (as a *taking out* or isolation), potentiality of potentiality itself, as Giorgio Agamben notes in *The Coming Community*, is derived from "the potentiality to not be"—the potential to not write, to not paint, to not play the piano—which directs the potential not toward some specific (representable) goal, but towards itself as pure, unexhausted (and yet material, embodied) potentiality.

> AGAMBEN: In the potentiality to be, potentiality has as its object a certain act, in the sense that for it *energhein*, being-in-act, can only mean passing to a determinate activity … as for the potentiality to not be, on the other hand, the act can never consist of a simple transition *de potentia ad actum*: It is, in other words, a potentiality that has as its object potentiality itself, a *potentia potentiae*.… [E]ven though every pianist has the potential to play and the potential to not play, Glenn Gould is, however, the only one who can *not* not-play, and, directing his potentiality not only to the act but to his own impotence, he plays, so to speak, with his potentiality to not-play.[4]

Webb could similarly be seen to have attempted to write her not-writing, to have simultaneously posited and withdrawn an "I" from her poetry in order to keep her poetry open to the other, the future, the "commune." Thus she might be seen to have attempted what

Agamben calls the "perfect act of writing," which "comes not from a power to write, but from an impotence that turns back on itself and in this way comes to itself as a pure act."[5] The real writing of the lyric is a writing of the not-lyric, and ultimately the real potentiality of writing lies in writing its not-writing. Abstraction can be this being-not-being—can be the potentiality of potentiality in the visual sphere. Like Laura Riding, Webb may have found that she had to "abdicate" her "authority"—had to give up the "real" (and representable) for the even more truly real—because truly potential—"unreal": the poetry only painting knows, the silence out—outside—language's walls. For Webb, poetry remained in the tension between silence and address: not-writing, while a pressing present absence, was mostly felt in actual absences from writing (the silence surrounding the minimal *Naked Poems*, the gap in publication between *Naked Poems* and *Wilson's Bowl*). Painting has given her the gift of wordlessness, of the full potentiality of writing, found in not-writing.

~

One cannot reduce the difference exposed in Webb's exile from poetry and her refashioning of herself as a painter. At the same time, it has been difficult to avoid seeing a sort of reversed *ut pictura poesis* in her transformation—an *ut poesis pictura*, where the painting of the former poet still traces the ragged and inarticulate edge of language (the empty crossword grid)—the point (which *is* poetry) at which language experiences itself as material, *embodied*, and resistant substance—where language "lives and moves and has being."[6] While one may regret a gifted poet's silence, there is no tragedy here, and Webb herself has characterized her "shift in consciousness to the visual" as a victory of the "colour-happy pleasure seeker" over the "verbal part of my brain, that cool, critical and boring superego."[7] If there are still "poems" of a kind coming from Phyllis Webb, they are bright in colour, sometimes awash in busy brush strokes, sometimes cleanly geometric, sometimes cut, collaged, folded, and deeply textured—a poetry, as Laura Riding hypothesized, "forced into a kind of outrageous, unnatural visibility."[8]

~

All this is perhaps a cruel undoing of an artist's desire to escape "the prison house of language" into the "wordlessness" of paint. But Riding's point is exactly that poetry only becomes abstract—becomes "absorbed by the medium of communication of sense"—by becoming something other than what poetry is *as a linguistic medium.* The two media twin in the modern turn from the semantic to the syntactic—from mimetic dependence to embodied independence—from *saying to being.* My argument is that that *being* of the abstract is a *being between*—a response and a responsibility—a *singular plural* anarchic array. Thus it is still communicative, still a telling, a sharing, a giving, a joining, a being together in the artifact of out meeting. The language poetry aspires to is a proto-linguistic proximity, a marking of horizon and companionship—and the abstract painting marks this same space.

It must remain an interesting mystery, rather than a problem disinterestedly solved—the reasons Webb left poetry for painting. In part it was a departure from the public sphere into the private—from the professional status of "established" poet to the amateur status of "a hobbyist."[9] This was an escape from fixed identity to the fluid futurity of the open road—a deft move in the face of death to rend creative potential out of the still untapped. I find it impossible not to admire her more and more. She enacts the impossible demands of the creative for freedom and belonging with each day on an island of paint. Her move from poem to painting she describes as "[a]lmost a Buddhistic withdrawl of identity."[10] Such a "withdrawal" by a lyric poet could not but leave the lyric behind. She chose. She became other.

If there is no outside of language, there is no point from which the linguistic sphere can be comprehended. Webb steps out of the poem to see if there is an outside, and to see if, after forty years of poetry, she can finally see what language is. It is full of silence. Visceral. Real. It is something the poet could not have foreseen—found in the "surprising doing in the hands."[11]

~

For the reader, there *are* the poems—engaging practices in the public sphere. We can respond to Webb's responses—this is in fact our *responsibility*. She has always positioned herself in a cabin on a cold margin—peering into "the common good." She peers through painting now. The poetry remains our commons—"Language is common," writes Antonio Negri—and "it is the immeasurable *to-come* that creates the common."[12] The multiple voices of Webb's poetry—the responses to other poems, the "scattering chips of dialogue" in their anarchic multiplicity—gather into the thick listening of paint—another otherness, another one-that-is-more-than-one—the "insurrectionary wilderness" of the lyric I become the common wood of the unicorns' "wilderness" "beyond the story" where the poet, not joining the journey into history and the word, remains inside outside, in her cabin, on her island of the "immeasurable *to-come*."

Notes

1. *Hanging Fire*, 67.

2. *The Vision Tree*, 54. *Wilson's Bowl*, 66.

3. Krauss, The Picasso Papers, 236.

4. Agamben, *The Coming Community*, trans. Michael Hardt (Minneapolis: University of Minnesota Press, 1993), 35–36.

5. Ibid., 37.

6. Jerome McGann, "Laura (Riding) Jackson and the Literal Truth," 472.

7. Webb, "What I'd be if I Were Not a Writer," 24.

8. Riding, *Anarchism Is Not Enough*, 37.

9. Webb, "What I'd be if I Were Not a Writer," 24.

10. Ibid.

11. Paul Goodman, *The Empire City*, 267.

12. Negri, *Time for Revolution*, 183, 189.

Acknowledgements

A shorter version of chapter three was published in *West Coast Line* 45 (2005), 79–95, as "Essay on Abstraction: Phyllis Webb & the Death of the Lyric."

Excerpts from chapter two have appeared in two previous publications: "A Duncan Etude: Dante and Responsibility," in *Jacket Magazine* 26 (January 2005), and "Another Duncan Etude: Empire and Anarchy," in *W* 10 (Summer 2005).

I extend my thanks to these editors. Gracious thanks also go out to the many who have helped along the way: Andrea Actis, Pauline Butling, Sharisse Dalby, Sandra Djwa, Roger Farr, John Hulcoop, Smaro Kamboureli, Glen Lowry, Lisa Robertson, Jordan Scott, Karl and Christy Siegler, Sharon Thesen, Betsy Warland, Lissa Wolsak, and Jerry Zaslove.

Thanks to Cathy, who always carries the load.

And thanks, above all else, to Phyllis Webb.

Works Cited

Adorno, Theodore. *Aesthetic Theory.* Trans. Robert Hullot-Kentor. Minneapolis: University of Minnesota Press, 1997.

———. "Lyric Poetry and Society." In *The Adorno Reader,* ed. Brian O'Connor. Oxford: Blackwell, 2000.

Agamben, Giorgio. *The Coming Community.* Trans. Michael Hardt. Minneapolis: University of Minnesota Press, 1993.

Ahmad, Aijaz. *Ghazals of Ghalib.* New York: Columbia University Press, 1971.

Altieri, Charles. *Painterly Abstraction in Modernist American Poetry.* Cambridge: Cambridge University Press, 1989.

Antliff, Allan. *Anarchist Modernism: Art, Politics, and the First American Avant-Garde.* Chicago: University of Chicago Press, 2001.

Arnold, Matthew. *Essays in Criticism, First Series.* Ed. Sister Thomas Marion Hoctor. Chicago: University of Chicago Press, 1968.

Avrich, Paul. *Sacco and Vanzetti: The Anarchist Background.* Princeton: Princeton University Press, 1991.

Bakunin, Michael. *Bakunin of Anarchism.* Ed. and trans. Sam Dolgoff. Montreal: Black Rose Books, 1980.

Barbour, Douglas. *Lyric/Anti-Lyric: Essays on Contemporary Poetry.* Edmonton: NeWest Press, 2001.

Berger, John. *Keeping a Rendezvous.* New York: Vintage, 1991.

———. *The Sense of Sight.* Ed. John Spencer. New York: Pantheon Books, 1985.

Bernstein, Charles. "The Revenge of the Poet-Critic, or The Parts are Greater Than the Sum of the Whole." In *My Way: Speeches and Poems.* Chicago: University of Chicago Press, 1999. 3–17.

Billington, James H. *The Icon and The Axe: An Interpretive History of Russian Culture.* New York: Knopf, 1968.

Blake, William. *The Complete Poetry and Prose.* New York: Doubleday, 1988.

Blaser, Robin. *The Holy Forest.* Toronto: Coach House Press, 1993.

———. "The Practice of Outside." In *The Collected Books of Jack Spicer.* Santa Rosa: Black Sparrow Books, 1975. 271–329.

Bloom, Harold. *The Anxiety of Influence: A Theory of Poetry.* Oxford: Oxford University Press, 1973.

Boone, Joseph and Michael Cadden. *Engendering Men: The Question of Male Feminist Criticism.* New York: Routledge, 1990.

Brooks, Cleanth. *The Well Wrought Urn: Studies in the Structure of Poetry.* New York: Harcourt Brace, 1947.

Brown, Norman O. *Love's Body.* Berkeley: University of California Press, 1966.

Butling, Pauline. "Phyllis Webb and CBC *Ideas*: Intersections of the Personal and Political." Vancouver, B.C. Typescript.

———. *Seeing in the Dark: The Poetry of Phyllis Webb.* Waterloo: Wilfred Laurier University Press, 1997.

Carr, Brenda. "Genre Theory and the Impasse of Lyric?: Reframing the Questions in Phyllis Webb's Lyric Sequences." *West Coast Line* 25: 3 (Winter 1991/92): 67–79.

Carr, E. H. *Michael Bakunin.* 1937. Reprint. New York: Vintage Books, 1961.

Chernyshevsky, Nikolai. *What Is to Be Done?* Trans. Benjamin Tucker. New York: Vintage, 1961.

Conte, Joseph M. *Unending Design: The Forms of Postmodern Poetry.* Ithaca: Cornell University Press, 1991.

Crawford, Robert. *The Modern Poet: Poetry, Academia, and Knowledge Since the 1750s.* Oxford: Oxford University Press, 2001.

Crossley, Nick. *Intersubjectivity: The Fabric of Social Becoming.* London: Sage Publications, 1996.

Culler, Jonathon. "Apostrophe." In *The Pursuit of Signs.* Ithaca: Cornell University Press, 1981: 135–54.

Derrida, Jacques. *The Gift of Death.* Trans. David Wills. Chicago: University of Chicago Press, 1995.

Dickinson, Emily. *Selected Letters.* Ed. Thomas Johnson. Cambridge: Belknap Press, 1958.

Diepeveen, Leonard. *Changing Voices: The Modern Quoting Poem.* Ann Arbor: The University of Michigan Press, 1993.

H.D. *Collected Poems, 1912–1944.* New York: New Directions, 1983.

Donne, John. *The Oxford Book of Seventeenth Century Verse.* Ed. Sir Herbert Grierson and G. Bullough. Oxford: The Clarendon Press, 1934: 111–12.

Duplessis, Rachel Blau. *The Pink Guitar: Writing as Feminist Practice.* New York: Routledge, 1990.

Duncan, Robert. "The Adventure of Whitman's Line." In *Fictive Certainties: Essays by Robert Duncan.* New York: New Directions, 1985: 194–210.

———. *Bending the Bow.* New York: New Directions, 1968.

———. "Changing Perspectives in Reading Whitman." In *Fictive Certainties: Essays by Robert Duncan.* New York: New Directions, 1985: 162–93.

———. *A Great Admiration: H.D. / Robert Duncan, Correspondence 1950–1961.* Ed. Robert Bertholf. Venice: Lapis Press, 1992.

———. "The H.D. Book." Part I, chapter 2. *Coyote Journal* 8 (1967): 27–35; part II, chapter 5. *Sagetrieb* 4: 2–3 (Fall/Winter 1985): 39–85; part II, chapter 7. *Credences* 1: 2 (1975): 53–94.

———. "An Interview with Robert Duncan." Michael Andre Bernstein and Berton Hatlen. *Sagetrieb* 4: 2–3 (Fall/Winter 1985): 87–135.

———. "An Interview with Robert Duncan." Jack Cohn and Thomas O'Donnell. *Contemporary Literature* 21:4 (1980): 513–48.

———. *Letters: Poems 1953–1956.* Reprint. Chicago: Flood Editions, 2003.

———. *The Letters of Robert Duncan and Denise Levertov.* Ed. Robert Bertholf and Albert Gelpi. Stanford: Stanford University Press, 2004.

———. "A Life in Poetry." Talk given at the 1963 Vancouver Poetry Conference. Transcribed by Charles Watts, Simon Fraser University Special Collections Library, Burnaby B.C.

———. "Man's Fulfillment in Order and Strife." In *Fictive Certainties: Essays by Robert Duncan*. New York: New Directions, 1985: 111–41.

———. *The Opening of the Field.* New York: New Directions, 1960.

———. "Pages from a Notebook." In *The New American Poetry, 1945-1960.* 1960. Reprint, ed. Donald Allen. Berkeley: University of California Press, 1999: 400–07.

———. Preface to "The H.D. Book." In The Poetry and Rare Book Collection, SUNY Buffalo, Buffalo, New York.

Eliot, T. S. *Collected Poems 1909–1962.* London: Faber and Faber, 1974.

———. "Tradition and the Individual Talent." In *Selected Prose of T. S. Eliot,* ed. Frank Kermode. New York: Harcourt Brace Kovanovich, 1975: 37–44.

Ellenwood, Ray. "The Autonomist Movement of Montreal: Towards Non-Figuration in Painting, Dance, and Poetry." *Canadian Literature* 113–114 (Summer/Fall 1987): 11–27.

———. *Egregore: A History of the Montreal Autonomist Movement.* Toronto: Exile Editions, 1992.

Farr, Roger. "The 'Insurrectionary Wilderness of the I': Phyllis Webb's Anarchist Poetics." *West Coast Line* 45 (2005): 63–76.

———. *Ventilation Flow.* Vancouver: Thuja, 1999.

Fer, Briony. *On Abstract Art.* New Haven: Yale University Press, 1997.

Findley, Timothy. *Not Wanted on the Voyage.* New York: Viking, 1984.

Friedman, Elizabeth. *A Mannered Grace: The Life of Laura (Riding) Jackson.* New York: Persea Books, 2005.

Gibson, Ian. *Federico Garcia Lorca, A Life.* New York: Pantheon, 1989.

Glickman, Susan. "Proceeding before the Amorous Invisible: Phyllis Webb and the Ghazal." *Canadian Literature* 115 (Winter 1987): 48–61.

Golding, Alan. "George Oppen's Serial Poems." In *The Objectivist Nexus: Essays in Cultural Poetics,* ed. Rachel Blau Duplessis and Peter Quartermain. Tuscaloosa: University of Alabama Press, 1999: 84–103.

Goldman, Emma. *Red Emma Speaks: An Emma Goldman Reader.* New York: Schocken Books, 1983.

Gooding, Mel. *Abstract Art.* London: Tate Publishing, 2001.

Goodman, Paul. *Empire City: A Novel of New York City.* 1959. Reprint. Santa Rosa: Black Sparrow Press, 2001.

———. "The Meaning of Abstraction in Literature." In *Art and Social Nature.* New York: Vinco, 1946.

Greenberg, Clement. *Clement Greenberg: The Collected Essays and Criticism.* Ed. John O'Brian. Vol. 2. Chicago: University of Chicago Press, 1986.

Grossman, Allen. *The Sighted Singer: Two Works on Poetry for Readers and Writers.* Baltimore: Johns Hopkins University Press, 1992.

Grosz, Elizabeth. *Becomings: Explorations in Time, Memory, and Futures.* Ithaca: Cornell University Press, 1999.

Guibault, Serge. *How New York Stole the Idea of Modern Art: Abstract Expressionism, Freedom, and the Cold War.* Trans. Arthur Goldhammer. Chicago: University of Chicago Press, 1983.

Hardt, Michael and Antonio Negri. *Empire.* Cambridge, Mass.: Harvard University Press, 2000.

Havelock, Eric A. *Preface to Plato.* Cambridge, Mass.: Harvard University Press, 1963.

Heidegger, Martin. *Being and Time.* Trans. John Macquarrie and Edward Robinson. New York: Harper and Row, 1962.

Hejinian, Lyn. "Two Stein Talks." In *The Language of Enquiry.* Berkeley: University of California Press, 2001. 83–130.

Howe, Susan. *The Birth-mark: Unsettling the Wilderness in American Literary History.* Hanover: Wesleyan University Press, 1993.

———. "Heterologies: Community of Form in Practice and Imagination." In *The Recovery of the Public World: Essays on Poetics in Honour of Robin Blaser,* ed. Charles Watts and Edward Byrne. Vancouver: Talonbooks 1999. 217–20.

———. *My Emily Dickinson.* Berkeley: North Atlantic Books, 1985.

Hulcoop, John. Introduction to *Selected Poems: 1954–1965,* by Phyllis Webb. Vancouver: Talonbooks, 1971.

———. "Phyllis Webb and the Priestess of Motion." *Canadian Literature* 32 (1967): 29–39.

Jameson, Frederic. *Postmodernism or The Cultural Logic of Late Capitalism.* Durham: Duke University Press, 1991.

Kadlec, David. *Mosaic Modernism: Anarchism, Pragmatism, Culture.* Baltimore: Johns Hopkins University Press, 2000.

Kamboureli, Smaro. "'Seeking Shape. Seeking Meaning': An Interview with Phyllis Webb." *West Coast Line* 25:3 (Winter 1991/92): 21–41.

Kandinsky, Vassily. *Concerning the Spiritual in Art.* 1912. Reprint. New York: George Wittenbom, 1947.

———. *Kandinsky: Complete Writings on Art.* Vol. 1 (1901–1921). Ed. Kenneth C. Lindsay and Peter Vergo. Boston: G. K. Hall & Co., 1982.

Katz, Michael and William Wagner. "Introduction: Chernyshevsky's What Is to Be Done? and the Russian Intelligentsia." In *What Is to Be Done?,* trans. Michael Katz. Ithaca: Cornell University Press, 1989.

Kelley, Paul. "'Destruction' and 'Experience': Four Notes on Walter Benjamin." In *Anarcho-Modernism: Toward a New Critical Theory,* ed. Ian Angus. Vancouver: Talonbooks, 2001. 21–33.

Knight, Lorna. "'Oh for the Carp of a Critic': Research in the Phyllis Webb Papers." *West Coast Line* 26: 2 (Fall 1992): 120–27.

Knutson, Susan. "Chiasmus, Chasm, Chi: Phyllis Webb's Semantic Geometry." *West Coast Line* 25:3 (Winter 1991/92): 118–21.

Krauss, Rosalind. *The Picasso Papers.* Cambridge: MIT Press, 1999.

Kropotkin, Peter. "Anarchist Communism: Its basis and Principles." In *Kropotkin's Revolutionary Pamphlets.* 1927. Reprint, ed. Roger Baldwin. New York: Dover, 1970. 46–78.

———. "Anarchism: Its Philosophy and Ideal." In *Kropotkin's Revolutionary Pamphlets,* 115–44.

Levinas, Emmanuel. *Entre Nous: On Thinking-of-the-Other.* Trans. Michael B. Smith and Barbara Harshav. New York: Columbia University Press, 1998.

———. *God, Death, and Time.* Trans. Bettina Bergo. Stanford: Stanford University Press, 2000.

———. *Humanism of the Other.* Trans. Nidra Poller. Chicago: University of Chicago Press, 2003.

———. *Time and the Other.* Trans. Richard A. Cohen. Pittsburgh: Duquense University Press, 1987.

Locke, John. *Two Treatises of Government.* Ed. Peter Laslett. Cambridge: Cambridge University Press, 1967.

McCaffery, Steve. "The Scandal of Sincerity." In *Prior to Meaning: The Protosemantic and Poetics.* Evanston: Northwestern University Press, 2001.

McGann, Jerome. "Laura (Riding) Jackson and the Literal Truth." *Critical Inquiry* 18 (Spring 1992): 454–73.

Malevich, Kasimir. *The Non-Objective World.* Trans. Howard Dearstyne. Chicago: Paul Theobald, 1959.

Marvell, Andrew. "The Garden." In *The Oxford Book of Seventeenth Century Verse,* ed. Sir Herbert Grierson and G. Bullough. Oxford: Clarendon Press, 1934: 751–52.

May, Todd. *The Political Philosophy of Poststructuralist Anarchism.* University Park: Penn State University Press, 1994.

Melfi, Mary. *A Queen Is Holding a Mummified Cat.* Montreal: Guernica Editions, 1982.

Mitchell, W. J. T. *Picture Theory: Essays on Verbal and Visual Representation.* Chicago: University of Chicago Press, 1994.

Mondrian, Piet. *Complete Mondrian.* Aldershot and Burlington: Lund Humphries, 2001.

Moore, Marianne. *The Complete Poems of Marianne Moore.* New York: Macmillan Co., 1967.

Moszynska, Anna. *Abstract Art.* London: Thames and Hudson, 1990.

Motherwell, Robert. *The Collected Writings.* Ed. Stephanie Terenzio. New York: Oxford University Press, 1992.

Nancy, Jean-Luc. *Being Singular Plural.* Trans. Robert D. Richardson and Anne E. O'Byrne. Stanford: Stanford University Press, 2000.

Neeson, J. M. *Commoners: Common right, Enclosure and Social Change in England, 1700–1820.* Cambridge: Cambridge University Press, 1993.

Negri, Antonio. *Time for Revolution.* Trans. Matteo Mandarini. New York: Continuum, 2003.

Ngai, Sianne. *Ugly Feelings.* Cambridge, Mass.: Harvard University Press, 2005.

O'Hara, Frank. *The Collected Poems of Frank O'Hara.* Ed. Donald Allen. New York: Knopf, 1971.

Olson, Charles. *Collected Prose.* Ed. Donald Allen and Benjamin Friedlander. Berkeley: University of California Press, 1997.

———. *Selected Poems.* Ed. Robert Creeley. Berkeley: University of California Press, 1997.

Oppen, George. *Collected Poems.* New York: New Directions, 1975.

Orlov, Henry. "Towards a Semiotics of Music." In *The Sign in Music and Literature,* ed. Wendy Steiner. Austin: University of Texas Press, 1981.

Osborne, Harold. *Abstraction and Artifice in Twentieth-Century Art.* Oxford: Oxford University Press, 1979.

Parsons, A. R. *Anarchism: Its Philosophy and Scientific Basis.* 1887. Reprint. New York: Krauss Reprint Co., 1971.

Perloff, Marjorie. *21st Century Modernism: The New Poetics.* Malden: Blackwell Publications, 2002.

Potvin, Liza. "Phyllis Webb: The Voice That Breaks." *Canadian Poetry* 32 (Spring/Summer 1993): 37–64.

Pound, Ezra. *The Spirit of Romance.* 1910. Reprint. New York: New Directions, 1968.

Proudhon, Pierre-Joseph. *What is Property? An Enquiry into the Principle of Right and of Government.* Trans. Benjamin Tucker. New York: H. Fertig, 1966.

Read, Herbert. *Poetry and Anarchism.* London: Faber and Faber, 1938.

Relke, Diane. "Feminist Ecocritique as Forensic Archaeology: Digging in Critical Graveyards and Phyllis Webb's Gardens." *Canadian Poetry* 48 (Spring/Summer 1998): 66–99.

Riding, Laura. *Anarchism Is Not Enough.* 1928. Reprint. Berkeley: University of California Press, 2001.

———. *Selected Poems: In Five Sets.* 1938. Reprint. New York: Norton, 1970.

Riding, Laura and Robert Graves, eds. *A Survey of Modernist Poetry.* 1927. Reprint. New York: Doubleday, 1928.

Rilke, Rainer Maria. *Selected Poems.* Trans. Stephen Mitchell. New York: Random House, 1982.

Robillard, Valerie and Els Jongeneel. *Pictures into Words: Theoretical and Descriptive Approaches to Ekphrasis.* Amsterdam: VU University Press, 1998.

Rogers, John. *The Matter of Revolution: Science, Poetry, and Politics in the Age of Milton.* Ithaca: Cornell University Press, 1996.

Rolfe, Edwin. *Collected Poems.* Ed. Cary Nelson and Jefferson Hendricks. Urbana: University of Illinois Press, 1993.

Sacco, Nicola and Bartolomeo Vanzetti. *The Letters of Sacco and Vanzetti.* Ed. Marion Denman Frankfurter and Gardner Jackson. New York: Octagon Books, 1980.

Said, Edward. *On Late Style: Music and Literature Against the Grain.* New York: Pantheon Books, 2006.

Scobie, Stephen. *Earthquakes and Explorations: Language and Painting from Cubism to Concrete Poetry.* Toronto: University of Toronto Press, 1997.

———. "I and I: Phyllis Webb's 'I Daniel'." *Open Letter* 6: 2–3 (Summer/Fall 1985): 61–70.

———. "Leonard Cohen, Phyllis Webb, and the End(s) of Modernism." In *Canadian Canons: Essays in Literary Value,* ed. Robert Lecker. Toronto: University of Toronto Press, 1991.

———. "The Poet of the Mind." In *Inside the Poem: Essays and Poems in Honour of Donald Stephens,* ed. W. H. New. Toronto: University of Toronto Press, 1992.

Scrivener, Michael Henry. *Radical Shelley: The Philosophical Anarchism and Utopian Thought of Percy Bysshe Shelley.* Princeton: Princeton University Press, 1982.

Sheehan, Sean. *Anarchism.* London: Reaktion Books, 2003.

Silliman, Ron. "The Dysfunction of Criticism: Poets and the Critical Tradition of the Anti-academy." *Poetics Journal* 10 (June 1998):179–94.

Spahr, Juliana. "Spiderwasp or Literary Criticism." In *Telling it Slant: Avant-Garde Poetics of the 1990s*, ed. Mark Wallace and Steven Marks. Tuscaloosa: University of Alabama Press, 2002: 404–28.

Spicer, Jack. *The Collected Books of Jack Spicer*. Ed. Robin Blaser. Santa Rosa: Black Sparrow Books, 1975.

Stein, Gertrude. *Selected Writings of Gertrude Stein*. Ed. Carl Van Vechten. New York: Vintage, 1990.

Steiner, Wendy. *The Colors of Rhetoric: Problems in the Relation between Modern Literature and Painting*. Chicago: University of Chicago Press, 1982.

Sujir, Leila. "Addressing a Presence: An Interview with Phyllis Webb." *Prairie Fire* 9: 1 (Spring 1988): 30–43.

Tallman, Ellen. "My Stories with Robert Duncan." Talk delivered at "Before the War: Returning to Duncan." Vancouver, B.C. April 2, 2005.

Thesen, Sharon. *The Pangs of Sunday*. Toronto: McClelland and Stewart, 1990.

Thompson, John. *Stilt Jack*. Toronto: Anansi, 1978.

Thoreau, Henry David. *Walden and Resistance to Civil Government*. Ed. William Rossi. New York: Norton, 1966.

Trepanier, Esther. *Marian Dale Scott: Pioneer of Modern Art*. Quebec: Musee Du Quebec, 2000.

Warland, Betsy. "Phyllis Webb and the Spirit of Inquiry." *Grain* 31: 1 (2003).

Watson, Scott. *Jack Shadbolt*. Vancouver: Douglas and McIntyre, 1990.

Webb, Phyllis. "Artist's Statement" from "Eight Visuals." *The Capilano Review* 2:37 (Spring 2002): 64.

———. *Even Your Right Eye*. Toronto: McClelland & Stewart, 1956.

———. *Hanging Fire*. Toronto: Coach House Press, 1990.

———. *Naked Poems*. Vancouver: Periwinkle Press, 1965.

———. *Nothing But Brush Strokes: Selected Prose*. Edmonton: NeWest, 1995.

———. "The Poet and the Publisher." *Queens Quarterly* 61 (Winter 1954–55): 498–512.

———. "Protest in Paradise." *MacLeans* 86 (June 1973): 38–39, 73–77.

———. "Radio Talks." *West Coast Line* 25:3 (Winter 1991–92): 95–100.

———. *The Sea Is Also a Garden*. Toronto: Ryerson Press, 1962.

———. "Script for Readings from 'The Kropotkin Poems.'" *West Coast Line* 25:3 (Winter 1991/92): 101–02.

———. *Sunday Water: Thirteen Anti-ghazals.* Lantzville: Island Writing Series, 1982.

———. Talking. Dunvegan, On: Quadrant Editions, 1982.

———. *The Vision Tree: Selected Poems.* Ed. Sharon Thesen. Vancouver: Talonbooks, 1982.

———. *Water and Light: Ghazals and Anti Ghazals.* Toronto: Coach House Press, 1984.

———. "What I'd Be if I Were Not a Writer." *Brick* 50 (Fall 1994): 24–25.

———. "The What Is to Be Done Poem." *In The New Romans: Candid Canadian Opinions of the U.S*, ed. A. W. Purdy. Edmonton: M.G. Hurtig, 1968.

———. *Wilson's Bowl.* Toronto: Coach House Press, 1980.

Weir, David. *Anarchy and Culture: The Aesthetic Politics of Modernism.* Amherst: University of Massachusetts Press, 1997.

Whitman, Walt. *Leaves of Grass: The First (1855) Edition.* New York: Penguin, 1959.

Williams, William Carlos. *Paterson.* New York: New Directions, 1963.

Winstanley, Gerrard. *Selected Writings.* Ed. Andrew Hopton. London: Aporia Press, 1989.

Woodcock, George. "In the Beginning Was the Question: The Poems of Phyllis Webb." *Queen's Quarterly* 93: 3 (Autumn 1986): 527–45.

Zizek, Slavoj. *Did Somebody Say Totalitarianism? Five Interventions in the (Mis)use of a Notion.* London: Verso, 2001.

———. *Welcome to the Desert of the Real!: Five Essays on 11 September and Related Dates.* London: Verso, 2002.

Zukofsky, Louis. *Bottom: On Shakespeare.* Austin, Texas: The Ark Press, 1963.

Index